Christianity, Social Change, and Globalization

Christianity, Social Change, and Globalization in the Americas

edited by
Anna Peterson
Manuel Vásquez
Philip Williams

Rutgers University Press
New Brunswick, New Jersey, and London

Library of Congress Cataloging-in-Publication Data

Christianity, social change, and globalization in the Americas / edited by Anna Peterson, Manuel Vásquez, and Philip Williams.

    p. cm.

    Includes bibliographical references and index.

    ISBN 0-8135-2931-X (hardcover : alk. paper) — ISBN 0-8135-2932-8 (pbk. : alk. paper)

    1. Christianity and culture—El Salvador. 2. El Salvador—Social conditions—20th century. 3. El Salvador—Church history—20th century. 4. Christianity and culture—Peru. 5. Peru—Social conditions—20th century. 6. Peru—Church history—20th century. 7. Latin Americans—United States—Religion. 8. United States—Church history—20th century. I. Peterson, Anna Lisa, 1963– II. Vásquez, Manuel A. III. Williams, Philip J., 1959–

BR625.S2 C47 2001
261.8'098—dc21
                                                    00–046873

British Cataloging-in-Publication data for this book is available from the British Library

Manufactured in the United States of America

Contents

Preface

On a blustery Saturday in October, more than a thousand people gather to participate in the procession of El Señor de los Milagros, the Lord of Miracles, patron saint of Peru, through the busy streets of downtown Paterson, New Jersey. El Señor is surrounded by beautiful flower arrangements, the most prominent of which are a U.S. flag and stands sporting the red and white of the Peruvian flag. Most participants are Peruvians who have come from as far away as Montreal to see the saint complete a course around Paterson's cathedral. One of Peru's main television stations has sent a crew to tape the event, which it will later broadcast to relatives in Lima. However, this celebration is not only Peruvian; Puerto Rican and Dominican Catholics also join the crowd. Many have brought their children to be blessed by the saint. The parents lift the children in the air to face El Señor, then trace the sign of the cross with the small bodies. In the meantime, vendors line the streets selling all sorts of things, ranging from cards and posters of El Señor, San Martín de Porres, and Our Lady of Guadalupe, to *uña de gato,* a plant considered to have miraculous powers. Inside the cathedral, two priests lament the fact that the religious fervor surrounding the Lord of the Miracles does not bring laypeople to participate fully in the life of the church during the rest of the year.

*   *   *

Avenida Tupac Amaru, the main thoroughfare in Comas, is a bustling, working-class district just north of Lima. Just off the avenue, named for the leader of an indigenous uprising in 1780, the "Great Rebellion" of colonial Latin America, the *hermanos* of the Evangelical Pentecostal Church of Peru, mostly people who have come to Lima from villages in the Andes, are gathered in worship. The pastor, Brother Julio, calls on the congregation to build up the church. Like most buildings in poor districts of Lima, the church is a collage of different building materials, added at different stages of a never-ending process of construction. However, Brother Julio was referring to the church's spiritual edification. Within the church, as in the world outside, there is "disorder, disobedience, disintegration," he proclaims; "the church cannot move forward this way." The solution, however, lies not in withdrawing from the evils of the world but in seeking to transform it to convert lost souls through personal effort and testimony. "If we isolate ourselves, separate ourselves, we're on the road to sin," Brother Julio continues. "How can we give our lives to others? If we brought food for the hungry it would be a blessing for our less fortunate brothers and sisters. We could go house-to-house evangelizing our neighbors."

The pastor stresses the capacity of each and every member to make good and just decisions, if only they believe in themselves. Raising his voice, Brother Julio reminds the congregation, "how many times have we heard the white people, the rich people in Miraflores refer to us as *cholos, indios,* helpless. Well, let me tell you something, we are more *[somos más]* than they are! Glory to God!" The congregation roars back, "Glory to God, Alleluia," and then breaks into boisterous applause and song. In Peru the term *cholo,* as the *hermanos* well know, usually carries a pejorative connotation, and many Limeños use it to dismiss migrants from the sierra as dirty, lazy, and backward. Brother Julio encourages his listeners to affirm their migrant identity, not only to build the physical church but also to construct a distinctive understanding of what it means to be both *evangélico* and cholo in Comas.

*   *   *

On January 16, 1992, thousands of people gather in San Salvador's central plaza to celebrate the end of eleven years of civil war. An endless series of individuals and groups steps up to a makeshift stage, some to lead songs acclaiming the left's success in forcing the government to negotiate a peace accord, others to remember the tens of thousands killed before peace came. Looming over the crowd is the skeleton of the national cathedral, unfinished since the late 1970s, when Archbishop Oscar Romero halted construction because, he insisted, the church ought to spend its money aiding the victims of violence. Romero was assassinated on March 24, 1980, and today his body lies inside the half-finished church that symbolizes his dedication to the poor. Young people have climbed up the cathedral and draped down its front flags with images of Farabundo Martí, a Salvadoran Communist executed in 1932, and the letters FMLN, acronym of the guerrilla organization that fought the government to a standstill. Even more than Farabundo Martí and the armed opposition, however, Romero dominates the celebration. Inside the cathedral, his tomb is covered with flowers, candles, and handwritten supplications and thanks. Outside in the crowd, his image—pastoral, serene—and his words—agonized, fiery, prophetic—are everywhere, on flags and bandanas, posters, and t-shirts.

Neither Romero's successor as archbishop of San Salvador, Arturo Rivera y Damas, nor any other members of the Catholic episcopacy are present. Instead, the only bishop present is Medardo Gómez, the head of El Salvador's Lutheran Church. He shares the stage with other leaders of the National Debate for Peace, an ecumenical group that has been working for the kind of dialogue between government and guerrillas which led to the negotiated peace. Thus the celebration presents a series of paradoxes: Archbishop Rivera first brought together the National Debate for Peace in 1987 but then abandoned it, leaving Gómez and Baptist pastor Edgardo Palacios to transform it into the country's most prominent peace organization. The only Catholics on the stage today are alienated from the episcopacy; many have left their parishes to work with the political opposition. The sole representative of the official church is the martyr Romero, whose legacy is so great that it almost seems the whole church is present for the fiesta.

*   *   *

At a Unitarian church near Mt. Pleasant in the heart of traditionally Latino neighborhoods in Washington, D.C., former gang members gather to read poems and short stories about their lives in the streets. The youths have formed an organization called Barrios Unidos, "Neighborhoods Together." A group leader tells us: "I have found my roots, *mi raza* [race] in sweatlodges and the spiritual talks I have here in church with my brothers in the Barrios Unidos. Before, all the white stuff, consumerism and drugs, just buried my real identity. Now, I have found my true nature in *rituales indigenas* that run in my blood and connect me with my brothers from all countries in Latin America."

*   *   *

These images reflect the diverse and sometimes unexpected faces of Christianity in the Americas today. Pastoral agents struggle to speak to gang members and guerrillas without losing the followers of the Lord of Miracles. Evangelical pastors debate the virtues of ecumenical solidarity versus withdrawal from *las cosas del mundo,* the worldly things that threaten believers' souls. In former war zones and in immigrant neighborhoods, centuries-old festivals for patron saints mix with commemorations of martyrs to political violence.

Everywhere, men, women, and children seek healing from different types of demons, spiritual and material.

This present volume examines the ways Salvadoran and Peruvian Christians interpret and respond to current social and political changes. Both El Salvador and Peru have recently emerged from years of political violence and are in precarious states of transition to democratic rule and neoliberal economic restructuring. In both countries, Roman Catholic and Protestant churches have played key political roles. Finally, both El Salvador and Peru sent thousands of immigrants to the United States during the period of social dislocation. Nevertheless, the two countries also differ significantly in their ethnic composition and in terms of the history, scale, and configuration of religious practices and institutions. Thus El Salvador and Peru offer excellent case studies for comparing and contrasting the varied roles of Christianity in the Americas today, especially in mediating social change.

Much social change today is initiated or exacerbated by globalization, which encompasses, among other aspects, economic adjustments, transitions to democracy, and the resurgence of religion in the public sphere, particularly in conflicts around locality and collective identity. Entering into this are growing immigrant diasporas, which do not melt into the host cultures but rather maintain multiple ties with their places of origin. These international, national, and regional shifts are felt in everyday and community life, where individuals struggle to understand and negotiate an increasingly baffling and threatening world. Religion offers important organizational, pragmatic, and symbolic resources that strengthen both the public sphere and people's capacity to confront the challenges of everyday life.

Acknowledgments

This project has been collaborative from its inception. It began March 1995 in Gainesville, Florida, with a meeting of the core team members Peterson, Vásquez, and Williams; Rosa Castro, Ileana Gómez, Cecilia Menjívar, Hortensia Muñoz, and Norys Ramírez; as well as Peruvian anthropologist Teófilo Altamirano. There we identified possible research sites, elaborated the survey and interview questions, and discussed the project's goals. We divided fieldwork by country. Williams, Muñoz, and Castro worked in Peru. In El Salvador, Peterson, Gómez, and Ramírez were joined by Francisca Flores and Lisa Domínguez. Manuel Vásquez coordinated research in the United States, working in Washington with Menjívar, Carmen Albertos, and Carlos Ruben Ramírez, and in New Jersey with Miguel De la Torre and Larissa Ruíz-Baia. From May 1995 to the end of 1998, we conducted surveys, interviews, and participant-observation in fourteen Catholic and Protestant congregations in Peru, seven in El Salvador, three in Paterson, New Jersey, and four in the Washington metropolitan area (see appendix for descriptions of the congregations studied). We conducted about forty surveys, interviews, and oral histories in each congregation. In this volume, we have given pseudonyms to all interviewees except a few pastoral agents. While conducting fieldwork, researchers in the same countries or cities often worked together and met to discuss their findings. The analysis of the data has also been collaborative. At a March 1998 conference in Gainesville, members of our team presented initial findings and engaged in discussions with other scholars of religion and society in Latin America and among U.S. Latinos. Since then we have written together and read and reread each other's work intensively. The three co-editors have read and revised every chapter in the book, and many of the other members of the team have also contributed to chapters other than those bearing their names. While most edited volumes consist of individually researched and written chapters, this book has emerged from a unified program of research and analysis. In a very real sense every member of the research team is a coauthor.

We are indebted to the people who spoke with us and opened their communities and homes to us in El Salvador, Peru, Washington, and Paterson. In El Salvador, we are especially grateful to Miguel Cavada, Noé Pérez, and Rosa Consuelo Acevedo. In Peru, we thank Teófilo Altamirano, Manuel Marzal, Catalina Romero, and José Sánchez at the Catholic University, and María Rosa Lorbés and the staff of the Instituto Bartolomé de las Casas. In the Washington area, Margarita Roque, the Capuchin Franciscans at Sacred Heart, and Fathers Francisco González and René Maldonado helped us enormously. And in New Jersey, thanks are due to Rev. Ezequiel Romero and to Fathers Peter Napoli, Gilberto Gutiérrez, and Luis Rendón. At the Pew Charitable Trusts, which provided the major funding for this project, we thank Edith Blumhofer and Luis Lugo. The Center for Latin American Studies at the University of Florida also provided support in the form of funding for our conference in March 1998. The center and the departments of religion and political science also supported graduate assistants, who deserve mention for their many contributions: Rony Behringer, Lisa Breglia, Vilma Fuentes, Mike Kenney, Marie Friedmann Marquardt, and Joann Sazama. We are also indebted to the efficient and patient work of many other people at the University of Florida, particularly Carmen Myers, Terry McCoy, and Charles Wood in the Center for Latin American Studies; Hazel Phillips, Marty Swilley, Debbie Wallen, and Les Thiele in the department of political science; and Julia Smith, Azim Nanji, and Shelly Isenberg in the department of religion. Numerous friends and colleagues at the University of Florida and elsewhere read drafts of chapters, spoke with us, participated in the conference, and otherwise helped us sharpen and clarify our thinking. In particular, we are grateful to Ed Cleary and Tony Oliver-Smith and to the participants in the conference at the University of Florida: Anna Adams, Phillip Berryman, Kathryn Burns, Carol Ann Drogus, Helen Rose Ebaugh, Orlando Espín, Rowan Ireland, Elizabeth Jelín, Peggy Levitt, Andy Orta, Miguel Ramos, Helen Safa, Dick Shaull, and Hal Stahmer. We must also thank colleagues at Wesleyan University, especially those at the Center for the Americas and the department of religion. Finally, thanks to Carmen Myers and Vilma Fuentes for their assistance in translating chapters 2, 4, 5, and 6.

Christianity, Social Change, and Globalization

Map by James Sloan

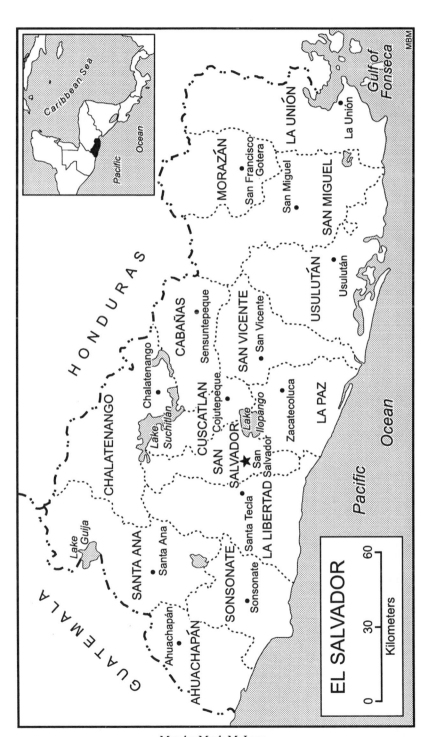

Map by Mark McLean

Anna Peterson, Manuel Vásquez, and Philip Williams

Introduction

Christianity and Social Change in the Shadow of Globalization

Christianity wears many faces in Latin America and U.S. Latino communities today: Pentecostal preachers in central plazas and black-robed priests in cavernous cathedrals, peasants leading "celebrations of the word," and teenagers singing rock-and-roll anthems to Christ. Amidst this diversity, certain common themes are evident. First, religion is changing but not disappearing. Greater religious pluralism has not led to secularization or religion's retreat from public life. If anything, religion has become more central to struggles around collective and individual identity and to the rearticulation of damaged civil societies. Second, while pluralism has challenged established religious institutions and elites, especially in the Catholic Church, it has also provided additional resources that help people manage severe crises in personal identity, in family stability, in neighborhood well-being, and in national civic life. Many of these crises are sparked or exacerbated by globalizing processes in economics, politics, and culture. As these pressures are felt in everyday life, people often turn to an increasingly diverse religious sphere. This book explores some of the complex links between religion and contemporary cultural, economic, and political changes in the Americas.

Recent History of Religion and Social Change in the Americas

The roots of our study of religion in Pan-American perspective lie in the transformation of Catholicism in the wake of the Second Vatican Council (1962–1965) and the follow-up meeting of the Latin American Bishops'

1

Conference (CELAM) in Medellín, Colombia, in 1968. Vatican II and its aftermath wrought profound changes in societies where the church was a major influence, including Latin America and U.S. Latino communities. The Council generated a wave of new Catholic pastoral and theological initiatives and also helped pave the way for growing religious diversity.

Perhaps most notably, Vatican II and the Medellín meeting gave rise to the popular church *(iglesia popular)*, a series of initiatives at all levels, from parishes to national and regional episcopacies. Its best-known aspects were liberation theology, a progressive rereading of the Bible and church doctrine, and grassroots Christian communities *(comunidades eclesiales de base,* or CEBs), neighborhood groups that read the Bible in light of their own experiences and, in many cases, mobilized for local improvements or social justice. At its 1979 meeting in Puebla, Mexico, CELAM outlined the "preferential option for the poor," which made people at the margins of society the locus for theology and pastoral work. Many Catholic activists, including prophetic bishops like El Salvador's Oscar Romero and Brazil's Dom Helder Camara, guerrilla priests like Colombia's Camilo Torres, and tens of thousands of ordinary women and men, directly confronted repressive governments (and sometimes died for their trouble). In many cases, progressive Catholics were the only significant critics of repression and the only defenders of its victims. Throughout Latin America, church initiatives sought to mitigate the effects of injustice, to provide space for the development of citizenship skills and the exercise of democratic processes, or to embody visions of a new society.

Progressive Catholic initiatives in El Salvador first emerged in the late 1960s, mainly in the archdiocese of San Salvador and rural areas such as Morazán and Chalatenango. In the face of growing political mobilization and government repression throughout the 1970s, Catholic activists developed ties to social movements and had a significant influence upon the political opposition, including the armed Frente Farabundo Martí para la Liberación Nacional (Farabundo Martí Front for National Liberation, FMLN). After Oscar Romero became archbishop of San Salvador in early 1977, a significant sector of the church "adopted a position of prophetic denunciation, speaking out against the military regime's human rights abuses and in support of far-reaching social transformation" (Williams 1997, 184). Many Salvadorans applauded Romero's public pronouncements, but economic elites and leaders in the government and military viewed progressive Catholics as "subversives." Against the backdrop of increasing political polarization, the government military and rightist paramilitary groups killed thousands of layworkers and nearly two dozen priests and nuns, including Archbishop Romero, between 1977 and 1989.[1]

Progressive Catholicism also flourished in Peru, with substantial support from the church hierarchy. In addition to the archbishop of Lima, Cardinal Juan Landázuri Ricketts, a number of bishops supported innovative pastoral programs, including the formation of CEBs and the training of rural lay leaders, and were outspoken on issues of human rights and social justice. The emergence of progressive Catholicism in Peru coincided with the reformist military regime of General Velasco Alvarado (1968–1975). During this period, many church leaders supported the reforms implemented by Velasco, while some local clergy encouraged parishioners to become active in popular movements linked to the left. When Velasco was replaced by a group of more conservative officers in 1975, many of the bishops distanced themselves from the government. Moreover, grassroots Catholic groups played an instrumental role in mobilizing opposition to the Morales Bermúdez regime (1975–1980).[2]

Thirty years after Medellín, the concrete achievements of progressive Catholicism generate debates among its adherents as well as its critics. On the one hand, liberationist Catholicism has profoundly shaped popular culture and politics throughout the region, including major political parties in settings as diverse as Brazil (the Workers' Party) and Nicaragua (the Sandinistas), as well as social movements and guerrilla organizations. The popular church also transformed Catholic ritual, theology, and ethics, making social justice and human rights central themes in all levels of church discourse, among moderates and conservatives as well as liberationists. Further, and perhaps most pervasively, CEBs and other progressive initiatives generated major shifts in laypersons' participation in and perceptions of the church. As a result, even the conservative initiatives of the late 1990s link doctrine to everyday life, encourage reading of the Bible, and prioritize lay education and leadership.

Progressive Catholic programs and concerns have spread well beyond Latin America. For instance, immigrants fleeing political violence in places like El Salvador and Guatemala sometimes inspired U.S. churches to adopt their own preferential option for the poor, often in direct opposition to U.S. foreign policy, as the experience of the sanctuary movement shows. Other, arguably more direct, connections between Latin American progressive Catholicism and churches in the United States include the adoption of CEBs as the central pastoral strategy to reach Latinos by the National Conference of Catholic Bishops and the emergence of Latino theologies that build explicitly on the insights of liberation theology (NCCB 1988; Elizondo 1983; Goizueta 1995).

Despite these successes, progressive Catholicism managed to institutionalize its goals in only a few places, most notably Brazil. Even there, current trends in the episcopacy, among other factors, threaten progressive initiatives. In El Salvador and Nicaragua, revolutionary Christians today are subdued and dispersed in the wake of growing conservatism in Rome and in their national hierarchies. Pope John Paul II's "conservative restoration" (Della Cava 1992) has, in Latin America, taken the form of the New Evangelization *(Nueva Evangelización)*, officially launched at the 1992 Santo Domingo meeting of Latin American bishops (Hennelly 1993; Peterson and Vásquez 1998). In the New Evangelization, spiritually oriented, clerically centered movements such as the Charismatic Renewal, the Neocatechumenate, and Opus Dei have replaced CEBs as pastoral priorities. To reinforce these pastoral trends, John Paul has undermined progressive bishops by moving them to obscure dioceses and replacing retirees with conservatives. Today, Catholic leaders speak more of "inculturation" and "a new civilization of love" than of liberation or the struggle to build the reign of God. A major exception is the state of Chiapas, Mexico, where recently retired Bishop Samuel Ruíz has been linked to popular movements for indigenous autonomy, land reform, and democratization. Ruíz's successor appears likely to continue his progressive approach.

The conservative restoration has made significant inroads in the Salvadoran and Peruvian churches. A dramatic symbol of the changes in the Salvadoran church is John Paul's naming of Fernando Saenz Lacalle, an Opus Dei member and a former military chaplain, as archbishop of San Salvador. In Peru, the pope replaced progressive bishops with conservative, noncontroversial ones. After stepping down in 1990, Cardinal Landázuri was succeeded by the conservative Augusto Vargas Alzamora, who in turn was replaced in 1998 by Juan Luis Cipriani, a member of Opus Dei. In both El Salvador and Peru, conservative bishops weakened the church's commitment to CEBs and social projects, focusing more on personal moral issues and questions of Catholic orthodoxy. Catholic pastoral workers seek to strengthen the church as an institution while also attending to urgent social problems.

Progressive Catholicism faces challenges from outside as well as within the church. Throughout the region, the secular left is experiencing a crisis of identity and participation. The 1990 electoral defeat of the Sandinistas in Nicaragua marks this crisis most dramatically, although it can also be seen in the continued isolation of Cuba and the failure of the parliamentary left, in Brazil and elsewhere, to win national elections. Revolutionary movements also face a crossroads. In Peru, the once-powerful Sendero Luminoso (Shining Path) and the MRTA (Tupac Amaru Revolutionary Movement), have suffered significant military defeats and become increasingly disconnected from the general population. The military stalemate in El Salvador ended with a negotiated peace in 1992, according to which the FMLN laid down arms and entered the electoral process. While the relation between the popular church and the secular left in Latin America has never been unproblematic, many Catholic activists in the 1960s and 1970s supported and drew inspiration from revolutionary movements, and the current crisis of the left forces progressive Catholics to rethink their goals and strategies (Vásquez 1998).

The crisis in the Latin American left is paralleled by the demise of military regimes and transitions to civilian rule throughout the region. Civil society has expanded, offering spaces for new social actors to stake their claims. Within this context, "new social movements" addressing local and neighborhood improvement, the environment, and identity have emerged throughout the Americas. These movements press the state for a decentralization of power and also challenge traditional opposition actors such as trade unions, leftist political parties, and the Catholic Church. Some progressive Catholics feel threatened by a shift away from class-based movements and toward everyday life concerns. Others, however, seek to integrate these concerns with their commitment to social justice. Many new social movements retain strong religious bases, but their affiliations are likely to be diverse, encompassing not only Catholicism but also Pentecostal Protestantism and African-based religions, among others.

Religious Pluralism

Religious pluralism in the Americas received a major boost from the internal diversification of Catholicism sparked by Vatican II. Transformations in Catholicism weakened the ties between church and economic and political elites, encouraged people to reflect on their religious choices and activities, and helped make it possible for diverse religious actors, both within and outside the church, to raise their profiles and expand their outreach activities. The most prominent of these new religious actors are evangelical, especially Pentecostal, Protestants. Although Pentecostal churches have been active in the region since the first U.S. missionaries arrived in the 1910s, most growth has come since the 1950s. Perhaps because of the dramas associated with the rise of the iglesia popular, however, few scholars (with exceptions such as Lalive D'Epinay 1968 and Willems 1967) paid much attention to Protestantism in Latin America until around 1990. In separate books published that year, David Stoll and David Martin suggested that Latin America might be "turning Protestant" and that this transformation heralded significant cultural, economic, and political shifts.

In the past decade, however, Protestant growth has slowed, and few observers predict a Protestant majority in Latin America, at least in the foreseeable future. Currently, probably 10 to 15 percent of Latin America's population is Protestant, although in some countries, such as Guatemala, Protestants might constitute as much as one-third of the population. Protestant growth is also significant among U.S. Latinos, leading Andrew Greeley (1988, 1997) to contend that the "equivalent of one out of seven Hispanics has left Catholicism in a little more than a quarter of a century. The annual loss is approximately one half of one percent. If this hemorrhage should continue for the next 25 years, half of all American Hispanics will not be Catholic." This represents "the worst defection in the history of the Catholic Church in the United States."

In El Salvador and Peru, as in Latin America generally, Protestantism encompasses a wide range of institutional forms, liturgical styles, theological and ethical concerns, and social profiles. Both countries house various Pentecostal groups, mainline or historic Protestant denominations such as Methodists, Lutherans, and Baptists, and newer churches like the Mormons, Jehovah's Witnesses, and Seventh-Day Adventists.

In El Salvador, as in most of Latin America, most Protestant churches were founded by foreign (mostly North American) missionaries, who began arriving in the country in the early 1900s. Salvadoran Protestantism was quite small in scope and mostly rural until the 1960s, when the largest Pentecostal denomination, the Asambleas de Dios (Assemblies of God), began intense recruitment programs in San Salvador. Throughout the 1960s and especially the 1970s, the Asambleas and other Pentecostal churches grew steadily, quickly surpassing the mainline churches. By the late 1980s, Protestants accounted for between 15 and 20 percent of the total population, three-quarters of them Pentecostal (Coleman et al. 1993).[3]

Most of Peru's Protestant churches were also established by foreign missionaries. Two of the most important early denominations were the Methodists and Adventists. The Methodists began work in Peru in 1889 and played a significant role in creating alternative educational opportunities, especially for women (Martin 1990). The Adventists concentrated on converting Andean communities while improving their basic educational and health infrastructure. With increasing migration to urban areas in the 1950s, other denominations became more important. The Assemblies of God experienced phenomenal growth during the 1970s and 1980s, catapulting it from the third to first largest denomination in the country. The Iglesia Evangélica Peruana (Peruvian Evangelical Church, IEP) was established in 1922 as a result of the efforts of a group of Scottish Presbyterian missionaries. In the IEP, as in the Assemblies of God, church administration eventually was taken over by Peruvian pastors. The Alianza Cristiana y Misionera (Christian Missionary Alliance, ACM) emerged from a split with the IEP during the 1950s to establish an independent denomination. Whereas the social composition of the Assemblies of God and IEP is largely working and lower-middle class, the ACM has concentrated its efforts mostly toward attracting middle- and lower-middle-class Peruvians. Over the last two decades, the Assemblies of God and the ACM have grown rapidly, the IEP more moderately (Kamsteeg 1991; Martin 1990). Today, about 7 percent of Peru's population is Protestant (INEI 1993).[4]

In the 1990s, much of the scholarly and journalistic energy previously directed toward transformations in the Catholic Church turned to the growth of Protestantism. Some observers insisted that evangelical Protestantism was inherently conservative, insofar as it encouraged believers to turn attention inward and upward and to reject participation in the "worldly" and therefore corrupt public sphere. Others, notably David Martin, saw evangelicalism as a harbinger of capitalism, democracy, and "peaceableness" in corporatist, authoritarian, and violent Latin American cultures.

More recent work has suggested an ambiguous role for Protestantism and has insisted on viewing Pentecostalism alongside other important religious developments, including the revitalization of African-based and indigenous traditions and the growing appeal of new-age religions. These seemingly disparate, competing religions share a focus on the reconstitution and redemption of the self. This is no small matter in an increasingly baffling and threatening world. As Alberto Melucci writes, we live "in a planetary society" in which "the accelerated pace of change, the multiplicity of roles assumed by the individual, the deluge of messages that wash over us and expand our cognitive and affective experience" are unprecedented. In this context, Melucci continues, "The points of reference used by individuals and groups to plot their life courses are disappearing. Answering the basic question 'Who am I?' becomes progressively more difficult. . . . The search for a safe haven for the self becomes an increasingly critical undertaking, and the individual must build and continuously rebuild her/his 'home' in the face of the surging flux of events and relations" (Melucci 1996, 2).

Part of the success of Pentecostalism and other non-Catholic religions may stem from their ability to provide this sort of "safe haven" from the fragmentation and confusion facing individuals and local communities, as early studies emphasized (Lalive D'Epinay 1968; Willems 1967). Congregational religions, in particular, offer institutional structures, practices, and narratives that help individuals navigate economic difficulties, sickness, and domestic troubles.

In the United States, parallel dynamics emerge in the therapeutic, individualistic emphasis of many religions, including Pentecostalism, which is especially powerful among marginalized Latino, African American, and rural white communities. Allan Deck (1995, 471, 469) argues that Latinos seek to "free themselves from the hierarchical, strongly communal, rural, traditional social and family structure, a system that seems more and more dysfunctional in the new circumstances of immigrant life in the United States." Pentecostalism provides a "more self-conscious, individualized faith," which dovetails with the "stress on human autonomy, mobility, personal freedom, and human rights" they face in the United States. In addition, as Leon (1998) writes, being "born again" helps many Latinos, especially young people, break with a past that might have included domestic violence, drugs, gangs, and political disenfranchisement. As we discuss later, the issue of gangs shows how religious and social life among U.S. Latinos is increasingly connected with reality in Latin America and how neither can be understood without an inter-American approach to religion and social change. The evolution of Pentecostalism provides signs of our globalized time: a religion founded by U.S. missionaries becomes indigenized and then travels back to North America with Latin American immigrants fleeing the political violence and economic dislocation of the 1970s and 1980s. Transformed yet again, Latino Pentecostalism returns to Latin America, as immigrant churches send their own missionaries to Latin America to start sister congregations in their sending communities (Garrard-Burnett 1998b).

Globalization as Contemporary Context

Contemporary religious life in the Americas must be understood in the context of globalization, in all its economic, political, and cultural dimensions. The current round of economic globalization in the Americas emerged as import substitution industrialization (ISI), which guided postwar development policy up until the late 1970s, gave way in the wake of the debt crisis to a technology-driven neoliberal capitalism. ISI stressed the importance of national markets, albeit connected to a capitalist world-system through tariffs and trade regulations. In contrast, the new economic order seeks integration into global markets through a laissez-faire approach opposed to protectionist measures. In this context, export-driven trading blocs, such as NAFTA and Mercosur have become central in the Americas.

These economic changes have had significant and often negative implications for everyday life, especially for poor people. In efforts to increase competitiveness in the globalized economy, the new economic policies have sought to deregulate and open local markets. The underlying logic here is that the sheer force of global competition will weed out ineffective, wasteful, and corrupt enterprises, leaving the national economies more streamlined and rationalized, capable of turning profits that will then trickle down through society. Politically, the deregulation of markets has meant the downsizing of the state, particularly welfare programs, now seen as wasteful and subject to patrimonial politics. The curtailment of welfare programs, together with the relative decline of the industrial sector and austerity measures like wage freezes and the devaluation of national currencies, has had a social cost, evinced by increases in poverty and inequality indices in many countries, including Peru and El Salvador (CEPAL 1992). Globalization also erodes the capacity of nation-states to control processes within their own borders. The increasing circulation of goods, capital, people, and ideas across national boundaries intensifies not only pluralism but also displacement and anomie.

Economic, political, and cultural globalization also affects U.S. Latinos, including both new and more established communities. The current period of economic expansion in the United States has been accompanied by a visible deterioration of the manufacturing sector, where many Latinos, particularly Puerto Ricans and Mexican Americans, found employment after World War II. Parallel to this decline has been the rapid growth of a service sector sharply divided between a small core of highly paid and highly educated workers in technology-intensive firms and a much larger group of "peripheral" workers, subject to job insecurity and low wages. Many recent Latino immigrants have entered this peripheral, subordinate part of the service sector, working as maids, nannies, gardeners, and laborers in *maquilas* and construction industries (Sassen 1998). With little hope for economic advancement and faced with persistent racism and declining public aid, many Latinos, like poor Latin Americans, turn to local, informal self-help initiatives to ensure personal and family survival.

In this context, churches have become critical resource centers. In the United States, both Democrats and Republicans have endorsed "faith-based" initiatives to mitigate the effects of welfare reform. Similar trends can be seen throughout the Americas, as child care centers, after-school programs, soup kitchens, and *comedores populares* (meal programs) form a precarious safety net which draws heavily on church resources, spaces, and personnel. Churches function as flexible networks of mutual aid, where poor people not only receive charity but also pool their resources and draw from institutional supports. These range from physical space to job referrals to the initial credit and vocational training for the poor to start their own micro-enterprises. In addition, some scholars have argued that evangelical churches "domesticate" Latin American men, encouraging them to spend their resources on family maintenance rather than gambling, drinking, and womanizing (Brusco 1995; L. Gill 1990; Mariz 1994). Among U.S. Latinos, Leon (1998) has observed how religion helps young men and women "take control of their lives" and "progress" spiritually, symbolically, and materially. As poor women and children have been among the sectors most severely affected by economic restructuring in both the United States and Latin America, these benefits cannot be ignored when making sense of the predominantly young and female face of grassroots evangelical churches. In sum, churches have proved to be an important resource for negotiating the changing challenges posed by economic pressures well beyond state control.

Women, Family, and Local Communities

Globalizing processes are often felt dramatically at the local level, where people must negotiate their effects by drawing from their cultural and religious resources. To make sense of their efforts, we must attend to the religious ideas and values that are embedded in the everyday lives of families and local communities. The chief actors in these local experiences are women, who have long formed the majority of most Catholic and Protestant congregations, in Latin America and among U.S. Latinos. However, scholars have only recently paid serious attention to the reasons for and consequences of this female presence. Recent studies have highlighted the ambivalence of religion's impact upon women and also of women's influence on the churches (Brusco 1995; Drogus 1997a, 1997b; Griffith 1997). Our research deepens these insights, showing religion's simultaneous potential to liberate women and to reinforce oppressive patterns of patriarchy, to generate solidarity and to tear apart families and communities.

The primary role of women in the religious traditions we studied paralleled and shaped the centrality of the family as a topic of concern and a unit of religious participation. For progressive Catholicism, the family and the married couple constitute, at least in theory, the fundamental unit of participation in base communities and other pastoral projects. Many CEBs, for example, began with *cursillos* (courses) open not to individuals but only to married couples, and many of the themes of discussion in cursillos and retreats focused on married and family life. Some scholars (especially Burdick 1993a) have criticized progressive Catholic interpretations of irresponsible male behavior in relation to social inequities, so that alcoholism, for example, is seen as partly a response to poverty and lack of opportunity. We found that progressive Catholics do link individual behavior and structural problems more often than Pentecostals, but also that many CEBs and progressive parishes provided as much support for women and men struggling with domestic problems and personal weaknesses as did their Pentecostal counterparts (Williams and Fuentes 2000).

Neither Catholic Charismatics nor Pentecostals display much interest in the social and economic sources of and solutions to family problems. The Charismatic Renewal and other conservative movements in Catholicism, however, remain grounded in the Catholic Church's corporatist tradition of social thought. Marriage and family, in this light, are crucial elements in the improvement of society as a whole, and, in turn, married couples and parents must direct their domestic lives to contribute to the common good. A purely privatistic vision of family life, in other words, has no place in any variant of the Catholic tradition. In contrast, Pentecostalism does not explicitly direct families to contribute to the common good. The latter is at best a by-product of the righteous lives of believers, as they enact the outward signs of personal salvation. Discipline, order, and piety in the family, as in the individual, serve precisely to distinguish believers from the chaos and sinfulness of *las cosas del mundo,* the worldly things, which will pass away.

The discipline and order of the family in Pentecostalism emerges from the emphasis on patriarchal authority in both the home and the church. The notion of the father as the caring but strict head of the household parallels the pastor's role as head of the church. The reinforcement of the nuclear family, in fact, is central to the vision (and the success) of Pentecostal churches throughout the Americas. In the face of disintegrating marriages, irresponsible husbands, and undisciplined children, Pentecostal churches often present appealing solutions: a place for each member of the family in an orderly, hierarchical, and stable structure, supported and mirrored by the church itself, and sharply opposed to the corrupt outside world. This contrasts with the mainline Protestant churches, which take a less sectarian approach to the outside world, often sharing the progressive Catholic tendency to link private and social problems. In both the United States and Latin America, the mainline churches emphasize the family the least of all the traditions we studied. It is worth exploring further whether this relative lack of emphasis on family matters has contributed to mainline Protestantism's crisis of participation in the United States and to its slower growth rates in comparison with Pentecostalism in Latin America and among Latinos.

Political Participation and Democratization

The wave of democratic transitions in Latin America during the 1980s brought hopes of stable democracies and expanded economic opportunities. At the end of the 1990s however, this optimism all but evaporated. Instead of solid democracies, most of the region's governments today are "incomplete" or "delegative" democracies (O'Donnell 1994), with powerful presidents, weak parties, and low citizen participation. Further, political transitions have occurred alongside economic restructuring in a process of "democracy with adjustment" (Jelín 1996a), which excludes much of the population. Guillermo O'Donnell (1993, 1361) calls this "low-intensity citizenship: A situation in which one can vote freely and have one's vote counted fairly, but cannot expect proper treatment from the police or the courts." Governments have abandoned socioeconomic rights in favor of political and civil rights. However, even recent progress in expanding political rights has often occurred in the face of widespread violations of civil rights.

While not subject to the authoritarian traditions of much of Latin America, the United States has also witnessed growing concern and debate about the health of American democracy and communal life (Bellah et al. 1985, 1992; Putnam 2000). Even amidst national prosperity, many sectors of U.S. society are excluded from meaningful political and economic participation. This is especially true for U.S. Latinos, who continue to experience a combination of low median family incomes and steep high school dropout rates. For example, in the Washington, D.C., area, where many Salvadorans have concentrated, Latinos have a median family income of $37,618, far lower than whites ($52,837) and Asian Americans ($46,430). Only African Americans have a lower income ($33,568). Latinos, however, fare far worse when it comes to education: 21.3 percent aged twenty-five or older have less than a ninth-grade education, compared to 8.1 percent of Asian Americans, who have the second highest percentage (Bates and Hall 1995). To the lack of economic and cultural capital, we can add the rise of technocratic policy making, the decline of trade unions, growing disillusionment with political parties and elections, and the dismantling of the welfare state to the list of factors that have widened the gap between government and citizens in the United States as well as south of its borders (Conaghan and Malloy 1994).

Within this new political landscape, religious movements have only a limited capacity to strengthen democracy. Progressive Catholicism played an instrumental role in weakening military regimes, but its influence has diminished in the wake of democratic transitions. In most cases, elites dominated the transitions to civilian rule and limited changes to establishing more open, pluralistic political institutions rather than sweeping socioeconomic transformations. In light of current conditions, some scholars have pointed out that even progressive Catholics, as well as evangelical Protestants, increasingly focus on local and everyday life issues. For example, proponents of liberation theology today are less inclined to speak of structural transformation and more likely to embrace pastoral approaches that focus on local community issues: drugs, gang violence, street children, family disintegration, domestic abuse, and inadequate local services. Even those who continue to insist on the need for structural change often believe that such change has to begin at the local level.

A local, even mundane focus does not mean that religion fails to contribute to the public realm. Numerous observers have pointed out religion's capacity "to foster patterns of civility in the actions of citizens in a democratic polity," as Alexis de Tocqueville recognized 150 years ago (Foley and Edwards 1996, 39). Building on Tocqueville's insights, Robert Bellah and colleagues (1985) described the "habits of the heart," including religious beliefs and practices, that can encourage cooperation and civic engagement in American life, although in other situations religion reinforces individualism and withdrawal. Scholars of religion in Latin America have highlighted religion's contributions to bonds of solidarity and trust, which in turn "lays a basis for broader arrangements of civic engagement, giving substance to the very notion of 'civil society'" (Levine and Stoll 1997, 74). However, bridging the gap between empowerment and power is a long-term process: the link between local religion and more inclusive and democratic national societies remains an open question.

El Salvador and Peru exemplify, with important variations, the severe economic inequities and political closure that have hampered democratic governance throughout the Americas. Both countries also illuminate the crucial role of churches in movements to change these conditions. In El Salvador, a number of militant opposition movements, many with close ties to progressive Catholics, emerged in the 1970s to challenge the power of military and economic elites. Religious as well as secular opposition activists and programs faced fierce retaliation by the Salvadoran government and military beginning in the mid-1970s. By the early 1980s, a full-fledged civil war was raging and political violence, ranging from individual death-squad killings to aerial bombings and massacres of entire villages, seemed to define Salvadoran society. The civil war continued until 1992, when United Nations–sponsored peace talks, made possible in part by a powerful guerrilla offensive in November 1989, led to a negotiated settlement between the government and the FMLN. The peace accords not only guaranteed a cease-fire but also provided for the transformation of the Salvadoran armed forces, the creation of a civilian police force, the incorporation of combatants into civilian life, limited economic reforms, and greater political openness, including the conversion of the FMLN into a legal political party. While the accords wrought very real changes in Salvadoran society, today the country still suffers from severe economic inequities, poverty, and elite domination of politics (Bird and Williams 2000; Montgomery 1995). It also suffers from widespread violence (much of it committed by former soldiers), perhaps at greater levels than during the war (DeCesare 1998). The lack of employment opportunities for the thousands of young men left jobless by the war's end, combined with a fragile judicial system, the wide availability of weapons, and the presence of transnational gangs, make it unsurprising that El Salvador now has the highest per capita homicide rate in the hemisphere. This leads some Salvadorans to look back on the war years as better, in some ways, than the troubled peace of the present.

One of the most important effects of the war was the massive displacement of Salvadorans from their homes, encompassing about a fifth of the national population. Most refugees were rural residents, many of whom went to nearby urban areas or to refugee camps in Honduras. Many other Salvadorans moved to the United States, including some peasants but also many urban residents, often opposition activists fearing for their lives. During the late 1970s and 1980s, Salvadoran populations emerged in most major cities in the United States, notably New York, Los Angeles, San Francisco, and Washington, D.C. (Mahler 1995; Repak 1995). According to the 1990 census, there were more than half a million Salvadorans in the United States, up from about 100,000 in 1980. Although reliable estimates are difficult to obtain, Repak estimates the Salvadoran population in the greater Washington, D.C., metropolitan area at more than 100,000, making it the second highest urban concentration of Salvadoran immigrants in the United States.

Massive out-migration has altered Salvadoran society almost as much as the war which prompted it. Migration has continued even since the war's end, due largely to hopes of economic improvement. For example, *remesas,* the money Salvadoran émigrés send back to their families, constitute the nation's largest source of foreign capital, surpassing coffee and other export crops. Virtually all the Salvadorans we surveyed, from middle-class residents of San Salvador to *campesinos* in Morazán, had at least one relative living abroad. El Salvador has become a fully transnational society, with a continual flow of people, ideas, money, and goods across borders.

Like El Salvador, Peru has faced prolonged political violence and economic instability. After military rule gave way to a democratically elected civilian government in 1980, deepening economic crisis led to growing frustration. Frustrated with the inability of traditional political parties to solve the country's most pressing problems, Peruvians in 1990 turned to a political unknown, Alberto Fujimori, in what some saw as a last desperate attempt to stave off total breakdown. Fujimori took office in the context of hyperinflation and a growing threat from the Sendero Luminoso guerrilla movement. During his first year in office, and contrary to his campaign promises, Fujimori implemented a draconian shock therapy program and joined his counterparts elsewhere in the region in embracing neoliberal economics. In the face of growing challenges from opposition parties in the legislature, Fujimori shut down the Congress in April 1992 and suspended the constitution. The "self-coup" *(auto golpe)* enabled Fujimori to intensify his structural adjustment program and his offensive against Sendero Luminoso. By the end of 1992, inflation was brought under control, and in the following year the economy began to grow again, even experiencing some of the highest growth rates in Latin America between 1994 and 1995. Finally, the capture of Sendero's top leader, Abimael Guzmán, in September 1992 resulted in a significant decline in political violence, especially in

Lima, where Sendero had established a firm foothold. Not surprisingly, Fujimori was reelected in 1995 with overwhelming support (Cameron 1997; Crabtree and Thomas 1998; McClintock 1993). The 1980s and the first half of the 1990s produced significant social dislocation in the country (Dietz 1998; Palmer 1992). The political violence perpetrated by the Shining Path was matched by a brutal government counterinsurgency campaign, especially in mountain regions such as Ayacucho. The violence fueled massive migration to urban areas, especially Lima's sprawling *pueblos jóvenes* (shantytowns; literally, "young towns"). By the early 1990s, Lima's poor districts were bursting at the seams. The increasing influx of migrants stretched the city's already inadequate infrastructure to its limits. Life in these districts was characterized by growing levels of violent crime, deteriorating infrastructure, lack of basic services, high levels of unemployment, housing shortages, pollution, and the growth of infectious diseases. While the war's intensity has diminished since the capture of Guzmán, continuing political repression and uncertainty, along with the harsh economic effects of structural adjustment policies on the poor, have led Peruvians to leave the country in record numbers. Teófilo Altamirano (1992) estimates the Peruvian population in Paterson, New Jersey, the oldest and most established in North America, at thirty thousand.

In the context of structural adjustment and political violence, popular movements and political parties in general have lost influence, if not collapsed altogether. Cameron (1997, 42) argues that the crisis of the formal economy and growth of the informal sector "undermined partisan loyalties, broke the tenuous linkages between parties and civil society, interrupted the traditional channels of communication between ruling elites and masses, and weakened the class cleavage by reducing the militancy of workers, undermining organization, and inhibiting collective action." Increasingly, poor Peruvians have become less inclined to believe the government would respond to public demonstrations or state-directed petitions. Consequently, many have turned to individual and family-based survival strategies or to new clientelistic networks established under Fujimori. Others have looked to their local church for direction and support.

Experiences in Peru and El Salvador, as elsewhere in Latin America, underline the fact that democratization requires not just the creation and consolidation of institutions and procedures but also a "culture of citizenship," as Elizabeth Jelín puts it (1996, 102). Religion plays a crucial role in this process of constructing moral, civil agents and strengthening bonds of solidarity. Progressive Catholicism and evangelical Protestantism may qualify as "new social movements," which are contesting and redrawing "the parameters of democracy . . . the very boundaries of what is properly defined as the political arena:

its participants, its institutions, its processes, its agenda, and its scope" (Alvarez, Dagnino, and Escobar 1998, 1). These movements suggest that the micro and the macro, the politics of everyday life and Politics with a capital *P*, are not two isolated, reified levels of social action. Rather, recent social-movement theorists use terms like *web* and *network* to suggest the diversity and multiplicity of linkages at various overlapping levels. Within the specific levels and in the links between them, religious organizations play vital roles.

Despite their potential contributions, religious movements face real limitations in fostering a culture of citizenship. For Pentecostalism, the ever-present tension between the things of the world and the things of God, sectarianism, and intra-ecclesial socioeconomic stratification made sustained, large-scale mobilization difficult (Garrard-Burnett 1998a). Even progressive Catholics vary in their willingness to assume responsibilities outside the church, with many declining to participate outside their parish. These experiences temper the optimistic belief of some theorists that the weblike nature of new movements can break their provincialism and transitory nature. It is also possible that religious movements are different (and necessarily more parochial) than their secular counterparts, privileged in the recent literature. At a minimum, religious movements can provide their members with important religious resources to help them make sense of and develop strategies for action in response to the challenges of everyday life. While such small steps may not produce the next great social revolution, they are nonetheless important, insofar as they constitute what Jelín (1998a, 66) refers to as an *"infrapolitics of the voiceless*, through which dignity and a sense of community are constructed."

Religion, Globalization, and Transnationalism

A principal effect of globalization has been the production of immigrant diasporas, which, while living in the host country, continue to sustain links with their home societies. Out of this diasporic condition emerges a "new conception of nation-state [that] includes as citizens those who live physically dispersed within the boundaries of many other states, but who remain socially, politically, culturally, and often economically part of the nation-state of their ancestors" (Basch et al. 1994, 8). As we discuss below, the "in-betweenness" experienced by many immigrants challenges fixed notions of nationhood and citizenship. This can fuel democratizing movements such as the pro-Aristide movement, which received widespread support from Haiti's "Tenth Department," the Haitian community in the United States (Basch et al. 1994, 210–224). Thus, in many instances it may be more useful to speak of "multiple citizenship" (Heater 1990) or "transnational citizenship."

The path toward a "postnational society" (Habermas 1996, 492–493), however, is not linear. In the United States and Europe, for example, movements are growing to restrict immigration and to exclude immigrants from the benefits of full membership in the political community. These struggles over the limits of citizenship in an increasingly globalized world are of great concern to U.S. Latinos, who have migrated north in greater numbers as a result of recurrent economic and political instability in Latin America since the 1960s. As Latinos create thriving and increasingly diverse communities in virtually all parts of the United States, new nativist movements have emerged, seeking to deny Latinos full membership in the national political community. This is illustrated more dramatically by the passage of Proposition 187 in California and the spread of the English-only movement (Perea 1997). Even Latinos who are U.S.-born citizens, as Flores (1997, 254) argues, "have been treated as second-class or third-class citizens." Faced with this challenge, Latino immigrants adopt a variety of strategies in developing a sense of belonging, and their religious organizations shape the ways in which they imagine their communities. They may help create a multicultural or pan-Latino identity, or they might reinforce national identities within a broader transnational field. Because of their simultaneous local focus and transnational character, churches are well suited to dealing with the dislocation and fragmentation produced by globalization. Churches can help open up possibilities for a robust "transnational civil society" (Rudolph and Piscatori 1997) rooted on notions of self and citizenship much richer than neoliberalism's *Homo oeconomicus*.

Civil society is also changed as a result of the altered experiences of immigrants. New technology has enabled immigrants to maintain strong connections with their places of origin and to resist assimilation into the "melting pot." Salvadorans and Peruvians, like many other recent immigrants, remain connected to and have influences upon their sending societies at the same time they adapt to and help transform their receiving communities. They are living transnational lives and building transnational societies. As Portes, Guarnizo, and Landolt (1999) define it, transnationalism encompasses activities and occupations that require a high volume of regular and sustained contacts over time across two or more national boundaries. These activities may include business networks, the political activities of national governments and nongovernmental organizations (NGOs), as well as sociocultural diffusions that involve the articulation of ethnic and national identities abroad. These activities may come from above, through the operation of institutional and corporate actors like multinational and multilateral organizations, or from below, as migrants and their family and community networks seek to manage their dual lives day by day.

Grassroots forms of transnationalism pose serious challenges to nation-states, insofar as the latter rely on images of a unified community with an overarching culture in a bounded geographical space. Latin American governments have responded with institutional initiatives designed to tap into potential economic and political benefits of transnational communities. Thus the frequent visits of former Salvadoran President Armando Calderón Sol to Mount Pleasant in Washington, D.C., and Dominican leader Leonel Fernández to Jackson Heights, New York. El Salvador is a particularly illustrative example here: Salvadorans abroad send $1.2 billion annually, a figure by far larger than what the country earns through coffee exports. This money has mitigated the social cost of—and thus reduced opposition to—neoliberal economic policies implemented by conservative administrations. The growth in transnational populations has also led some countries, including Colombia, Peru, and Mexico, to permit "brothers and sisters in foreign lands" (*hermanos y hermanas en el extranjero*) to vote and run for office in local elections.

Because of their liminality, however, transnational migrants can sometimes escape the reach of nationalist projects and agendas. This does not necessarily lead to enhanced agency for immigrants, as they may experience not dual citizenship but "dual disenfranchisement." On the one hand, immigrants are not fully accepted in the United States, often living under the stigma of illegality, especially now at a time of widespread nativist sentiment. On the other hand, they no longer accept the persistent patrimonial politics in their sending countries, since they have learned new rules and adopted new roles to navigate U.S. society. In this process of negotiating change, adapting ideas and institutions, and constructing novel communities and identities, religious life plays a central role.

The Structure of the Book

The book is divided into three parts, beginning with "Women, Family, and Community." In chapter 1, Anna Peterson explores the complex relationship between religion and women's lives through oral histories from women in CEBs, the CCR, and Pentecostal and Lutheran congregations in San Salvador. On the basis of these data, she draws several conclusions. First, in El Salvador, as elsewhere in the Americas, women are the majority of members and perform most of the maintenance tasks, despite the fact that few churches ever address women's gender-specific concerns explicitly. Second, despite theological, pastoral, and organizational differences, in all instances religion plays a central role to the women's identity as women and citizens. Further, despite the general lack of attention to explicitly feminist issues in their churches, women find in their religious participation moral support, intellectual stimulation, and practical assistance that help them both in their personal lives and in their concern for women's social position more generally. Religion, then, is doubly embedded in everyday life for women: they perform the everyday work of the churches, and the churches enter into and transform their everyday lives in turn.

In chapter 2, Rosa Castro Aguilar explores the relationship between religious faith and new forms of family life among Peruvian Catholics. Drawing from the oral histories of Catholics in both urban and rural parishes, Castro highlights the growing pressures on the institution of marriage and the increased educational and employment opportunities for women. She also points to the growing gap between the values embedded in family life, especially solidarity and dialogue, and the consumerism and individualism reinforced by an increasingly globalized Peruvian society. Within this new landscape, Castro examines the ways that Catholicism contributes to new perceptions of self and the development of new values and styles of family life.

In chapter 3, Philip Williams outlines the ways that religion has contributed to the literal as well as metaphorical reconstruction of community in Yungay, an Andean town rebuilt in the wake of a devastating earthquake and avalanche in 1970. Prior to 1970, global forces of change had barely affected the traditional social relations and patterns of authority in Yungay. However, post-disaster reconstruction opened the way to a period of major social and religious transformation. Williams shows how the accelerated process of rural-urban migration, the agrarian reform program in the countryside, and the influx of foreign priests and religious all stimulated new pastoral initiatives that often conflicted with traditional approaches. In the context of these dramatic changes, local expressions of popular religion took on new and different forms, sometimes complicating the local church's efforts at community-building. Williams's exploration of the distinct pastoral approaches and expressions of popular religiosity that emerged during the reconstruction of Yungay highlights both the diversity within traditions and the interdenominational and sometimes international character of certain trends.

Part 2, which focuses on citizenship and political participation, begins with chapter 4, in which Hortensia Muñoz discusses the mobilization of Pentecostals for the founding of a *barrio popular* in Huaycán, Peru. Muñoz shows how social action is closely intertwined with the articulation of collective and individual identity among evangelicals, challenging the distinction made earlier between "new," identity-based actors and old, class-based ones. The construction of the new community in Huaycán drew evangelicals into the political arena and forced them to define themselves in relation to Catholics. As evangelicals made their presence felt, they challenged the automatic identification of Catholicism as the lingua franca in the public sphere, thus making religious difference an important variable in forging a unified neighborhood movement. Evangelicals also found that the exercise of citizenship—negotiations among competing projects and interests, including those of the left-wing municipal administration and of the Shining Path, in order to advance communal interests—was not always fully compatible with their religious identity.

Catholic theology and organizational style may have more affinities for social activism. This is suggested by Rosa Castro Aguilar in chapter 5, which documents how Peruvian Catholics in both urban and rural settings developed an expanded notion of family that came to include their local community. For many, "being Christian" implied not only church involvement but also a commitment to work for social justice, which propelled them to become active participants in an array of community-based organizations. This participation takes place in the context of the neoliberal emphasis on individual rights and the corresponding marginalization of many poor Peruvians. Castro documents the transformation of political culture among Peruvian Catholics who increasingly demand equal treatment and opportunities from public and private institutions even as they sometimes question the very legitimacy of political institutions.

In former war zones in El Salvador, diverse churches have contributed to repairing the fabric of civil society torn apart by the war, as Ileana Gómez shows in chapter 6. Gómez examines the political dimensions and implications of religious participation in Morazán province in eastern El Salvador, a major battleground in the civil war. Political repression during the late 1970s and 1980s virtually destroyed community life in Morazán, including the religious as well as economic and physical networks that had sustained rural life. Since the war's end, both Catholic and Pentecostal pastoral agents have been seeking, in different ways, to rebuild these systems. While Catholics often emphasize collective solidarity and economic development, many Pentecostals stress personal discipline and faith as the solution to social problems. Despite their differences, both Catholic and Pentecostal churches help "fill the void left by the still weak mechanisms of local social representation and helped strengthen these institutions, such as community directorates and peasant associations," Gómez concludes.

Part 3 focuses on globalization and transnationalism. In chapter 7, Larissa Ruíz Baía explores Peruvian Catholic lay brotherhoods (hermandades) in Paterson, New Jersey. The brotherhoods exemplify the enduring vitality of pre–Vatican II Catholicism, with their strong emphasis on devotion, preserving traditions, and maintaining hierarchical religious and social arrangements. However, the challenges of organizing the festivities outside Peru have led the brotherhoods to modify some key ritual aspects, like allowing women to carry the image of the saint during the annual procession. This in turn has altered the balance of power between men and women within the brotherhoods in North America and also in Peru as immigrants visit sister organizations in Lima. Ruíz Baía examines the various relations, formal and informal, institutional and personal, involved in forging transnational linkages. However, most important is how she problematizes the concept of transnationalism by pointing to the interpenetration of transnationalism, cosmopolitanism, and pan-ethnicity among Latino immigrants.

In chapter 8, Ileana Gómez and Manuel Vásquez examine the growth of transnational gangs, often associated with violence and organized crime, in El Salvador and in U.S. cities such as Washington. They interpret gangs as an attempt by young people to deal with the social dislocation produced by recent political and economic changes. More specifically, gangs enable young people to assert personal identity (through a subculture), locality (the neighborhood), and kinship (the extended family) over and against encroaching structural and systemic processes. The success of different churches in evangelizing gang members is predicated on their capacity to offer alternative ways for youth to negotiate the links between the personal, the local, and the global. These links are particularly tricky for young, second-generation Latinos, who are often "bifocal," as Roger Rouse (1991) puts it, dwelling simultaneously in two cultures.

Chapter 9 focuses on Catholic Charismatics in El Salvador and among Salvadorans in Washington, D.C. Manuel Vásquez and Anna Peterson see the CCR as incorporating several central features of Pentecostal Protestantism—including an emotive, intensely personal style of worship and the central role played by the Holy Spirit in healing and glossolalia—with a continuing, distinctive Catholic identity. The parallels to Pentecostalism may be especially strong in the United States, where Latino Catholics find themselves in an environment that sees success as issuing from a Protestant ethic. However, the CCR is not a mere copy of Pentecostalism. Most notably, Charismatics reject the dualism of much of Pentecostal theology. Rather than a sharp distinction between insiders and outsiders, the saved and the damned, the CCR focuses, in typical Catholic fashion, on an ongoing progression toward fuller involvement and knowledge. This process offers the distinctive resources of both rupture and continuity to women, immigrants, and others struggling to negotiate the challenges of globalization.

Numerous challenges face scholars of religion and society as well. In the final chapter, we outline some of the ongoing questions that future research on religion in the Americas might address. Some of these issues arise when we consider the common themes that link our case studies. One of the most important of these issues concerns linkages among different spatial levels, such as the local and the global. We also explore some of the difficulties and surprises we encountered in our own fieldwork, including access and the role of researchers and the larger methodological issues that these raise.

Notes

1. On progressive Catholicism in El Salvador, see Berryman (1986), Cáceres Prendes (1989), and Peterson (1997).
2. On progressive Catholicism in Peru, see Fleet and Smith (1997), Klaiber (1992), Peña (1995), and Romero (1987).
3. For additional sources on Protestantism in El Salvador, see Williams (1997).
4. For additional sources on Protestantism in Peru, see Escobar (1981) and Marzal (1989).

Part I
Women, Family, and Community

Chapter 1

Anna Peterson

"The Only Way I Can Walk"

Women, Christianity, and Everyday Life in El Salvador

Ana Cristina López rises every day at 5:00 A.M. to bathe, dress, and prepare *café con leche* for her husband and five children.[1] On weekdays, she catches the bus to work at 5:45, arriving at 6:30. She returns home around 5:45 P.M. to begin dinner for her family. Often she leaves the meal out for them so she can attend church meetings: catechist training on Tuesdays, parish council on Wednesdays, pastoral training team on Fridays, and, on weekends, theology and catechism classes in addition to mass. After these activities, Ana Cristina returns home to wash and iron until 11:00 or 11:30. Her life reflects the *doble jornada* (dual workday) of many poor and middle-class Latin American women. In addition to performing most of the household tasks, an increasing number of women from all classes work outside the home, either to supplement a male partner's income or because the woman is the only or primary breadwinner.

It may be hard for outsiders to understand why women like Ana Cristina would fill their evenings and weekends with church activities. In fact, the multiple pressures of life as mothers, wives, heads of household, and workers are precisely what makes religious activities so valuable and even necessary for many women. This logic becomes apparent only when we try to understand religious participation from the vantage point of women's own experiences, priorities, and commitments.

Women in the Popular Church

Ana Cristina's story exemplifies the struggles of many Salvadoran women. Originally from Suchitoto, a small city north of San Salvador, she fled the political violence in the region and moved to the capital in the early 1980s. With her husband and children, she lives in the tin-roofed house they built in a working-class neighborhood in Mejicanos. The house is so small, she says, that the first time a church group held a meeting there she feared the participants "would not even find a place to sit." She works at one of San Salvador's universities as a laboratory assistant, a position that is poorly paid and demanding but better than her prior job as a janitor at the university, which in turn was better than taking in washing, her earlier source of income. She worries about the difficulties her children will face finding decent work in the future. When asked whether she believes the country will be better in five years, she replies, "I have faith that it will be better, because I sure don't want it to get worse than what it is now."[2]

Ana Cristina began participating in the Catholic parish of San Francisco de Asís in 1991. Since then she has assumed responsibilities as a catechist, family pastoral agent, member of the liturgy team, and other positions. Before she became active in the church, she remembers, her life lacked meaning and was marred by conflicts with her children and husband. Now, she claims, she does not know what would have happened had she continued that way: "my routine was that on Sundays I was stuck washing, and I never had time for anything else. I learned that through the things of God, God helps to plan everything and put it in order." The life that God has helped Ana Cristina to put in order is extraordinarily demanding but, she insists, also rewarding. She credits her church participation for her success in obtaining paid work outside the home, not an easy accomplishment for a poorly educated, middle-aged woman, especially given El Salvador's chronic shortage of jobs. She credits the church for bringing her out of the narrowness and pessimism of her previous life.

> When I began to work there in the university, I had already been participating for three years in the parish, and I already felt that opening, that gladness, that self-confidence, because before, when I didn't ever leave my house, I didn't even like to get dressed up at all, I would just say, why bother . . . so through the church I began, and when the lady told me to go that Friday to have a job interview I got dressed up as well as I could [*yo me arreglé lo mejorcito que pude*] and I went, and I felt faith that God was helping me, because I had recently stopped working at my mother's and had been taking in washing and ironing so as not to leave my children alone, I would go give

them lunch and then finish washing, and that was how my life was then, running from here to there, and I felt exhausted. So I feel that the church has helped me a lot, the communication I had there, the participation in the community, although often one doesn't participate because when you start, you feel shy and all, but thanks to God now, [I have] a job and the church, as I say to my mother, if I didn't have that little job or my meetings I would have died from so many troubles, so many things.

Although there are many exceptions, Ana Cristina's experiences illustrate a number of important characteristics common to progressive Catholic women in El Salvador. Like her, most are from what we might call the working poor, a very large group in El Salvador. In these families, at least one and often two adults bring in a small but steady income, usually as skilled blue-collar workers or in the service sector. Like Ana Cristina, many have little formal education past high school or even elementary school, but they nurture the hope of higher education for their children. Women from this sector perform most of the parish's day-to-day work: attending meetings, serving on committees, teaching classes, and undertaking the service projects that define progressive Catholicism. Further, they do so at no small cost. They dedicate themselves to their church not in their free time but in hours that might have been for relaxation or sleep.

Insofar as women constitute the large majority of its members, the popular church is a church of women. In what sense is progressive Catholicism a church for women, meeting women's gender-specific concerns? Do women simply serve as workhorses for male-dominated institutions out of masochism or lack of self-esteem? The Catholic Church continues to deny women many leadership opportunities beyond the local level, due to the maintenance of an exclusively male priesthood. As another member of the San Francisco parish, María Guadalupe Roca, explains, "there is a lot of resistance," even in the base communities, to gender issues. Although progressive Catholic discourse criticizes oppressive political and economic structures, it rarely addresses issues such as domestic violence, family planning, pay equity, or political representation. Nonetheless, a number of men in San Francisco and elsewhere emphasized that their participation in CEBs altered their approach to male and female domestic roles. Antonio Castillo, a Mejicanos resident, explains: "since I've participated in the church my moral life changed, because my thinking about having a family and being responsible is different now . . . [and] the machismo that I might have had before has disappeared to a certain extent, not completely."

Although even the most progressive sectors of the Catholic Church continue to limit women in various ways, it would be a mistake to judge the popular church simply as alienating to women. Progressive Catholic women's religious participation serves as the foundation for their identities as individuals, as members of a community, and as women. Because their sense of self rests on their church involvement, the women conceive their long hours of work for the church not as self-sacrifice but rather as the fulfillment of a richer sense of self (Welch 1990, 165). This does not mean that women's church participation is liberating in an unproblematic sense, but it does suggest that these women's religious involvement is more contradictory and more multidimensional than most previous studies have assumed.

In Brazil, Carol Ann Drogus found that while the popular church is not feminist, it has contributed to such feminist goals as heightened self-esteem and awareness of gender discrimination among some Catholic women. Experience in CEBs also helps women move toward greater public participation, authority, and equality, at least in limited spheres. Still, Drogus cautions, gender-based values and activism in Brazil cannot be encompassed within terms familiar to North American and European feminists, who often understand women's activism as a challenge to tradition. In contrast, many Brazilian women view their activism as "an extension of their traditional roles," which "is justified by a continued belief in women's essential nature and role as care giver and mother" (Drogus 1997a, 165). In El Salvador, similarly, women in CEBs blend public activism and traditional values in ways that seem paradoxical to many outsiders. This approach is exemplified by mothers' groups, based on the Mothers of the Plaza de Mayo in Argentina, which use maternal imagery and values as the basis for demands such as the release of political prisoners and reform of the judicial system.

What is most telling, perhaps, is Drogus's description of the progressive church as a "revelatory experience" for many women, opening up possibilities for public participation that they never before imagined (Drogus 1994, 13). In El Salvador, many women describe how participation in CEBs caused them to "open their eyes" or "wake up" and perceive a world beyond the drudgery, stress, and immediacy of household and paid employment. This awakening stems in part from progressive Catholic ideology, which interprets personal and domestic problems such as alcoholism, unemployment, or gambling in the light of larger economic and political forces. Participation in the popular church reveals a new world, with transcendent dimensions linked to both everyday life and political events. Progressive Catholicism also offers women a way to participate in, even to help transform, their worlds. For many, the church mediates between private life at home and the larger, public realm of work and community participation. Participation in the church literally took Ana Cristina from the washboard into a collective sphere where she shares problems, explores ideas, evaluates possible solutions, and participates in joint projects to improve conditions not only for herself and her family but also for her neighbors and, perhaps, her country.

This sense of being part of something larger and more meaningful than the individual household strengthens many women's self-esteem and desire to "do something more" with their lives. The popular church provides an entry into a larger world in two senses: it connects them to the public sphere and, through its efforts to link faith and life, illuminates the sacred dimensions of present events. The central CEB activity of collective Bible reading, for example, provides women with the opportunity to relate biblical stories to their own lives, as Rosa, a member of a CEB in Ciudad Segundo Montes, highlights: "As women we meet once a month and we've been reflecting on the issue of women's participation in the life and work of Jesus, in Jesus' passion also. And it's very interesting how in the Bible there's a whole line of women who accompanied Jesus. So to discover these women, discover their values and their talents, their participation, and to share it is something that really encourages us a lot."

This experience is life-changing for many women. Isabel González explains the impact of her participation in CEBs in San Francisco: "Before, I lived more in the material and the social, I mean they were more superficial commitments, and in contrast in the church I feel it is deeper, more real, more substantial. One knows what one wants, sees things as they are, and is no longer enslaved to certain norms and conventions." It is more common, however, for progressive Catholic women to say that their religion has not freed them from tradition but rather helped in their efforts to improve their traditional lots, including both material assistance and, equally importantly, moral support and reinforcement of their self-esteem. María Guadalupe Roca says the church helped her "to value" herself after her husband left her, and Paula Ríos recalls how the base community in San Francisco helped her family cope with her husband's alcoholism and supported his efforts to stop drinking.

These accounts contrast sharply with John Burdick's argument that CEB members "do everything they can to avoid making concrete connections between the Word 'and life'" (Burdick 1993a, 195). For Burdick, "life" means personal and family concerns. The problem with progressive Catholic discourse is that it "presents domestic problems as secondary to the 'really important' issues of the world beyond the household" (Burdick 1992, 176). According to Burdick, economic and political issues do not interest most poor and working-class people, particularly women, for whom only domestic issues are "really important." CEBs either ignore them or place responsibility for domestic conflict on women. In contrast, he argues, Pentecostalism and Umbanda create socially safe spaces and shift blame for conflict away from women (Burdick 1993a, 115).

While Burdick's account might be accurate for the CEBs he studied in Brazil, it does not hold true for progressive Catholicism in other settings. In El Salvador, we found that progressive Catholic communities offer many women support, both material and moral, for their efforts to cope with domestic problems such as a husband's departure or alcoholism. Further, we found that while domestic problems are important to women, they are not the only concern women bring to church. Many Salvadoran women are interested in personal and social issues, and in CEBs they explore both. Burdick's emphasis upon domestic issues obscures the extent to which women, no less than men, can engage national issues and local community improvement. Certainly, it denigrates women's concerns to avoid domestic issues as irrelevant, as many leftists have long done. However, it seems no less sexist to suggest, as Burdick does, that women care only about domestic problems. The most radical aspect of CEBs might be precisely their assumption that all Christians, male and female, are citizens of a larger community, held accountable by God for their efforts to create a more just society.

The Catholic Charismatic Renewal

The lack of an outward turn is precisely what some progressive women criticize in the Catholic Charismatic Renewal (CCR). According to María Guadalupe Roca, who formerly participated in the Charismatic Renewal in another parish, the CCR lacks community spirit and concern for others there. Charismatics, she says, are "closed in their prayer circles." While her criticism may be unduly harsh, it is true that the CCR often focuses on prayer groups and religious celebrations and pays little attention to "good works," at least beyond small-scale charity projects such as visiting the sick. Many CCR groups also emphasize the authority of the priest and do not encourage laypersons, particularly women, to take leadership roles except under close clerical supervision. In this sense, the movement is squarely within the letter and spirit of the New Evangelization, a broad set of initiatives established by Pope John Paul II to reaffirm the authority of the clergy and hierarchy and turn attention away from the democratizing tendencies unleashed by Vatican II and realized most fully in base ecclesial communities (Peterson and Vásquez 1998).

One similarity between the CCR and CEBs is that their members are primarily women, for whom the movement makes paradoxical but real contributions to their everyday lives. In both programs, women are often the only members of the family to join the movement. Few of the women we interviewed had succeeded in bringing their husbands to the movement, although we did see a few middle-aged men at CCR services. While women are often the only family members to participate, when men participate, they usually do so with their wives or other relatives.

A majority of the CCR members we interviewed in Don Rúa and elsewhere in El Salvador described themselves as always having been relatively religious and concerned with a Roman Catholic identity, although many did not participate actively in the church except for Mass prior to joining the CCR. Few CCR members consider Pentecostal or other non-Catholic groups to be viable options for religious participation. Further, few find CEBs appealing, even though some parishes include both options. Class and political differences also shape Catholic women's decisions to join CEBs or the CCR. Most of the Charismatic women we interviewed and observed were politically traditional and wary of "radical" options, and many were lower to upper-middle class, with a smaller representation from poorer or wealthier sectors. This is not due solely to the parish itself, since participants come to Don Rúa from throughout the metropolitan area. Neocatechumenate activities bring wealthier people from different neighborhoods to Don Rúa, and ordinary Sunday mass attracts very poor people as well as the working and lower-middle class, who predominate within the parish's geographical boundaries.

While the Charismatic movement in Don Rúa seems primarily middle class, this characterization needs to be qualified in several respects. Some participants travel from poorer neighborhoods, including Mejicanos and Soyapango, to Charismatic services and activities at Don Rúa. Further, Charismatic movements in Don Rúa and other parishes, such as the Iglesia El Carmen, have organized prayer groups and other lay movements in poor neighborhoods. For example, some Charismatic lay leaders from Don Rúa were undertaking, with variable success, outreach activities in a very poor neighborhood, called La Fosa (The Grave) at the northern edge of the parish boundaries. The Charismatic movement, like CEBs, varies widely, based on clerical leadership, local concerns, and the interests and energy of lay leaders. Different groups, or the same group at different times, can attract different sectors and experience varied degrees of clerical supervision, lay autonomy, and social activism.

Most of the women in the CCR are middle-aged, with their children grown and without paid work to occupy them, either because they are retired or because they have never worked outside the home. Religious participation provides these women with an outlet for energies that otherwise were focused on the home and, in a few cases, on unrewarding work outside the home. Their identity has come primarily from motherhood and marriage. Many find, after the children leave home, that their marriages are not that satisfying and their horizons seem very small indeed. Many have a maid to cook and clean, so they don't even have household activities to occupy them. Eva, a retired social worker, explains: "I began to have a series of problems when I retired, here at home, because I was used to working and when I arrived home, well, we had the maid who does everything, and so I did very little. I said when I retire I'll dedicate myself to my garden, I'll do all these things, I said, and I didn't do any of it."

Like Eva, many of the women in the CCR have little to occupy their time and energy, in contrast to the poorer women in parishes like San Francisco, who lack domestic help and usually do some sort of paid work as well. The middle-class women often find that what is filling their time is domestic conflict, usually fights with their husbands or children. They seek changes in frustrating personal situations but do not look to sociopolitical issues, as the CEBs demand, or to a radical break from the Catholic Church, which represents continuity with their personal, family, and class background. For such women, the structured courses (*crecimientos*, literally "stages of growth"), prayer groups, and celebrations in the Charismatic movement provide opportunities for personal transformation within carefully constructed and maintained religious and social boundaries. The most distinctive elements of this transformation seem to be their concern for the woman's own character and its consequences for her family relationships. A number of Catholic Charismatic women recalled, in tracing their paths to the movement, that they had "strong characters" or bad tempers that led them to fight with relatives. Several say that only the church, God, or Jesus helped them become less proud and aggressive and make peace with their relatives. (Several CEB members also reported that church participation had improved their domestic relations, but it was not such a striking focus.) Eva recalls that when her problems with her grown daughter became unbearable and her husband offered little support, she turned to her younger sister (already involved in the CCR in another, wealthier church), who told her, "'you have always been arrogant, you've been proud, you've never wanted to ask for help from anyone, and so now I'm surprised that you're telling me this.' She told me: 'now is the time for you to get closer to the Lord and to see how wonderful he is and how he can help you.'" Eva began to attend Charismatic services and classes, and, she recalls,

> I began to change my personality, I began to be more flexible, I began to be more tolerant, more understanding . . . I began to soften myself, and I asked God, "Lord, Lord, give me humility," because that is what I need, to be humble, not to be so arrogant or proud, because what do I get from that? I just get bitterness, and a bad life. . . . My change was slow . . . but by the second crecimiento, I was a new person, I was no longer that person who at-

tacked for just about anything or answered back if someone said something. They taught me that one has to be humble and pardon and ask for forgiveness. . . . What the Lord wants is a humble heart, and when I asked the Lord, I said, "Lord, give me a soft and humble heart like yours, how can I fight with all those people if you don't help me, take my hand because that is the only way I can walk."

Echoing her, Raquel Rivas says, "I have a very strong character, and only the Lord has helped me soften it." Now, she says, in a difficult situation, "You remember that Christ is in your heart and ask the Holy Spirit for help. Undoubtedly it's God who is working in that instant and so, instead of giving an angry response, you give a loving one, because now it's the Lord acting in one . . . In my life no one could ever dominate me, not my father, my mother, my husband, not anyone, because I've had a strong character, but the only one who has been able to dominate me has been Jesus, . . . he is the only one who controls my character, who controls my temper."

The experiences of Raquel and Eva reveal some of the appeal of the Charismatic Renewal to the middle-class, middle-aged women who are its main constituency. They are frustrated with the limitations of their lives, but their personal and class backgrounds prevent them from joining a group, religious or not, that suggests any sort of rebellion against their status. While CEBs often attribute domestic and personal issues to structural injustices, the CCR puts these problems in a different kind of context: their own failure to meet the ideals of their faith. They would not have problems, the message seems to be, if they were more like Jesus: patient, humble, and ever-forgiving and loving even in the face of opposition and disappointment. The Charismatic movement, in a sense, domesticates women, teaching them to "conform" themselves *(conformarse)* to their relationships, their households: in short, to their lots in life.

The accounts of Eva and Raquel resemble the experiences of members of the Women's Aglow Fellowship, a Charismatic Christian group in the United States which is mostly Protestant but almost a tenth Catholic (Griffith 1997, 59). Both movements stress personal, especially emotional, transformation rather than changes in other people or social structures. R. Marie Griffith describes a Women's Aglow member whose "failure consists of harboring resentment and anger against those who abandoned her . . . to be healed and released from bondage, she had to bring these hidden feelings to the surface, confess them humbly to God in prayer in the presence of her friends, and let them go." This creates "a wholly renewed relationship with God, bringing with it the renewed capacity to experience life as a gift of love rather than a bitter trial" (Griffith 1997, 112). Raquel and Eva understand their experiences in almost the same terms, as a way to substitute peacefulness and humility for resentment and anger.

Some scholars view movements such as the CCR or the Women's Aglow Fellowship as simply a reworking of *marianismo,* the female counterpart to machismo. Marianismo presents an ideal of women as long-suffering and morally superior, particularly in their capacity to forgive endless hurts and still nurture their families while never complaining or asking anything for themselves. The CCR emphasizes Jesus rather than Mary as the model for Christian women, a shift probably influenced by the more Christocentric theology of post-Conciliar Catholicism. Still, the message remains essentially the same: be humble, gentle, loving, and nondemanding. The CCR does not contend that men are naturally inclined to sow wild oats, but it does reinforce the idea that women should solve their problems through personal discipline and attitude adjustment rather than changing problematic conditions. This leads to criticism from some feminists and progressive Catholics in El Salvador.

The Salvadoran women in the CCR, however, do not find its message oppressive. As noted earlier, many of these women lack other acceptable (to them) outlets for their energy. They are strongly disinclined to seek more radical alternatives, due to their religious conservatism and middle-class status. Significantly, they also lack the economic independence to reject their lots as wives and mothers. While feminists might want these women to shake off their chains, they are extremely unlikely to do so and even less likely to improve their socioeconomic status if they did. They may need precisely what the Charismatic Renewal offers: personal transformation in the context of religious and social continuity. The CCR does not ask members to break with the church of their youth or to critique the socioeconomic system. Instead, it encourages them to look inward and upward, to ask God's help in achieving personal rather than social transformation. The changes encouraged by participation in the Charismatic Renewal are small but crucial: rethinking their identities and the causes of their suffering and gaining a modicum of control over them by placing them in a broader religious framework.

This parallels Griffith's finding that participants in the Women's Aglow movement "believe that their true liberation is found in voluntary submission to divine authority" (Griffith 1997, 199). They view this submission not as mere acceptance of domination but rather as a liberation. The emancipating effect of self-control parallels the experiences of Catholic Charismatic women and some Pentecostals, for whom, as Cecilia Mariz notes, "One is free when one is able to give up bad habits. Pentecostal liberation is a personal transformation" (Mariz 1992, 50). This holds true as well for many women in the Catholic Charismatic Renewal in El Salvador, for whom freedom means not escaping but rather coming to terms with the conditions of their lives.

Pentecostalism

The CCR emphasizes personal change while strengthening members' ties to the Catholic Church and, through it, to the social and political status quo. In contrast, Pentecostalism demands a radical break with "the world." Believers are born again into a community that stresses separation from the corruption of both secular society and the Catholic Church. Despite this contrast, in some ways the CCR and Pentecostalism resemble each other in a number of ways. First, both movements emphasize the power of the Holy Spirit, in contrast to progressive Catholicism and liberal Protestantism, which are more Christ-centered, and also to folk Catholicism, with its emphasis on Mary and the saints. Another similarity between the CCR and Pentecostal churches is their emotional worship style and the dominant role both give to music, physical movement, and personal expression. Sharp swings from rapture to agony and back, however, seem more typical of Pentecostal services. This might be because priests tend to control Catholic Charismatic celebrations much more closely than Pentecostal pastors do their own services. In fact, at one Sunday service at La Redención Assemblies of God church in Mejicanos, the pastor watched in apparent bemusement as a visiting preacher, a Salvadoran woman who lived in Los Angeles, led a long and enthusiastic session of speaking in tongues, healing, and spiritual cleansing. From our research, at least, it appears that the Holy Spirit is more likely to burst institutional bounds in Pentecostal services.

The continuities between Protestant Pentecostalism and Charismatic Catholicism run into further ambiguities in their attitudes toward the domestic sphere. Women in the CCR often seek to improve their personal relations and their own performance as wives and mothers, but they do not make the domestic sphere their primary source of identity and value. Rather, their church participation extends them into a larger religious and social community, which transforms their private as well as public identities. Pentecostal discourse, however, elevates the private sphere and the church as part of its larger rejection of the corruption of the public sphere and the secular world. Observers are divided on the implications of this central Pentecostal theme: some see it as "a symptom of political alienation and a hindrance to social transformation," while others believe it represents "a cultural innovation that fosters social change" because it breaks with machismo and militarism (Mariz 1992, 43). Thus Elizabeth Brusco, for example, argues that Pentecostalism enhances female status, promotes female interests, and provides an antidote to machismo by bringing men's priorities in line with women's and forcing men to fulfill their household responsibilities (Brusco 1995, 6). Pentecostalism also offers women new ways to interpret destructive male behavior, such as adultery or alcoholism, as the work of the "powers of darkness" rather than the wife's failure (Griffith 1997, 212; Mariz 1992, 47, 52).

Burdick agrees that Pentecostal affiliation provides women with benefits of domestic peace and financial stability, which most see as worth the subordination demanded by the church's patriarchal ideology (Burdick 1993a, 110). Burdick pushes the argument further and argues that women's subordination involves "contested models of gender relations." Women make household work into proof of their sex's moral superiority; for example, because women have spiritual power, they do not require material power (Burdick 1993a, 111). Pentecostal women also insist that they are subordinate, in the end, to God and not to men. This inverts what Sharon Welch calls the "erotics of domination," in which men contend that they dominate not for themselves but in God's name. Welch points out that this serves to reinforce the value of absolute power and domination at the same time that it shifts responsibility from the ones actually holding power (Welch 1990). We might term what occurs in Pentecostalism in Latin America an "erotics of subordination," in which women claim to be subordinate to divine power rather than male power. (This echoes, also, the claim of Raquel, the Charismatic Catholic, that "the only one who has been able to dominate me has been Jesus.")

Many Salvadoran Pentecostals view the nuclear family not as a vehicle of male power but as a divinely ordained structure in which both women and men find their greatest (worldly) fulfillment and can pursue their ultimate spiritual ends. The importance of family surfaced often in our interviews with Pentecostal women in El Salvador. For example, Angela Díaz of La Redención explains that "God founded the family as the base of society, God truly founded the family because in his plan the family should be united, he founded marriage as something basic . . . so we teach people that the family is in God's plan." This is tied to an elevation of domestic chores as an appropriate way of serving God. Many women remarked that they found satisfaction in even the most mundane tasks by reconceiving of them as dedicated to God and fulfilling God's will for their own lives. This is not the same thing, however, as saying that domestic chores are the only way for women to serve God, a view that we did not find among women we interviewed.

Although the divinely ordained family follows a patriarchal model, few of the women we interviewed equate the father or husband's role with God's lordship as strongly as the other studies suggest. Rather than a gender dichotomy,

Salvadoran Pentecostal women emphasize a sacred/profane dichotomy. Thus they contrast God's absolute lordship more often with the worldly rule of secular authorities than with men's role in the family. María de Jesús, for example, explains, "I think that God installs the government that He wants, whether people vote or not, God removes whoever he wants and also installs his government because those people, really, are mistaken in thinking that they are going to govern. It's not that way. Rather, God has a purpose for humanity." This insistence on God's lordship goes along with a strong emphasis on staying out of politics as much as possible. María de Jesús continues, "It's true that the church is part of society, but I think that we have more important things to do than to get involved [in it], since the one above is the one who's going to take all this into account, because if the Bible itself says that if we judge, we also will be judged, so I think that it's better to leave things for God to decide and judge." This claim was repeated by a large percentage of the Pentecostals we interviewed, regardless of sex, geography, class, or age and is perhaps the most distinctively and typically Pentecostal conviction. True Christians should concern themselves with spiritual matters and with the personal transformations wrought by accepting Jesus as one's lord and savior in Evangelical terms. Silvia de Guerrero explains: "When we let God enter our being, let him be the lord of our lives, we feel a big change because we aren't the same persons as before."

The element of personal transformation in Pentecostalism, as in progressive and Charismatic Catholicism, seems to be a major factor in its appeal generally and especially to women. However, the character of this transformation and its social implications vary greatly for the three traditions. For progressive Catholics, personal changes coincide with an awakening of community spirit and a conviction that personal life, faith, and civic responsibilities cannot be separated in the life of a Christian. Charismatic Catholic women, in contrast, often emphasize the way their religion has helped them control their characters as a way, essentially, of coming to terms with their personal and social situations while at the same time providing an emotional and collective outlet for energies they cannot express in other spheres. Pentecostalism, in turn, presents a dualistic vision of life as divided between the sacred and the profane, the things of God and those of the world. It explains the cause of both domestic and political problems and prescribes a clear-cut solution to them. Achieving eternal salvation, the only prize worth seeking, requires keeping one's own house in order and obeying God's rules. This makes mundane tasks provisionally valuable—every task becomes dignified as a service to God—and also puts them in perspective as not ultimately meaningful.

The Lutheran Church

All three traditions discussed above operate within deeply sexist institutions. The Catholic Church and most Pentecostal churches in Latin America prohibit female ordination and prevent laywomen from rising higher than local leadership roles. When they do speak to women's gender-specific concerns, further, these denominations do not address the social, economic, and political issues central to North American or European feminists but rather focus on strengthening the family, cleaning up male behavior, or improving local living conditions. The notable exception to this trend, within the Salvadoran religious arena, is the Lutheran Church, headquartered at Resurrection Church in San Salvador's San Miguelito neighborhood. Alone of the churches we studied in El Salvador, the Lutherans have an office for women's concerns, ordain women, and explicitly address issues such as domestic violence, pay equity, shared household responsibilities, and even feminist theology.

The Lutheran Church in El Salvador, headed by Bishop Medardo Gómez, has been at the forefront of activism for human rights, peace, and social justice since its founding in 1972. In fact, due to their denunciations of government violence and support for war refugees, Lutheran leaders have been victims of violence more often than any religious sector except progressive Catholics. A Lutheran pastor was assassinated in the early 1980s, and a number of pastors and layworkers were imprisoned, threatened, or deported in the wake of the November 1989 FMLN offensive. This progressive stance has attracted many of Resurrection's members. Vilma Ibarra, in her fifties, migrated to San Salvador from Atiquizaya in 1978 because of political violence. She joined the Lutheran church because "it was a progressive church, a church that was in tune with the people . . . a church that didn't mind suffering." The dominant image of the Lutheran Church in El Salvador is dominated by its progressive political commitment, leaving the specifics of Lutheran doctrine and liturgy sometimes obscure.

The church's political and humanitarian work has strengthened its ties to progressive religious and secular groups in El Salvador, the United States, and Europe. These links replaced the church's denominational ties to its U.S. sponsor, the conservative Missouri Lutheran Synod, from which it separated in the late 1970s. While a number of issues prompted the division, one of the most important was Medardo's support for female ministry (which is permitted by the Evangelical Lutheran Church in America, with which the Salvadoran Church is now affiliated). In fact, his Mexican-born wife, Abelina Centeno de Gómez, is an ordained minister. At present, perhaps as many as a third of Salvadoran Lutheran pastors are women, as are at least half of the missionaries who have come to El Salvador from the United States, Europe, and other parts of Latin America. However, since few of the Salvadoran women working as pastors are seminary graduates and formally ordained, they lack the prestige and opportunities given to ordained, seminary-educated male pastors.

Since the founding of La Resurrección, women have played a central role in both pastoral and social activities. During the early 1980s, the Ladies' Society (Sociedad de Damas) that had been started by the Missouri Synod missionaries was renamed the Women's Society and, in 1990, it was established as a formal office within the church, called the Women's Pastoral. During the war, the women's group worked not only on gender-specific issues but also on human rights issues and support for war victims. Currently it pays particular attention to the economic difficulties facing women, especially single heads of households. Abelina de Gómez explains:

> We have always seen women in the home and this role raises no problems, no questions or anything, the woman is in the house sweeping, mopping, washing, ironing, raising children, and this is the role and in regards to it there are no questions, if a woman does that, it's fine. But if a woman doesn't do that and is doing something else, and stops doing the other, then the questions start, because it's something new. And I think this is the situation, because women have been required to leave the home . . . because in our society there are many single women. . . . For women it has been a little hard to leave [the home] because it has been out of necessity . . . but also within this necessity, we have realized that God does not reject us and that God is always at our side. So we can see, then, whom we need to question, the system or someone else . . . I think it's hardest for the man, because he has always been the one with all the privileges, for example to train himself and study. He has always had a woman to take care of him, he comes home from studying, from work, and is welcomed and taken care of in his house, but when a woman goes out to study or to work and comes home, who takes care of her? No one takes care of her.

Inés Hernández, a Lutheran seminary student who works as a pastor in a poor community while finishing her studies and awaiting ordination, agrees with much of Abelina's analysis of women's plight but also emphasizes the difficulty of fitting church activities into the demands of everyday life. Inés uses her own life as an example: "[When is there time for church activities?] Not in the morning, because I have to put on the beans, I have to cook the corn, I have to go to the market . . . to buy perhaps the pound of beans to cook that day, and the next day it's the same problem. [The women] have to go to buy the pound of beans to cook the next day and so on, because they don't have the money to buy for the whole week. So all their time goes to this struggle for subsistence; they don't have time to reflect, because their priority isn't reflection, it's survival."

While women face special pressures, Inés recognizes that men also must spend most of their time working or looking for work, which further complicates pastoral work. Sometimes a planned Bible study group fails because people do not come, for example. Other times, she fears, people get involved in the church for social rather than religious reasons. Sometimes, however, the campaigns that draw people in do help awaken, as Inés hopes, to profound religious commitment. Victoria Infante, initially attracted to the church for its political stance, explains that what she likes best about her church involvement now is "preaching, talking about the word of God." Her faith helps her in her work and other aspects of her life because "my faith has opened me up, it has given me clarity to be able to share, to teach, you know, or to study the Bible, the good news." After two of her sons and her brother were killed and her husband fled to Nicaragua, she recalls, she despaired, "I asked God to let me die. But not now . . . now I am happy, because God has helped me and has given me the opportunity to serve." Victoria's testimony echoes that of other Salvadoran women who identify their religious life as a source of meaning, dignity, and even joy in the midst of extraordinarily hard lives.

The Lutheran church pays special attention to the particular ways in which women's lives are hard. Most women we interviewed acknowledged the problems of single motherhood and economic hardships facing women, but the Lutherans were distinctive in their attention to equity and structural sexism. While CEB members cited structural problems as the causes of unemployment, poverty, and other widespread social inequities, they rarely pointed to sexist or patriarchal structures in particular. Their analysis focused, in other words, on socioeconomic or class injustices rather than on gender-based ones. In contrast, Lutherans discussed gender issues as related to but not subsumed into issues regarding class. Lutherans also emphasized the theological dimensions of gender issues much more than Catholic and Pentecostal women. Many Lutheran women, for example, are interested in women's role in the Bible, which a number of laywomen cited as one of the best aspects of theology and liturgy at La Resurrección. Bible readings also lead to religiously based denunciations of sexism, as Abelina explains, "Now we see that God does not want [machismo], but rather in the home or wherever they need to work, the man and woman should have the same privileges and the same value." The notion that God calls for equality between women and men is reinforced in church publications and by the Women's Pastoral Office, which sponsors both analyses of sexism and efforts to change women's social and religious roles, on the one hand, and practical programs, especially classes in areas from literacy to job skills, on the other.

Most of the Lutheran women we interviewed emphasized the importance of female pastors. Even women who are not particularly active in the church notice this quality, as Margarita Mendoza comments: "The role of women in the church is very important, because there is more space. We have women pastors. For example, the wife of the bishop is a minister. There are many women who have trained and who are being trained to be ministers. And just as there are women getting this education, there are also classes for women to learn how to work with the base communities" (one of many innovations the Lutherans have borrowed from progressive Catholicism).

Because of its distinctive qualities, the Lutheran church attracts certain women, and these women in turn shape the church. Lutheran women have a high degree of involvement in church activities and professional pastoral work. Many, but not all, of these women have substantial formal education. Several women who are now leaders in different pastoral programs "rose through the ranks," moving, for example, from a job as a cook to active leadership and paid employment in the women's pastoral office. While not perfectly egalitarian, the Lutheran church appears to offer significant mobility and leadership opportunities to women who might have been hindered not only by their sex but also by their educational and class background. This contrasts sharply with the restrictions on women's leadership in the Catholic Church and most Pentecostal churches. Access to leadership has helped the Lutheran church attract a number of talented and energetic young women who may find the church appealing as the only site where they can bring together religious commitments, political activism, and professional ambition.

Although the Lutheran church is exceptional as an institution, not all of its members embrace female leadership. Women's performance of the sacraments seems to be an especially controversial issue. Abelina de Gómez recalls that the first time she performed communion, around 1985, over a decade after she had come to El Salvador as an ordained minister, one woman left the church. Most of the Lutheran women pastors commented on this issue and related it to the larger issue of sexism in Salvadoran culture generally, rather than a problem unique to the Lutheran Church. Inés, another Lutheran pastoral agent, explains: "I think it is necessary for us to change the way women and men interact, and that is reflected in our work. As long as we don't get rid of those habits, which we can call *machista,* we won't move ahead in our work, as men or as women ministers, because in our work in the parishes . . . there is deep alarm at seeing a woman in the altar and even worse giving the host or bread, the wine. So I think this is something very important we need to get over."

Sexist attitudes in the church are tied to structural issues. Despite the growing number of women pastors and the national prominence of Abelina and a few other women, most high-ranking church leaders are male. Even Abelina, an extraordinarily capable and energetic woman by any standards, works in the shadow of her husband, the bishop, who for many symbolizes the Lutheran church in El Salvador. Some members of the younger generation critique the male-dominated character of the top leadership. Elena, a well-educated young woman involved in a variety of activities in the church, replies thus to the question about how the church addresses women's problems: "Passively." She continues, "In the first place, [this is] because we have a very patriarchal and *machista* hierarchy. The people who direct it aren't to blame, obviously they were educated in a society that demands continuity with the machismo of the whole culture . . . I think that there are spaces for women, but some of us don't always take advantage of them. I think we should be more aggressive, more determined and more educated, in order to have a base and make concrete proposals to our hierarchy."

While tensions remain, La Resurrección has made remarkable progress toward women's full participation, especially in light of its short history and the severe gender inequities of Salvadoran society. Most of the Lutheran women we interviewed recognized this, praising their church's openness to women and the opportunities it provides them to work. Although they recognize the need for further progress, most have faith that the Lutheran church is capable of these changes, not only because of its political commitments but also because of its theological roots. The church can meet the challenges of incorporating women in theological terms, Abelina explains, because "the Reformation means that the Lutheran Church itself needs to be reformed constantly."

Comparative Issues

In the end, the experiences of Salvadoran women reinforce some generalizations about religion's roles in Latin America and challenge others. Regarding the best-known groups, Pentecostals and progressive Catholics, we agree with Carol Drogus's conclusions regarding women in Brazil: "The key difference seems to be that Pentecostals do most to promote equality in the private and religious spheres, while CEBs demand women's public-sphere participation as well as providing some opportunities to act on that demand. Perhaps as a consequence, CEB women seem more successful in pressing for public power rather than in pursuing private equality" (Drogus 1992, 66). This echoes Cecilia Mariz's assertion, regarding Brazil, that CEBs bring women into the public sphere, while Pentecostal churches bring men into the private sphere (Mariz 1992). Our research in El Salvador also confirmed Drogus's finding that progressive Catholic women rarely played leadership roles beyond the local parish. To a lesser extent, we found support for the claims made by Elizabeth Brusco and Cornelia Butler Flora in Colombia, Hanneke Slootweg in Chile, and John Burdick in Brazil regarding Pentecostalism's strong appeal to women with domestic problems. Overall, however, Salvadoran Pentecostal women, like Pentecostal men, expressed greater interest in the duality between "the world" and the church than in the differences between men and women or even between the public and private spheres. This emphasis may have much to do with the distinctive features of our specific research sites and of Salvadoran society overall.

Compared to Pentecostalism and progressive Catholicism, the Catholic Charismatic Renewal and mainline Protestantism have received little scholarly attention, especially in relation to women's roles and attitudes. In El Salvador, the CCR appears most distinctive for its capacity to combine personal transformation with social and religious continuity. We also found that the Lutheran church offers a striking exception to the general tendency for Latin American churches to avoid explicit challenges to women's traditional domestic roles, their inferior social position, and even their limited leadership opportunities in the religious sphere. The Lutheran case, however, reveals that a more liberal position on women's roles inside and outside the church does not guarantee a greater appeal to women. While Lutheran women clearly value their church's attitudes toward women, La Resurrección had the lowest percentage of female members of all the churches we studied, with around 60 percent female attendance, in contrast to 80 percent or more in other churches. It might be argued that given the heavily female character of most other congregations in El Salvador, the Lutheran church is disproportionately male. (This may well reflect a greater appeal to men rather than a failure to attract women.)

In sum, women do not measure what a church does for them simply in terms of gender-specific projects. More generally, we cannot explain a religion's appeal or an individual's conversion only in utilitarian terms, as we might if people selected a faith based solely on rational, voluntaristic, and self-interested calculations that outsiders could assess. Women clearly recognize and appreciate the benefits they gain from church participation and take them into account in decisions to join, leave, or continue with a particular congregation. However, these benefits are often intangible or paradoxical. This is evident, for example, in the way Charismatic Catholic women praise the way the movement has been able to "dominate" their "strong characters." To an outsider, particularly of feminist inclinations, this might seem a dubious benefit. The advantages are much less obscure, however, for women who lack the financial resources, job skills, personal histories, and social conditions necessary for ringing declarations of independence. A faith that explains the reason for their frustrations and offers ways to reduce them enhances their lives significantly. More generally, the fact that all the churches we studied appeal to women, despite their significant ideological and institutional differences, suggests that Salvadoran women seek diverse kinds of assistance in negotiating the highly unequal and difficult conditions of their everyday lives. It is not clear, of course, whether any of the churches will, in the long run, transform these conditions.

Notes

1. Norys Ramírez's paper, presented at the University of Florida Center for Latin American Studies conference in Gainesville, Florida, in March 1998, provided a starting point for this paper. The discussion of the day of Ana Cristina comes from her presentation.
2. All quotations from individuals are from personal interviews conducted by Francisca Flores, Ileana Gómez, Anna Peterson, and Norys Ramírez in San Salvador and San Francisco Gotera between June 1996 and November 1997.

Chapter 2

Rosa Castro Aguilar

Religion and Family

Catholic Experiences in Peru

Faith and pastoral involvement constitute crucial aspects of personal identity for many Peruvian Catholics. Religion nourishes believers' understandings of the world and their values, hopes, and relationships with others. Religious participation also has a significant effect on the family, as our research in three diverse parishes in Peru has shown. Specifically, we have found that laypersons' involvement in grassroots Christian communities can contribute to changes in self-perception, improve family relationships, and help redefine the roles of women in both the home and the larger community. Moreover, by forging more egalitarian families, these Catholics help foster the construction of a democratic culture, in which family members recognize their rights and responsibilities as citizens within the larger community.

The Family in Peru

The family is not only a group of individuals united by marriage and blood ties but also an institution. The classical sociological definition of an institution is "a pattern of expected action of individuals or groups enforced by social sanctions, both positive and negative" (Bellah et al. 1991, 11). However, institutions do not exist apart from individuals and their social interactions. Instead, "we form institutions and they form us" in our everyday lives. In Peru, one of the most important institutions is the family, the basic nucleus in which socialization begins. The family influences not only individual identity, values, and choices but also other institutions. Families prepare individuals to live in their society in particular ways and thus to shape that society. As Violeta Sara-Lafosse puts it, the family seeks the creation and support of a "common culture" (Sara-Lafosse 1996). Just as social changes influence the family, the values, expectations, and behaviors that families inculcate affect society.

The last decade has witnessed much debate about the crisis of the family in Peru, based on perceptions of family instability, often tied to economic difficulties, and to a presumed decrease in the subjective importance of the family, especially for younger Peruvians. Some observers argue that the crisis of the family results from the difficulty of navigating between the instrumental values of Peruvian society (for example, efficiency, consumerism, and hedonism) and the expressive values of the family sphere (for example, protection, love, confidence, authority, and tradition) (Fabbri 1994). Some also contend that the contemporary crisis of the family stems from the growing emphasis on individual rights, which makes commitment to larger groups secondary (Comblín 1994). This argument attributes the crisis of the Peruvian family to tensions between individualism and solidarity and between tradition and contemporary values.

Family structures in Peru today correspond to two general types: patriarchal and egalitarian, distinguished primarily by the roles of women and men and their attitudes toward these roles. As Violeta Sara-Lafosse (1988) notes, many Peruvian families are in transition between these two models, moving from patriarchal to more egalitarian structures. In order to understand family structures, we must take into account various factors, especially the division of labor and authority within the family and the feelings that unite members of the family (Sara-Lafosse 1996, 140). In addition, we must consider the educational level, age and place of residence of household members, as well as women's participation in the labor market, even though these factors do not determine the transition from one type of family structure to another. This transformation requires changes in the culture within which the family develops. These social changes occur only gradually and are a consequence of changes in the perceptions, common sense, and practices within the family.

The present crisis in Peruvian families is related to cultural changes in the relations between individuals and the larger society and also among individuals, especially men and women. Women's domestic roles have changed substantially in Peru during the past thirty years, due largely to women's increased access to education and their greater participation in the labor market and social organizations. Although women's gains have been significant, the discourse about the place of the male and female in both the family and society has moved faster than in practice. Both discourse and practices are undergoing an uneven transition from an authoritarian, *machista* culture that subordinates women to a more egalitarian culture in which responsibilities are shared. As noted above, families play an important role in the broader civil society. This suggests that families which support and inculcate more egalitarian values and ideals can contribute to the consolidation of a democratic society, a crucial task in Peru today. By acknowledging and asserting the rights of each and every member of a family and promoting communication and consensus in family decisions, egalitarian family values can also promote individuals' sense of responsibility toward society. Because the family is the first sphere of socialization, its members must assume responsibilities within it, adapting its traditional function of creating culture and generating meaning to the present situation. This means continuing to offer protection, love, education, and culture to its members and respecting their rights.

During the present period of profound changes in popular worldviews and in global economies, cultures, and politics, families often seem to lack clear direction as they help create a "common culture" (Sara-Lafosse 1996). The challenge becomes whether to turn toward values that encourage work for the common good or toward values that encourage individuals who live for the present without assuming social responsibilities. Both global and national changes create new knowledge, different feelings, and different interpretations of the world. Simultaneously, some groups, in Peru and elsewhere, seek to recover and re-create older traditions. In this context, traditional institutions such as the family change their way of socializing people and the cultures they create.

Perspectives on Marriage

Peruvians' perspectives on marriage differ by age group. According to the 1993 census, Peruvians over forty tend to believe that marriage is the best way to live as a couple; those in their twenties think it best simply to live together; and those in their thirties are divided. The lower incidence of marriage among younger adults suggests either that marriage as a rite or formality has less weight among this age group or that people are increasingly waiting to achieve financial security before marrying. It could also mean that younger adults prefer to live together as a trial period before formalizing the relationship in marriage. More people over forty are married, although some lived together first.

While most Peruvians continue to respect the institution of marriage, the search for personal fulfillment and happiness prompts many young adults to live together before formalizing their relationships through matrimony. Many young people believe that the older generations "sacrificed their happiness" in order to maintain a life as a couple. They want to be sure that they are going to find happiness before committing themselves to marriage. However, people may find it easier to back out of a relationship rather than struggle to maintain it when faced with the first obstacle. The relativizing of marriage as a social institution is evident among younger generations, who often prefer to be free to decide whether or not to maintain a personal relationship with another individual.

Most Peruvians want their relationship or marriage to contribute to personal growth. This can be interpreted, on the one hand, as an affirmation of personal happiness without concern for others. This critique, coming from within and outside the church, ties changing expectations of marriage to increased individualism and irresponsibility. From another perspective, though, the insistence on satisfaction in marriage can be seen as an increased exercise of personal freedom and a recognition that the rights, desires, and aspirations of others are fundamental for personal growth.

Values and Ethics in Peruvian Families

The principles that rule and guide the lives of individuals are learned and acquired in the family. Family values can promote tolerance, respect, and equality, or they can produce attitudes of intolerance that exacerbate conflicts with others. Of course, people often change and sometimes outright reject the values and identities they learned in their families. Still, as Berger and Luckmann (1966) put it, individual identities emerge first through interactions with family members and only later, and under the influence of family relationships, in interactions with the public sphere. Because the values that guide social behavior are closely associated with the culture of families, it is important ethically to "think carefully about the ideals or objectives" pursued by families (Moreno Rejón 1984, 96).

In regard to the present crisis of the family in Peru, some critics argue that the family does not transmit the values that individuals need in order to identify themselves with a changing society. Critics claim that the family, which is in charge of transmitting traditional values such as reliability and dignity, is in tension with contemporary values such as pragmatism and individualism (Fabbri 1995). Others argue that the solidarity that exists among family members does not lead them to develop communication with, responsibility toward, or a sense of belonging to society (Fabbri 1994). However, it is important to note that for poor and working-class people in Peru, family solidarity facilitates the establishment of networks based on extended kin relations and shared places of origin. These networks help rural migrants move to and settle in cities. Thus, reciprocal relationships are established between families that do not live together or share finances. In critical moments, these networks play an important role in solving problems of basic subsistence (Ponce and Marfil

1985). Thus, some observers claim, for migrants the family is the human face of the city (Comblín 1994).

In various ways, the family develops values that help individuals either strengthen their sense of belonging to society or lose interest in it. However, the present conflicts between dominant social values and those prized by families correspond to the fact that established values now need to be reinforced or re-created in the context of globalization. In this process, religion can play a decisive role, significantly influencing the individual's socialization "that develops in diverse intermediary groups, beginning with the family and continuing in economic, social, political, and cultural groups" (John Paul II 1991, 13). In this way, religion can contribute to the consolidation of a democratic culture of respect, recognizing the diversity and equality of individuals. This is certainly true for the Catholics we interviewed in Comas, Huaycán, and Yungay. For many, religion has enriched marital relationships, enabling couples to get to know each other better and to develop dialogue and tolerance, which improves their communication. And in some cases, religious experiences have helped strengthen women's roles in the household and in society and have initiated changes in the values that guide their family life.

Participation in the Parish

Peruvian Catholics become actively engaged in their parishes for various reasons. In cities, women usually take the initiative to join a church, often to prepare for their children's first communion or to find help meeting their family's subsistence needs. In some instances, urban women join the church because they are invited to by others. In rural areas, men are the first ones to join the church. Since many of them can read and write, they join a parish in order to become catechists. Rural women generally do not take the initiative to join a parish: young women often migrate to cities, while older ones tend to be illiterate and, consequently, are inhibited from undertaking pastoral work.

Children are a frequent cause for greater church involvement. Catechism classes for first communion allow parents to participate with other parents. They share their experiences and reflections about the family, the children, the church, and the community. Diego, a lay celebrant in Comas, explained how he became active in his parish through his wife's concern for the children's religious education. When Diego's older daughter was old enough to receive first communion, his wife signed them up for the responsible parents program *(paternidad responsable)*. As a result, Diego began participating in the parish. Celia, also a lay celebrant in Comas, recounted a similar experience, explaining that her son's desire for a first communion led them to approach the parish.

In Peru, women are generally given responsibility for the children's education and for the family's religious life more generally. Diego's experience corroborated this: "[My wife] Lucila was more attached to religion. She belonged to the Legion of Mary in her town. It seems that in her town there was a steady priest. But my situation was different. In my town the Bishop arrived only when he was going to confirm the children; and here [Lucila also] looked for the Church, wanting to go to mass during Easter Week, [while I wanted to be] with my football game."[1] Women's concern for children's religious education reflects an interest in transmitting the family heritage and providing identity and culture, in addition to the desire for children to become full members of the church (Gonzáles 1987).

While sacramental life is very significant, women sometimes join a parish for a more instrumental reason: to satisfy the basic needs of their family. Labor insecurity and low wages make it difficult for families to cover all their needs. Most workers in Peru do not enjoy permanent salaried employment, and the minimum wage is only one hundred dollars a month. These two factors force many women to work outside their homes, either for a salary or by participating in a subsistence organization. Church-based projects often provide aid to families who otherwise could not cover their basic needs. These organizations also have encouraged the personal growth of women and helped them both learn about and affirm their rights. Martha, a member of a parish *comedor* in Huaycán, told us: "Yes, almost eight years I had been selling food in Huaycán, and afterwards I was not well. From then on I came here to the *comedor.* I asked if they could do me the favor of receiving me . . . and [they told me] 'Yes, there are openings. You can come in.' That's how I started to participate." After joining the parish *comedor,* Martha began participating in other aspects of parish life: masses, Christian communities, religious education courses.

In addition to concerns internal to the family, Peruvian Catholics, especially women, also became more involved in their parishes for social and community reasons. Often, invitations from neighbors or other active laypeople bring people into church life. These invitations sometimes prove life-changing. Sara, a lay leader in Huaycán, came to the church after an invitation to participate in the Christian community. At the beginning she was not interested in joining the parish because she had other interests and preoccupations. However, she grew tired of the constant invitations from parishioners. "Well, for the third time they invited me, and then I said [to myself], 'I am going to go a while so that they stop coming' . . . [When] I started participating I felt something. The second time I already felt impatient about the time to come. No one had to come to my house to remind me." At church, Sara found the human warmth and solidarity that was missing from her life: "I saw how [members of the Christian community] talked with such enthusiasm. They shared their experiences, their testimonies, and this helped me a lot."

When a Christian community is established, pastoral agents or lay leaders usually invite the participation of neighbors, especially those who express an interest in parish life. Hilda, a lay celebrant in Comas, always went to Sunday mass with her husband. She explained:

> They invited us to participate, and then I signed up for the [family catechism] course and we went to a meeting, but my husband, since he worked, said, 'No, I do not have time for that. That is for those who do not work.' Since I had never gone out of my house, I did not know [what to expect]. 'Oh,' I said, 'How am I going to leave my children? Who is going to serve them their meal? Who is going to do the ironing? Who is going to help in the household chores?' So that year we missed out.

Many women believe that they should dedicate their time to household chores and the family and view "going out" of the house as an abandonment of their traditional responsibilities. This causes women to be insecure when faced with the unknown, with what lies beyond the frontiers of the domestic sphere. This is why Hilda did not participate in the responsible parents program without her husband. However, the following year they came back and found something unexpected: they came to know themselves better and improve their relationship as a couple. Sara, Inés, and Hilda all received invitations they did not expect, and their acceptance initiated processes of personal growth. As a result of their participation in church life, these women began to change their perceptions regarding their traditional gender roles and to improve their family relationships. Today they combine multiple commitments to their household, work, and parish.

While most lay leaders in the cities are women, men are more likely to assume leadership roles in rural parishes in Peru. The position of catechist is a social and religious function that is highly valued among the members of the community. However, such positions of authority require literacy and a command of Spanish, and rural women are more likely to be both monolingual Quechua speakers and to be illiterate than rural men and urban women and men (Ugarteche 1998). As a result, rural women rarely become catechists or community leaders. Many rural women also believe they are incapable of undertaking a public role because they can be misled and thus jeopardize their community or family. However, a number of different organizations offer opportunities for growth and personal development to rural women in Peru. In many cases, after acquiring a better command of Spanish and learning to read and write, women become more active in community and church projects.

In the countryside, catechists organize religious education and celebrations and also offer advice and spiritual support to all the members of their community, advise community authorities about matters of collective interest, and invite others to become catechists. Because of the respect and authority catechists enjoy, being invited to become a catechist is considered an honor. This is especially the case in rural areas with a small public sphere and few prominent organizations. Although the catechist receives certain privileges, he may also be held to a higher standard of behavior. For many catechists, this requires a change in their daily lives in the family and community. Men, for example, may feel compelled to reduce their time in bars or the streets and to fulfill the image of an upright Christian man.

The few female catechists in rural areas know how to read and write and sometimes learn Spanish in the school for rural catechists. Some women become catechists after their husbands do. Esther, for example, saw changes in her husband's behavior and decided to undertake pastoral work herself. As a translator describes, "Before [Esther] became a catechist, when her husband used to come home she was always upset, she argued. But now she has changed. [Now] she also [wants] to help others, her neighbors, her family, her children . . . She wants to follow this life" (oral translation from Quechua to Spanish). By serving as lay leaders, rural women have the possibility of fulfilling both a social and religious role in their community. This helps women gain confidence in their own abilities and capacity to serve, and it causes men to see women as individuals with their own capabilities and voices.

New Life Perspectives

Participation in parish groups often enables both men and women to encounter new outlooks toward life, often radically different from those they inherited and reproduced. Most important, perhaps, religious participation enlarged the framework in which participants interpreted their own lives. They became convinced that their actions had implications beyond the frontiers of the family. As a result, many began learning about the needs of their neighbors, and some became active in the public sphere. The parish provides a space in which people of all ages and life circumstances can become involved with helping others. Fanny, a single mother and coordinator of her Christian community in Comas, found a place for herself in the parish. "Once family catechism is over, once the child receives the first communion, the parents have the option to stay in the community. They can be *parejas guías* (model couples), be in the pastoral health [program], join any group. Then I saw my possibility.

I said, 'If I join the parejas guías . . . I am an odd couple. I do not qualify for that.' But I continued coming on Fridays to prayers. I kept coming. Why? Because I liked it."

Like Fanny, most of the Catholics we interviewed have found a sense of belonging in their parish. There they do not experience the alienation that they might feel in other places because of being a single mother, a senior, youth, or illiterate. If they are committed to participating, they can do so without any restrictions. In the parish, people feel accepted and are able to develop their personal capabilities.

Participation in parish life has enabled our interviewees to understand the importance of testimony in Christian life. Testimony and consistency are especially important in the daily lives of rural catechists, since relationships in rural communities are direct and personal. In a culture that values practicality, the lessons that catechists learn and teach are viewed by others as norms to follow. Catechists must demonstrate consistency between what they preach and how they live their lives. Otherwise, they are immediately questioned. In urban settings, where relationships are more distant because of the larger numbers of inhabitants and their different urban lifestyles, testimony tends to be more public and less personal. Still, even in urban settings active lay participation often requires adoption of behavioral norms and values that reinforce the new life perspectives that they discover in their pastoral work.

Church activities such as family catechism offer parents the personal experience of closeness and friendship with other couples. These activities allow Christians to share their problems, orientations, and visions about family life; to build brotherhood and solidarity; and to help each other in times of need. People reflect on and discuss family, work, and neighborhood matters through church organizations. José, a catechist in Yungay, indicated that family catechism strengthened his relationship with his wife: "Last year, my wife was somewhat [distant], but when we [went] through these preparation classes, this grabbed our attention. Afterwards, we reconsidered [our relationship] in our conversations, as well as during moments of conversion. It has really helped."

Participation in different pastoral groups where there is reflection, exchange, and discussion about everyday experiences can enrich the personal and family lives of the members of the Christian community. Together people find a way to be Christians in their own daily lives, to be consistent with their evangelizing work. Diego explains, "We have been through all those [parish] groups; it has been twenty-two years. But it is very good. I have received a lot, a lot of instruction. I have also received the grace of the Lord, and this voluntary commitment and with the grace of God has allowed us to be in a stable family."

Finding a view of life that requires service to others and a concern for the common good has altered the lives of many Catholics we interviewed. Their experiences reflect the concrete consequences of Catholic social thought on communities and individuals. This is clear in the experience of Héctor and his wife, both of whom participated in a parish youth group in Huaycán when they were younger. After marrying and starting a family, they wanted to help other young couples solidify their relationships. Héctor explains: "Then we started working in the parish, but this time as a married couple. . . . We now wanted also [to share with] other young couples. . . . In this way we began little by little joining the work of the baptismal catechism [group]. At the moment we are a pareja guía in the parish."

The experience of serving others has given new meaning to the lives of many Catholics, enabling them to live differently, to value themselves, and to recognize their capacity to change. Sara, who coordinates a Christian community in Huaycán, experienced a dramatic change in her life as a result of her participation in church activities. She explains: "It was not easy. It did not happen from one day to the other. A long time has passed, but in the long run I did begin to see that change. I had stopped being that swearing, yelling woman that wanted to control everything with a shout, with a whipping."

For many, participation in the Christian community often leads to a more communal understanding of faith, as communion not only with God but also with one's neighbors. Solidarity and service to others are highly valued in the Christian community. In addition, participants discover new horizons and apply them to their personal and family life. This new approach to life gives them confidence in their capabilities and possibilities. It shows them a new way to achieve personal realization based on commitment to a group, be it a family, parish, or local community. The communal experience of prayer and Bible study encourages Christian community members to adopt new ways of relating to their family and community, as individuals with the capacity to contribute to the construction of the Kingdom of God. Their faith is not limited to a discourse that promotes social justice, as Burdick claims (1992); rather, when put into practice, it gives new meaning to people's lives.

Changes in Personal and Family Life

Participation in Christian communities and other pastoral projects has led many of the Catholics we interviewed to modify their attitudes about gender roles. Religious experience has led many women, in particular, to affirm their own dignity, to change their understandings of both family and society, to value gender equality, and to seek new lifestyles for their families. These changes, while often small in scale, help establish the necessary conditions for a transition to a more egalitarian family structure in Peruvian society as a whole. In patriarchal cultures like Peru, there is a strict division of labor in the home, and most women depend financially, emotionally, and socially on husbands, fathers, or brothers (Sara-Lafosse 1988). Men make family decisions, and, until recently, only men have worked and studied outside the home or participated in social organizations. Men have controlled not only the life of the family but also the public sphere. With the passage of time, however, many Peruvian men and women have altered their attitudes about family structure and gender roles. Even though gender inequality persists, women have attained a higher educational level and income and have participated increasingly in social organizations. Despite these gains, women remain marginal in various social settings and continue to depend financially and psychologically on men.

Today, a number of different social spaces, including many Catholic parishes, help inculcate more democratic or egalitarian values. Participation in pastoral work sometimes helps women learn to value themselves, to depend less on their husbands, and to make their own decisions. Sara explains that before joining the parish, "I did not value myself. That was my problem. I always saw myself lower than my husband. I saw myself as small. Back then I always saw him above me and always would say to myself, 'Why did he set his eyes on me?' I would not give myself any value, but I always felt lower than others. But after participating in [the parish] we are taught to understand the value that we have, that we are not less than anybody."

In order to acknowledge the equality of men and women, women must first value themselves as having rights and the ability to confront problems and find solutions. Irma, a lay leader in Huaycán, has suffered repeated abuse at the hands of her husband. Nevertheless, her active involvement in pastoral work has helped her to find the strength necessary to confront her domestic problems. "I have encountered the same suffering, but I feel good. I feel happy. I am not even afraid, nor anything. I have improved my life a lot from what I used to be. I learned to be strong. I learned to deal with individuals and conquer, to decide also. A woman has rights also. An individual has rights. One cannot be like that, alone, mistreated. I have met many like that, but they do not understand me. On many occasions my family does not understand me either." As Irma makes clear, changes in women's attitudes are not always understood or accepted by their families. Acceptance also requires changes in the whole family culture. However, it is a step forward for women with little formal education and little or no experience working outside the home to acknowledge their capabilities and possibilities as individuals. This realization enables them to redefine their role in the family and to begin transforming their family culture and structure.

By discovering their capabilities within the family and public sphere, our interviewees have been able to grow in self-esteem, increase their educational level, and improve the quality of their family relationships. While increased self-confidence and the feeling of belonging to a larger community are sufficient rewards, some women also experience greater equality in their family relationships as a result of participation in church projects. Women sometimes stop seeing their role as that of the sacrificial mother who postpones her aspirations in order to raise her children and provide them with a good education. Instead, they strive for self-realization and try to achieve goals in other areas of their lives.

Religious participation, among other factors, sometimes helps women realize that the best way of life is not a violent family but a family that supports the personal growth of all its members, even if that means the absence of the father from the home. Separation is generally decided by the mother or, sometimes, by the father and mother together. Such decisions, made possible by women's conviction that they can survive without male support, help undermine the attitude of the "macho" who abandons the family (Sara-Lafosse 1995). The experiences of Peruvian Catholic women suggest that there are a variety of ways in which religious participation can help transform weak or struggling families. Increased male participation based on an authoritarian model is one option, but women may also gain self-confidence and practical skills that enable them to challenge male dominance. Of course, without the capacity to provide for their children economically, few women can separate from even the most abusive husbands, since Peru's government, like most others in Latin America, does not enforce payment of child support.

Gaining practical skills and earning one's living require self-confidence, which sometimes comes through church involvement. Some Catholic pastoral programs teach women about their rights as well as more general notions of equality between men and women. Participation in Christian communities and other pastoral projects also allows women to assume leadership roles that give them transferable skills and social legitimacy. Through these roles, women display their capacity to work in social promotion programs and to make decisions about their education and work. They begin to value their condition as individuals, to recognize that they deserve to be treated with respect, and to begin relating to others in the same manner. Along the way, women cease to be submissive and begin asserting their rights to express an opinion and decide their future and that of their families.

Pastoral activities affect the real world in which they are carried out. Church programs can encourage people to participate with neighbors and to get to know the needs and demands of the community. People cease to be self-absorbed in their daily problems and discover that life has a greater meaning. They discover that Christians must embody the Kingdom of God and build a strong community in the present. Sara learned to speak in public in her Christian community. She learned to share her life and dreams with others and to listen to their experiences and hopes, and to share opinions about family and community matters. This taught her to be more tolerant. "Little by little, [my husband] began noticing this change [in me] and he started to change. Yes, he would notice that I turned talkative. That is, I was not solving problems by shouting or getting nervous and sometimes even slapping. He was noticing that now I had the patience to ask, communicate, and understand."

Similarly, Silvia's work in the church gave her a different outlook on life. She became increasingly active in parish life and today coordinates the parish *comedor* program in Huaycán. For Silvia, as for many women, experience as a lay leader and the discovery of new ways of making sense of the world freed her of everyday struggles. Becoming concerned about the problems of others, paradoxically, answered some of her own difficulties. The liberating nature of pastoral experience for Silvia and other Peruvian women we interviewed echoes the experience of Salvadoran women described in chapter 1, who insist that their religious involvement has transformed their lives and become central to their happiness and even their survival.

Local communities benefit when people associate with neighbors, other parents, fellow workers, and friends at the *comedor* and when they work together toward achieving common benefits. This experience encourages active participation in the Christian community, in schools, and in neighborhood organizations. Sara, for example, discovered a sense of service that prompted her to make a commitment not only to her Christian community but also to her neighborhood. This new image of herself and of her responsibility as a believer and as a neighbor inspired her to share her experience with others: "I learned to be joyful. I learned to laugh, which I had not done much. I had become too bitter. I felt full of happiness that I was spilling from every corner. Things were going well with my husband, with my children at home, then I accepted this responsibility with the hope to be able to do good. Because of my experience I wanted to reach other people that had the same problems that I had had [and help them] find the peace and serenity that I have been able to have and that I have until now."

There is yet another source of personal change that many Peruvian Catholics have experienced through social organizations and pastoral work. Women and men have learned to value each other in concrete tasks. Church-sponsored subsistence organizations have enabled families to recognize the value of the work that women carry out in the home. In the pastoral programs, men and women have listened to each other and expressed their opinions as equals. Although these experiences are not without difficulties, the benefits achieved have contributed to a family culture that fosters communication and equality between couples.

When the woman assumes a position within a social organization, her family—and the woman herself—often worries that her participation will take away from her domestic responsibilities. Women try to dedicate themselves to both their families and their pastoral responsibilities and to make these two tasks compatible. Rita, a parishioner in Comas, tried to meet this challenge when she assumed a position in a woman's organization in her district. "My children at the beginning, like their father, would say, 'no, now my mother is not going to be in the house' . . . When I was chosen district leader, I did not want them to know." By exercising leadership positions, women discover the qualifications that allow them to be not only good housekeepers but also excellent administrators. Women learn to excel in a number of activities without help from their families. They feel capable of performing in the public sphere and asserting their identity in the family. This experience, with time, brings changes to the image that husbands and children have regarding women's traditional gender roles. Rita, for example, stood up to her family. "Then I told him, 'Look Jorge, do not worry. I am going to continue in the organization because that is what I like, and I think I have already fulfilled my duties with you.' I told my children, 'Some of you are already married. I have no babies now. Now let me live my own space. It is my time to have my identity as an individual, to value myself and define the place that belongs to me.'"

Women who are engaged actively in pastoral work sometimes feel pressure to be "superwomen": they must be efficient in everything, in the family as well as outside of it. This *doble jornada* leads many women to assert their rights and equality. While church involvement can help strengthen women's assertion of equal rights, the demands of work should not lead them to uphold the image of superwomen. Instead, participation in pastoral work often seems to facilitate a redistribution of labor within the family by helping family members acknowledge that they all have equal rights. According to the traditional distribution of labor in Peruvian families, men perform duties related to production and women engage in activities of reproduction. Productive labor is valued socially and is thus remunerated. Reproductive labor, on the other hand, is not acknowledged in society and is given no monetary value. The redefinition of this division of labor depends on a couple's educational levels, the woman's entrance into the labor force, and both partners' attitudes toward women's equality. Redefinitions can also come as a result of church involvement, especially when religious education teaches the value of more egalitarian relations between men and women. Silvia explains that women must learn "to love ourselves . . . not be so submissive to the man. [Women] also must learn to work, to go out to work, because now it is not only the man who works, the woman also." Thus, many women realize that paid work is a right and a possibility for them. Social organizations have helped women consider paid work as an option. This offers them security and confidence. Pastoral work also gives women the ability to try to modify their family relationships, to have their opinions heard, and to make decisions with their partners.

Besides facilitating changes in women's attitudes, active participation in parish life can encourage men to view women in a different light. Because of his participation as a catechist in the parish of Yungay, Sebastián now realizes the importance of his wife's work and her role in the family. He now sees her as a rock upon which family life is built:

> Yes, this year [my wife] is attending the catechist school. And, in truth, brother, I have an excellent wife. During my whole life she has helped me always, and at one time, brother, I almost was demoralized with my illness from the accident. I suffered, because then we did not have anything to eat because for three years, four I was resting, almost five years it has taken for my bone to heal, my clavicle. I have not had it operated on, only like that it has repaired. We did not have anything, and so then my wife was very faithful, and she has helped me a lot not to lose my faith.

The increasing presence of women in various occupations encourages them to assert their condition of equality with men. Sara's testimony is significant:

> [At church] we also learn that both men and women have the same rights, because today we are seeing how women have been liberated so much that even in the job they are at the same level, doing the same job. How was I going to be working? When I would say that I wanted to work, [my husband] would say "No," that . . . it was the man who should sustain the home even if I felt pinched for money. . . . Not now. Now I depend on my work because I decide to do this. I am working—well, without telling him, "I make more money than you." Nothing like that, but it is a type of liberation for women.

Women's participation in church and social organizations can transform the relations between women and men in the family by increasing awareness about equal rights and recognition of women's abilities to play productive roles in the public sphere. However, families have not undergone a total transformation. That would require a greater number of women to enter the labor market and an improved level of education among both men and women. Likewise, in life it is important that family members share the household responsibilities, abandon the idea of the superwoman, and learn to value the work of the mother in both the private and public spheres. Patriarchal culture, in short, must be transformed at multiple levels: in both domestic and public realms, in large structures, and in everyday activities.

New understandings and practices of faith learned in parish groups have compelled many Peruvian Catholics to change their lives. One of the first changes that people experienced is the desire for consistency between what is taught or preached and what is practiced. This desire has encouraged many to formalize their relationship with their partner through a religious ceremony. Fausto, a rural catechist in Yungay, decided to marry the woman with whom he had lived for many years. He believed this was necessary for his status as a catechist. This conviction had more weight than the tradition in his community of having a big celebration after the wedding. Because they are poor, Fausto and his wife did not have the big, post-wedding celebration. Only their parents and godparents attended the wedding. Nevertheless, they were happy to comply with their faith and to be consistent with Catholic teaching. Their participation in church activities has led Fausto and his wife to modify old cultural norms in favor of religious ones, giving new meaning to traditional culture.

Although changing traditional cultural norms can take years, participation in pastoral work has encouraged many of our interviewees to reconsider the old ways and to adopt new modes of family life. Sebastián explains:

> If I had not started in this school, for sure my life would have been different. I have realized this because when I was fifteen or sixteen, I had the same incorrect idea as my father's because my uncle told me that my father had ten women. I personally have met three [of these] women. [My father] has had children with them but hasn't supported any of them. We have not received anything, neither food nor clothing, nothing from my father. I [used to think], "My father has had fun that way and I probably will have more fun." . . . But then, after I received this training in the catechist school, I [have come to] live differently. I am very grateful to my school because at the age of seventeen, I made a commitment with this school and to this date I like it. I have attended [the catechist school] for thirty years . . . I am an old man, and I am the father of a family.

Paternal abandonment, common in Peru, results in part from machismo. Like patriarchal culture, machismo assigns high status to men, but the latter also encourages men to avoid family responsibilities, to seek numerous lovers, and to father children with all of them. Participation in parish groups encouraged many Peruvian Catholic men and women to recognize and change those attitudes and customs that negatively affected their family life and to take seriously their family responsibilities. As Diego explains, "Never again [have I bet on horse races] nor bought lottery tickets, nor anything. Once I joined the [church] classes, that was it. Little by little I gave [it all up] . . . Now we plan the finances, things [have] changed."

Conclusion

The experience of faith and the involvement in pastoral work gives many Catholics an opportunity to reflect on their lives, which in turn encourages them to deepen the faith that they have inherited from their parents, to give it new content, meaning, and expressions. The experience of living their faith within a Christian community or parish encourages people to relate to others differently, to look at reality in a new way and assume new challenges. Diverse pastoral programs, including biblical reflection and collective experiences of sharing, listening, and offering advice, can motivate laypeople to change their attitudes toward central dimensions of their lives, including their families as well as their commitment to the church. Pastoral experiences can open up other ways of life within the family, in turn bringing changes in people's relationship with members of the opposite sex and views toward society and family. The trajectories of the Catholics we interviewed varied according to the individual and community, the timing of their incorporation into community life, and the particular characteristics of their neighborhood and family life. Consequently, to understand the extent to which the Christian community's message of solidarity, justice, peace, and equality has taken root, we must look at individuals' life histories.

We also found that participation in pastoral work helps men and women develop their potential as individuals. It encourages them to adopt leadership roles, develop their public speaking skills, coordinate groups, and discuss daily life in light of God's word. All of this helps individuals strengthen their self-esteem and acknowledge their rights and responsibilities in their church and community. In particular, pastoral experiences have allowed women in a patriarchal culture with little formal education and only a minimal participation in the labor market to become literate and develop their public speaking and leadership skills. These achievements have encouraged women to view themselves differently—to believe that they are equal to men, that they have a right to their own opinions, and that they are able to make decisions on their own. By allowing women to become active in church activities, parishes have simultaneously encouraged men to alter their authoritarian behavior and view women in a different light. Although these achievements represent a step forward in Peruvian culture, they are not without limits.

Thus, pastoral and social responsibilities are helping to change aspects of the patriarchal culture in Peru and facilitate the transition toward an egalitarian family and society. This cultural transformation also may serve as an important foundation for the consolidation of a more democratic society. Recognition of women's rights and the equality of men and women in family life can lead to the formation of engaged citizens who form part of a political community that guarantees the rights of all citizens and that promotes the common good. Likewise, more egalitarian families can contribute to the development of democratic practices and culture, thereby strengthening the process of democratic consolidation. Faith and pastoral experience that strengthens the individual can foster values of solidarity and justice and promote the development of leadership capacities that help lay a new cultural foundation for the family. At the same time, by generating a "concrete commitment to solidarity and charity" (John Paul II 1991, 49), these experiences can foster individual responsibility toward the larger community and provide guidance at a time when the tension between individualism and solidarity is producing great disorder and uncertainty.

Note

1. All quotations from individuals are taken from interviews conducted in Comas (May–August 1996), Huaycán (October 1996–June 1997), and Yungay (June–August 1997).

Chapter 3

Philip Williams

Popular Religion and the (Re)Construction of Community in Yungay

In Yungay's Campo Santo (Holy Ground), the tops of the old palm trees that once graced the town's central plaza are still visible. So are the twisted remains of a bus and a truck and the bricks from the old church. Huge boulders are scattered about between rose gardens and rows of white crosses. To the east, staring down on the Campo Santo stands the traitorous Huascarán. Looking up, one tries to imagine that fateful Sunday afternoon in 1970.

Willy, a resident of Musho, at the foot of Huascarán, recounted the tragic day: "I saw the snow, it fell like a huge mass, as if a bomb had exploded, expanding on all sides," Willy said. "We thought that it was coming toward us, so I threw myself on the ground to await my death. But it didn't come, the rumbling sound passed by over there, it continued toward Yungay."[1]

When Socorro, a resident of Yungay, heard the noise, she ran out of her house. "Neighbors were running everywhere. One neighbor shouted to me to run toward higher ground. I decided to run down the hill. The *aluvión* (avalanche) swept away my neighbor. I was saved when it stopped two meters from where I was running."

On May 31, 1970, at 3:23 P.M., a powerful earthquake (7.7 on the Richter scale) shook the Callejón de Huaylas, a picturesque valley nestled between the towering Cordillera Blanca and Cordillera Negra in the north-central Andes of Peru. The sheer magnitude of the earthquake dislodged a huge mass of ice from the northwest face of Huascarán, Peru's highest mountain. "This immense mass of ice, mud, and rock careened down the mountainside at a velocity varying between 217 and 435 kilometers per hour" (Oliver-Smith 1992, 11–12), carving a path of death and destruction that completely buried the town of Yungay and most of its residents. Because the avalanche took place on a Sunday, the town was particularly crowded with Indians from the upland communities who had come down for market. Only about 300 to 500 of the town's 4,500 residents survived the disaster (Oliver-Smith 1992).

The efforts to rebuild Yungay in the wake of the disaster are a testament to the will and determination of the survivors. Initially, government authorities wanted to relocate the city some fifteen kilometers away from its original site; however, the survivors, who viewed relocation as "a challenge and a threat to Yungaíno identity," successfully pressured the government to rebuild the city just north of the old Yungay (Oliver-Smith and Goldman 1988). By remaining close to Campo Santo, survivors preserved a symbolic connection to their past and reaffirmed their allegiance to the old community. Nevertheless, while the struggle to maintain continuity with the past would provide a source of unity in the initial aftermath of the disaster, it would not be sufficient in reconstructing a sense of community and shared identity in the new Yungay.

The disaster and subsequent reconstruction of Yungay provides a unique window through which to explore the role of popular religion in fostering collective identity in the context of dramatic social change. Prior to 1970, popular religion, as expressed through traditional devotions and the religious fiesta cycle, contributed to a shared Yungaíno identity and to a strong relationship between the town and upland rural communities. Global currents of renovation that were beginning to transform the Latin American Catholic church had not yet made themselves felt in Yungay. Moreover, while the global forces of economic modernization were slowly transforming the "traditional, almost feudal, life-style" of Yungay (Oliver-Smith 1992, 39), the pace of change was slow. The aluvión, however, was a major catalyst for social change. The disaster opened the way for military reformists in the Velasco government to use the reconstruction process as a way to bring economic and social modernization to the Callejón (Oliver-Smith and Goldman 1988). In addition to planning new urban developments, the Velasco government implemented an agrarian reform program that completely transformed traditional social relations and patterns of authority in the countryside. The disaster also accelerated the process of rural-urban migration, both within the Callejón and toward coastal cities. Finally, the influx of foreign priests and religious, influenced by reformist currents in the Catholic Church, stimulated new pastoral initiatives that often conflicted with traditional approaches. In response to these dramatic changes, local expressions of popular religion took on new and varied forms.[2]

The concept of popular religion has generated significant debate among both scholars and practitioners of religion. Earlier approaches to popular religion have been criticized for "overemphasizing the disjuncture between clerical and lay religion" and for "equating popular religion with forms of religiosity that are unsystematic, superstitious, and inauthentic" (Kselman 1991, 6). On the first score, Harline (1990) argues that while the boundary between popular religion and official religion is clear in the abstract, it becomes fuzzy when studying specific groups. For example, in some cases it is difficult to determine whether parish priests are representatives of official dogma or local beliefs and practice. Furthermore, as Carroll (1996) points out, official religion is not unproblematic, since there is often a divergence of opinion within church hierarchies regarding doctrinal and devotional issues. On the second score, Davis (1974) criticizes those who portray peasants as being passive recipients of what is transmitted from above and as being incapable of religious innovation. Instead, she argues that popular religion arises from the creative processes of ordinary people, not distortions of official religion, and can form a consistent system of symbolic meanings in its own right.

Similarly, within the Catholic Church in Latin America, the concept of popular religion has produced heated debate. During the 1970s, many progressives attacked popular religion as encouraging "fatalism, conservatism, and a concern for otherworldly salvation" (Kselman 1986, 30). The emphasis on traditional saint worship, processions, and pilgrimages was seen as detracting from Christians' obligations to struggle for social justice and liberation. Conservative critics, on the other hand, were concerned with maintaining orthodoxy and with the impact of popular religion on structures of authority within the church. By the time of the Latin American Bishops' Conference in Puebla in 1979, a more accommodationist view appeared to prevail. The bishops, while stressing the negative aspects of popular religion, praised the positive elements of traditional devotions (Kselman 1986). During the 1980s, progressive theologians began to reassess popular religion, emphasizing its positive, potentially liberating aspects. Instead of denigrating popular beliefs and practices, progressive priests and pastoral agents looked for ways to revalue popular religion while giving it new content and meaning (McGovern 1989, 91). Nevertheless, despite this newfound respect for popular religion, the new thinking still tended to underestimate the capacity of ordinary people to engage in religious innovation. Rather, church elites, while accommodating local conditions, were ultimately responsible for renewing popular religion.

A more fruitful approach to popular religion would consider the interaction of popular religious beliefs and practices with religious institutions: "new beliefs and devotions, constantly emerging, sometimes from above, but very often from below" (Carroll 1996, 7). Thus, while the boundaries between popular religion and official/institutional religion are not always clear, the logic of each can shape, and sometimes constrain, the other (Kselman 1983). While "a logic that guides the creative responses of ordinary people must have as its origins the local experiences of those same people" (Carroll 1996, 242), popular religion, for all its spontaneity, does occur within an institutional and even global context. Global processes impact local communities, including everyday expressions of popular religion. For example, popular devotions, which are considered a key element of popular Catholicism in Latin America, were introduced to the Americas by European missionaries during the colonial period (Kselman 1986). Moreover, both national and global religious forces continue to shape new religious movements and ideas at the local level. As was discussed in the introduction to this volume, the conservative restoration under Pope John Paul II has contributed to the weakening of pastoral strategies associated with the iglesia popular in favor of more spiritually oriented and clerically centered movements (see Hennelly 1993; Peterson and Vásquez 1998).

Although the religious/institutional context influences local elaborations of religion, it should not be seen as defining what is allowable. As Peterson (1997, 8) argues, popular religious groups "usually operate within traditions and certain broad guidelines set by the official church, but their practices and beliefs do not always conform closely to church orthodoxy." In the case of Catholics, the local parish provides only one source of ideas and spiritual support, since Catholics often participate in lay associations that are highly autonomous or in religious movements outside of the parish. Moreover, the process of expanding religious pluralism means that Catholics are increasingly exposed to religious ideas and practices from a variety of sources. However, as De Theije (1999, 118–119) points out, instead of simply "reacting" to these alternative influences, laypeople are "self-conscious actors in the construction of everyday Catholicism" with "substantial liberty to give form and meaning to their local expressions of Catholicism."

It should not be surprising, then, that within a single parish like Yungay, a variety of pastoral styles and priorities can coexist. In the period after the disaster, two distinct pastoral approaches emerged, as well as a variety of new expressions of popular religiosity. As Peterson (1998, 399) discusses, the tremendous diversity of popular Catholicism can produce "much contestation, among laypeople, between laypeople and pastoral agents, and between these groups and officials of the institutional church." While such conflict may undermine efforts by the local church to foster a sense of shared identity, it can also create new opportunities for community-building.

The Identity Crisis

*Yungay has no soul. The old Yungay disappeared and very
few survived. Only ten families still remain, the rest came
from here and there, they came to find something for themselves. The majority works here in Yungay, they work for
their livelihood, and that's it.*

—María

During our interviews with Yungaínos, both survivors of the disaster
and those who migrated from rural areas, we were struck by the absence of a
strongly shared Yungaíno identity. Many of those we interviewed commented
on the lack of unity, the widespread apathy, and the general unwillingness to
participate in collective endeavors. Even after twenty-seven years, Yungay was
still a new town, struggling to create new traditions and an identity of its own.

The crisis of identity is related to the disaster and subsequent reconstruction of Yungay. For survivors and their descendants, the 1970 earthquake represents a historical marker, dividing time into "before" and "after" the disaster.
Survivors look back to the old Yungay with great fondness and allegiance.
Teresa, who lost most of her family in the disaster, remembers: "Yungay was
beautiful, the people were warm, the town had a lot of commercial activity, a
town of hard-working, progressive people." Teresa's nostalgia for the old
Yungay has made it difficult for her to identify with the new town that has
emerged in its wake. When she returned to the Callejón de Huaylas from Lima
a few months after the disaster, she refused to believe that Yungay had disappeared: "All of us that returned had this idea that Yungay had not disappeared,
in our minds we had an image of how Yungay was, with its streets and economic activity . . . today we find ourselves living in some other place."

Besides the nostalgia and emotional suffering of the survivors, the process
of reconstruction contributed to their identity crisis. Initially, the struggle
against government efforts to relocate Yungay far away from its original site
helped to unify survivors and other victims of the disaster who had congregated in the survivors' camp. According to Oliver-Smith and Goldman (1988,
112): "Resistance which began with the core of urban survivors quickly spread
to the new peasant immigrants and ultimately to the peasant hinterlands of
Yungay, forming a powerful bloc of opposition to the government relocation
plans. Survival as a sociocultural entity and as the paramount urban center of
the province became the raison d'être of the population."

Throughout the rebuilding period, survivors felt abandoned by the government agency responsible for reconstruction (CRYRZA—Commission for
the Reconstruction and Rehabilitation of the Affected Zone), as aid was slow
to arrive and insufficient to cover the needs of the survivor camp's growing

population. The Velasco government viewed the earthquake as a unique opportunity to implement some of its plans for national transformation.[3] Besides
rebuilding the damaged infrastructure in the Callejón de Huaylas, the military
modernizers in CRYRZA hoped to address the existing socioeconomic and political inequalities, thereby creating a "new social order" (Bode 1989). Nevertheless, despite the government's rhetoric about popular participation,
CRYRZA's failure to consult residents about reconstruction plans was a constant source of conflict.

The urban development plan for Yungay unveiled in 1974 was greeted with
great skepticism by residents. Neither the physical layout nor construction of
the new city's principal buildings bore any resemblance to the old Yungay.
While commercial, residential, and industrial areas were clearly demarcated,
buildings ranged from the massive two-story concrete and glass municipal
building, to the hundred or so wooden prefabricated houses *(casas rusas)* donated by the Soviet Union, to the haphazard *auto-construcción* of residences
utilizing a mixture of building materials (Oliver-Smith 1992).

Despite a number of setbacks, the planned and unplanned reconstruction
of Yungay proceeded apace. By the 1990s, Yungay had recovered and surpassed
its pre-earthquake population. Declining from 3,543 in 1961 to 1,537 in 1972,
Yungay's population grew to 2,850 in 1981 and 4,646 in 1993 (Doughty 1999;
INEI 1993). Much of the population growth was the result of rural migrants.
Immediately following the earthquake, people from surrounding rural communities migrated to the survivor camp, where emergency food and shelter were
available. Given that many of the 300 survivors of the old Yungay moved to
Lima or other coastal cities, the social composition of the new Yungay was completely transformed. "The avalanche surgically excised the conservative, urban,
mestizo elites who had previously controlled affairs. For the new Yungaínos,
it was a unique opportunity for social mobility in a frontier-like scenario"
(Doughty 1999, 245).

The initial unity in opposition to government relocation plans soon gave way
to division and conflicts (Oliver-Smith and Goldman 1988). Traditional tensions
between mestizos and Indians reemerged and were exacerbated by the competition for scarce resources during the reconstruction period. Oliver-Smith
(1992) describes the hostility of the town's survivors toward rural migrants,
whom they considered "imposters, exploiters of the tragedy, seeking to get
something for nothing" (136). Many of the townspeople felt "surrounded" by
Indians and resented them benefiting from the disaster aid. While there had
always been an antagonistic relationship between mestizos and Indians, "there
never was anything like an effective caste system" (Bode 1989, 223). According to Bode, the vertical relationship between town and country was shattered

by the earthquake: "The patterned flow of life up and down the mountainsides was interrupted. Indians were no longer settled for the night in the surrounding mountains, and mestizos on the valley floor. Many Indians moved down into the valley to occupy the deserted ruins of a town house or to avail themselves of free shelter and provisions being distributed" (1989, 223). The tensions were especially visible during the allocation of temporary housing, when urban mestizos were unwilling to allow Indian peasants to be housed in nearby modules. Moreover, townspeople viewed the influx of rural migrants as contributing to the overall backwardness of the new Yungay. Teresa explained: "Yungay is very backward in the cultural aspect . . . the town has been formed by people from the countryside, so it will take many years for Yungay to reach its former level."

The antagonistic relationship between mestizos and Indians may explain to some extent the failure to forge a collective identity in the new Yungay. In contrast, in popular districts of Lima, people's participation in collective struggles for basic infrastructure and recognition by the central government have contributed to a sense of community and belonging among residents. As Muñoz and Castro Aguilar point out in chapters 4 and 5, even though migrants in Comas and Huaycán did not share a common place of origin, during the 1970s and 1980s they asserted their rights as residents and joined local community organizations to obtain access to housing, basic services, and education. Although there were differences in the socioeconomic status of migrants, most were very poor, and those who were better off enjoyed few privileges in the new squatter settlements. As popular districts became more established, as in the case of Comas, socioeconomic differentiation increased; however, this did not produce the degree of antagonism evident between mestizos and Indians in the countryside.

The level of citizen participation in the reconstruction of Yungay differed significantly from that of squatter settlements in Lima. The reconstruction efforts of CRYRZA and its successors in the Callejón de Huaylas were highly centralized and carried out in an authoritarian fashion with little input from the victims of the disaster. Doughty (1999, 250) explains: "Despite the governmental rhetoric about public participation, outsiders controlled and manipulated decisions at many levels . . . In no case did the rehabilitation administration appreciate the need to fortify or create municipal organization as critical to the recovery process, or indeed, as part of a future mitigation strategy." Consequently, local government institutions, important channels for citizen participation, were weakened as a result of the reconstruction process.

In Yungay, migrants from the rural communities were content to establish an urban residence but not much interested in participating in the town's development and progress. Instead of becoming active participants in the construction of the new town, many of the new residents were more likely to follow the lead of urban mestizos. Moreover, urbanite *prepotencia* (prepotency) tended to discourage participation by people of rural origin.[4] This legacy of the reconstruction process is still evident today in the low levels of citizen participation in community affairs. For example, when the municipal government organized a *cabildo abierto* (town meeting) to discuss the town's chronic water shortage, attendance was disappointing. According to Silvia, who operates the parish pharmacy, "only about twenty people attended this last *cabildo abierto,* twenty people to defend the needs of all of Yungay."

Survivors of the aluvión express ambivalent attitudes about the development of the new town. As was discussed above, many yearn for the Yungay that once was (at least as they remember it). At the same time, they exhibit pride for what has been accomplished but are reluctant to embrace it as their own. For example, Teresa boasted that Yungay was the only town in the Callejón to have two normal schools and a police training facility. According to Teresa, these accomplishments are a testament to the courage and determination of the survivors: "The Instituto Pedagógico was the result of the efforts of ten people who struggled against all odds, including opposition from residents, but we continued forward despite the opposition until we achieved our goal, and now the Instituto serves not only the people of Yungay, but the entire Callejón de Huaylas."[5]

Paralleling the transformation of the urban area of Yungay were significant changes in the countryside. The Velasco government's (1968–1975) sweeping agrarian reform program dispossessed *hacendados* of their large estates in the Yungay countryside, leaving in their place a number of *comunidades campesinas* (agricultural cooperatives) and small individually owned farms. Despite the promise of improving living conditions in the countryside, the agrarian reform achieved mixed success. *Campesinos* in Yungay no longer had to work as peons on haciendas; however, the small size of their plots and the government's failure to provide them with adequate support services (credit, technical assistance) forced many to work a few months a year on the large commercial farms along the coast, as had been the case before the reform was enacted.

Despite difficult conditions in the countryside, 73 percent of the population of district of Yungay lives in rural areas and 27 percent in the urban area (INEI 1993). In the rural communities, Quechua is the dominant language. While most of the men are bilingual, having attended a few years of school, many of the women have difficulty communicating in Spanish. Increasingly, though, women are attending primary school in their local communities, and some travel to Yungay to attend secondary school. For young people in both the urban and rural areas of Yungay, education is highly valued and seen as a way out of poverty. Nevertheless, because of the limited postsecondary educational opportunities (with the exception of the normal schools) and the small labor market in Yungay, most young people have to migrate to Huaraz (the department capital) or Lima to pursue education or work opportunities, and few return to Yungay.

The Death of a Fiesta

Yungay doesn't have anything that it can call its own . . . the majority of the towns [in the Callejón de Huaylas] have their fiesta patronal, almost all of them, and Yungay doesn't have a fiesta patronal; its patron saint is Santo Domingo, the fiesta is the 8th of August, but it passes by almost unnoticed.

—María

Prior to the earthquake, the fiesta of Santo Domingo de Guzmán was celebrated with great fervor. Along with feast of Santa Rosa, it was one of the most important events in the religious calendar. The surrounding upland communities descended upon the town of Yungay in a celebration of religious devotion, mixed with drinking, dancing, and revelry. The rural communities were organized into two barrios (Mitma and Huambo), each with an *alcalde pedáneo* (Indian or "petty" mayor) appointed by the mayor of Yungay. Competition between the two barrios was intense. Each barrio tried to hire the better band, design the most elaborate costumes for their dancers, and put on the best fireworks show. On the central day of the fiesta, the two barrios entered the plaza from different streets, processing around the plaza before entering the church side by side. After the mass, from the balcony of the municipal palace, the mayordomos (sponsors of the fiesta) lowered gifts of sheep, bread, and liquor with a rope to the alcaldes pedáneos waiting below.[6]

According to Oliver-Smith (1992), the indigenous fiesta cycle was a ritual expression of allegiance to the town and contributed to maintaining the town's domination of rural communities. Indigenous communities were responsible for organizing and assuming financial responsibility for fiestas, in addition to their normal role in providing unpaid labor crews for municipal and district projects. The fiestas of Santo Domingo and Santa Rosa also provided an important source of income for townspeople, as it brought thousands of people to town for the central activities. However, from the perspective of the Indian communities, their participation was not simply a reaffirmation of their allegiance to political and religious authorities in the town. Assuming ritual obligations was a way of according status in the community, redistributing economic surplus, reaffirming *compadrazgo* (godparenthood) ties, as well as keeping *promesas* (promises) to Santo Domingo to assure good harvests and other blessings.[7] Moreover, Indian participation in the fiesta represented a symbolic inversion of power and status. Despite the town's traditional domination of the countryside, at least during the few days of celebration, Indian peasants "invaded" and "occupied" the town, engaging in behavior normally prohibited any other time of the year. Finally, despite the rivalry between the communities organized into the two barrios, their participation in the fiesta contributed to a heightened sense of ethnic identity vis-à-vis the townspeople.

After the 1970 earthquake, participation in the fiesta declined. According to Oliver-Smith (1992, 213), for the 1971 celebration, the bishop of Huaraz issued a decree "condemning all activities associated with religious festivals which were not of a specifically religious nature." The parish priest of Yungay preached against the excessive drinking and revelry associated with the fiesta. These attacks on the more "profane" aspects of the fiesta were part of a more general critique of popular religion within reformist currents of the Catholic Church in Latin America during the 1960s and 1970s. In addition to the clergy's exhortations against the excesses of traditional religious celebrations, the diocese of Huaraz began a program to train rural catechists as a way of reestablishing Catholic orthodoxy in the rural communities and suppressing superstitious beliefs and practices.[8]

Also contributing to the decline in participation was the withdrawal of the Mitma barrio from its ritual obligations. The avalanche completely destroyed nine communities of Mitma and cut off others from the survivors' camp. Moreover, the alcalde pedáneo and several other authorities perished in the disaster. When Yungay authorities attempted to appoint a replacement for the alcalde pedáneo, none of the candidates accepted. According to Oliver-Smith (1992) the remaining Mitma communities used the disaster as an opportunity to resist the traditional control exerted by authorities in Yungay and to withdraw from the dual village system. Given the extent of the destruction, Mitma leaders viewed their ritual obligations as an additional burden. Consequently, for the 1971 fiesta, the Huambo barrio assumed exclusive financial responsibility, while the participation from the Mitma barrio was much diminished.

Another factor that contributed to the decline of the fiesta was the physical infrastructure of the survivors' camp and the new town. Prior to the disaster, the layout of the city "reaffirmed the social and ritual division of the province in that the special alignment of the central plaza, adjacent streets, and church entrance demarcated pre-conquest moiety boundaries between the *waranqas* or barrios of Huambo and Mitmaq" (Doughty 1999, 246). In contrast, the survivor's camp was a random collection of temporary dwellings, with none of the splendor of the old central plaza and church (Oliver-Smith 1992, 208). Even when the new Yungay eventually took shape, the town's layout bore no resemblance to the old Yungay. Construction on the church did not begin until after 1980 and was still not completed in 1997.

By the 1990s, the fiesta had all but disappeared in Yungay, except in some of the upland communities of Huambo, where it was still celebrated with some fervor. In 1996 there was no celebration in Yungay because of the failure to recruit a mayordomo. In 1997 there was an attempt to revive the fiesta; however, according to participants, the festivities paled in comparison to earlier times. Approximately four hundred people, mostly from Huambo communities, attended the central Mass and participated in the procession around the plaza. Many of the old traditions were absent. While the alcalde pedáneo was accompanied by his staff-bearers *(varayoq)* during the initial procession, there were no traditional dancers *(shaqshas* and *pallas)* and only a small band. The lowering of the gifts never occurred because the alcalde pedáneo had forgotten to bring a rope. There was no great fireworks display and only fairly modest drinking and revelry after the Mass. As if symbolic of its diminished importance, when the procession returned to the church to replace the image of Santo Domingo, a funeral mass had already begun. Participants in the two rituals became intermingled, with both groups jostling one another as they tried to leave through the front door of the church.

The Fiesta of Señor de Mayo

The Señor de Mayo has renewed people's faith in Yungay.
Nobody pays attention to Santo Domingo anymore.

—Teresa

At the same time that the Fiesta of Santo Domingo was in decline, a new popular devotion began to spread among Yungaínos. During the 1970s, a Yungaíno family with ties to the upland community of Rayan Shuyup began promoting devotion to the Señor de Mayo (Lord of May). The image of the crucified Christ was originally housed at the family's hacienda in Shuyup before being donated to the community's tiny chapel. According to local residents, the image dates back to the early colonial period and was one of the first images brought to the Callejón de Huaylas by the Spaniards. People attribute supernatural powers to the image. For example, while the other images of saints in the Shuyup chapel were destroyed during the earthquake, Señor de Mayo survived intact, with only slight damage to one of its arms. Devotos (devotees to the saint) turn to the Señor de Mayo in times of personal or family crisis and often interpret the resolution of such crises as resulting from the Señor's intervention on their behalf. José, a catechist and one of approximately eighty devotos in Shuyup, attributes his success in the catechist school to the miraculous power of Señor de Mayo: "When I attended the catechist school for the first time, the *procurador* of Señor de Mayo asked me to become a devoto and I accepted . . . and since then he [Señor de Mayo] has helped me; for example, since I entered [the catechist school] how many catechists have I left behind that are still in the first cycle. Yes, I believe it's as we say, miraculous, yes."

Devotos hope that by offering promesas to Señor de Mayo, such as participating in processions or sponsoring a Mass, they will benefit from his "miraculous" protection during difficult times. José explains the obligations of the devotos: "Well, every Saturday the devoto takes a flower and places it in front of the image, every eight days he changes it for a new one . . . later when the day of the fiesta arrives, he helps prepare the fiesta, organize the Masses." Each year a *procurador* (manager of the fiesta sponsors) is appointed to organize the festivities. His duties include recruiting mayordomos to assume financial responsibilities for all aspects of the fiesta, including the bands, dancers, the food and drink, fireworks, and the Masses. The fiesta takes place during the last two weeks in May.

In 1973 a small group of devotos in Yungay asked Shuyup authorities permission to bring the image to town to be venerated prior to the main celebration. According to one of the devotos (Teresa), following the earthquake there was a general decline in the religious faith of Yungaínos. Many of the survivors had lost their entire families and interpreted the disaster as God's punishment. Feeling abandoned by God, many turned to alcohol and away from their faith: "there was a time when people didn't want to go to church, didn't want to go to Mass either. My husband's grandfather used to have the image on his hacienda [before giving it to the community]. So we succeeded in convincing the people there [in Shuyup] that the image would give us strength, that we should bring it here. Each house would have it for a day and a night, and we would arrange the most beautiful altars." From 1973 to 1982, a group of devotos from Yungay would bring the image to town for two weeks in early May and then return it for the fiesta in Shuyup.

In 1982 a devoto in Yungay had the idea to make a replica of the image that would be housed in the church in Yungay. This way, the townspeople would be able to venerate the image year round. However, in Shuyup rumors began to spread that the townspeople wanted to switch the images, keeping the authentic Señor de Mayo for themselves.[9] The ensuing dispute prompted Shuyup authorities to limit the "visit" to two days each year. The conflict highlighted the traditional tensions between town and country and demonstrated the unwillingness of indigenous communities to be manipulated by townspeople.

Since 1982 participation in the two-day celebration in Yungay has increased significantly. According to Teresa and her husband, devotion to the Señor de Mayo has helped revive the religious faith of Yungaínos and has brought more unity to the town. Since Santo Domingo was always considered a fiesta of the "country people," townspeople never had a fiesta that they could claim as their own. In contrast, the fiesta for Señor de Mayo is a religious celebration organized and sponsored by townspeople, particularly original Yungaínos. For these Yungaínos, Señor de Mayo gives the town a new religious foundation upon which to rebuild a sense of community. In recent years, the fiesta has attracted a growing number of participants from the Yungaíno migrant community in Lima and other coastal towns. For migrants, the fiesta represents an opportunity "to meet family and friends, exchange news, and be 'home' for awhile" (Otter 1985, 238). The participation of migrants in the fiesta of Señor de Mayo parallels the experience of other Andean communities. In addition to transplanting Andean religious fiestas in their migrant communities in Lima, many migrants return to their place of origin during the *fiesta patronal,* in what becomes a kind of homecoming (Doughty 1968; Marzal 1989). For example, in our surveys of migrant laypeople in Comas and Huaycán, we found that 41 percent travel frequently to their hometowns, often to visit relatives during the fiestas. Similarly, as Ruíz Baía demonstrates in chapter 7 on transnational *hermandades* in Paterson, New Jersey, the centrality of traditional popular devotions to immigrants' sense of "Peruvianness" encourages some to return to Peru for important religious fiestas.

Over the past few years, Yungaíno migrants have been recruited as mayordomos for the fiesta of Señor de Mayo. For those who assume sponsorship of the fiesta, it is "an opportunity to demonstrate economic wealth and gain personal prestige" (Paerregaard 1997, 216). Besides reconnecting migrants with their Yungaíno roots, the fiesta also has encouraged some migrants to help raise funds for completion of the church in Yungay. One of the honored guests for the 1995 celebration was a Yungaíno working in the president's office in Lima. He lobbied successfully to provide a large subsidy for the completion of the roof. During the 1997 celebration, when the new roof was inaugurated, he served as mayordomo.

The Local Parish and the Identity Crisis

*The priests here generally spend their time celebrating
Masses. If someone dies, Mass; if someone has a birth-
day, Mass; if it's the anniversary of some institution,
Mass . . . the parish priest celebrates three Masses a day
minimum in Yungay.*

—María

Prior to the earthquake, the local church attempted to utilize the indigenous fiesta system in support of the town's traditional domination over the
surrounding rural communities. However, the arrival of Catholic reformers to
the parish in the aftermath of the disaster contributed to the emergence of two
very distinct pastoral orientations. One is represented by the parish priest, the
other by a group of Franciscan sisters and the French-Canadian religious. The
parish priest adopts a traditional sacramentalist approach, concerned primarily with administering the sacraments in the town and surrounding rural communities. He puts little emphasis on evangelization and supports the training
of lay leaders only insofar as it helps prepare parishioners for the sacraments
of baptism and first communion, and as a means of enhancing church control
over rural communities.

The Franciscan sisters and the French-Canadian religious represent an alternative pastoral approach. The Franciscan sisters run a school for rural catechists to promote the role of laity in rural, pastoral work. The program to train
rural catechists in the diocese of Huaraz dates back to 1967, when the first
catechist school was established. Catechists were to replace the traditional religious practitioners *(doctrineros)* in the rural communities, assuming responsibility for religious education and celebrations.[10] The *doctrineros,* who had
some expertise in leading prayers and hymns, did not receive training in the
parish and were not subject to church control. Hence, the purpose of the original catechist program was to evangelize rural communities and reassert institutional control.

After the earthquake, the program to train rural catechists in the diocese
gained momentum. A number of clergy and religious, influenced by reformist
currents within the church, arrived to the Callejón de Huaylas to participate
in the reconstruction effort. In Yungay, a group of Franciscan sisters helped
found the catechist school in 1974. Over the years, the program has grown
considerably. By 1997 there were fifty catechists covering thirty communities
in the parish. The catechists participate in monthly training sessions in Yungay,
where they receive instruction on church doctrine, liturgy, sacraments, and
social issues. They are responsible for running catechism programs and presiding over religious celebrations in their communities. In addition, the cat-

echists are recognized leaders in their communities, sought out for advice and counsel.

The French Canadian religious—a priest and two brothers of the San Viator order—support the school for catechists in addition to teaching religion courses in the Instituto Pedagógico and directing the Juventud Agraria Rural Católica (JARC). The JARC is affiliated to the International Movement of Catholic Rural Youth (MIJARC—Movimiento Internacional de la Juventud Agraria Rural Católica), which was founded in Europe in 1954. The movement, which traces its origins to the Catholic Action movement, began its work in Peru in the early 1960s with the help of a group of French missionaries.[11] From 1965 to 1970 the upsurge in peasant mobilization in the Peruvian highlands, as well as the agrarian reform program under the military government of Velasco Alvarado, encouraged several of the JARC's leaders to become involved in revolutionary movements. The increasing radicalization of the JARC leadership created tensions with the church hierarchy, which withdrew its support from the movement during the 1970s. After a period of decline, the JARC began to renew its leadership and rebuild its base organizations during the 1980s. By emphasizing its pastoral dimension and avoiding more political activities, it also succeeded in regaining official recognition by the church hierarchy.

The presence of transnational religious movements like the JARC in Peru highlights the importance of global religious influences, particularly the role of foreign missionaries in shaping local pastoral initiatives. Foreign priests and sisters bring with them a diversity of experiences and ideas that encourage new pastoral styles and priorities. However, because their access to rural communities is often limited by language or distance, they rely on lay leaders (catechists) to transmit religious doctrine. In many cases, catechists communicate what they learn in the catechist school in a highly selective fashion, adapting it to local customs and rituals (Siebers 1999). In turn, religious innovation at the local level can reverberate back, shaping the pastoral orientations of foreign missionaries and transnational religious movements.

In Yungay the JARC has been active since 1991. The French Canadian religious have been especially instrumental in promoting the movement and recruiting young campesinos to become leaders in their communities. JARC members are to "give witness to their faith" by working to improve the economic, social, and spiritual conditions of their communities. They also participate in local, regional, and national workshops and conferences, where they receive religious instruction and courses on human rights, agricultural technology, and other social issues.

The two conflicting pastoral orientations have made it difficult for the local church to speak with one voice. This contrasts with the parishes that we studied in Comas and Huaycán (see chapter 5). In those parishes, local clergy and religious transmitted a fairly coherent communitarian worldview based on the notion that believers are called upon to construct the Reign of God here and now. Consequently, the church emphasized local transformation and played an instrumental role in propelling community-based movements (Williams and Fuentes 2000). In Yungay, on the other hand, the local church was ineffective in fostering greater citizen participation in the reconstruction process. As was discussed earlier, the low level of civic engagement carried over into the post-reconstruction period.

Given their sacramentalist approach, the parish priests in Yungay did not attempt to establish Christian communities or promote other forms of lay participation in the town. A program to train urban catechists, directed by the Franciscan sisters, provides one of the only opportunities for lay participation. However, most of the catechists are in their early twenties, study and work full-time, and often leave Yungay to pursue educational or job opportunities. Consequently, few laypeople in the town develop the leadership skills and confidence that might encourage them to become more active citizens.

In contrast, rural parishioners have more opportunities to develop leadership skills. In fact, given the decline of rural-based organizations in the Callejón de Huaylas, participation in both the JARC and the school for catechists provides one of the only venues for campesinos from different communities to meet and share their experiences. According to José: "When we come down for our workshop we share with one another, we pray together, we share our understandings . . . what we learn we then try to share with our communities." Likewise, Willy feels "more connected" as a result of his participation in the school for catechists. According to Willy, during the period of the agrarian reform under Velasco, and to a lesser extent during the García government (1985–1990), there were greater opportunities for participation in rural movements. However, with the disappearance of the Ligas Agrarias (Agrarian Leagues), the catechist school became the only opportunity for campesinos to participate in organizations that extended beyond the community level.

The self-confidence and leadership skills that catechists develop enable them to hold their own in mestizo-dominated settings and institutions. Isaías, president of the JARC in the Callejón de Huaylas, spoke of the marginalization experienced by young campesinos when they go to town: "When the young campesino goes down to the town, he's marginalized, sometimes because of his social class, because when someone comes down from the *altura* (high altitude), since they have a different social life in the countryside, they don't act like the townspeople and they feel marginalized." Participation in the JARC has enabled Isaías and other leaders to overcome this feeling of social exclusion. As a JARC leader, Isaías has had a number of opportunities to attend regional and national JARC conferences, interacting with leaders from other regions of Peru. He has also attended theology courses at the Catholic University in Lima during the summers. As a result of these experiences, Isaías no longer feels intimidated in mestizo settings. For example, in 1997 Isaías attended the VIII Pastoral Assembly of the Diocese of Huaraz as the representative of the JARC. During the assembly, Isaías criticized the work of parish priests: "the parish priests should comply with their evangelizing mission, not just celebrate Mass, not just perform a service for profit but also when it's not profitable."

The skills and competence acquired in the JARC and the catechist school also encourage younger rural parishioners to pursue additional educational opportunities. Isaías's participation in the JARC reinforced his desire to pursue postsecondary studies. He is currently studying at one of the normal schools in Yungay and hopes to work as a mathematics and religion teacher in a rural community. Fausto, from the community of Masra, decided to go back to school soon after becoming a catechist. He thought that by completing his education he could improve his communication skills so essential in his pastoral work. To attend night school in Yungay, Fausto had to walk one and a half hours each way, after working all day on his farm. Eventually, Fausto decided to move to town, where he and his family lived in a kiosk in the market. To support his family, Fausto had to abandon his farm and work full time in the market repairing shoes while studying in the evenings. Upon completing high school, Fausto received a scholarship to study at the Instituto Pedagógico in Yungay. Fausto believes that as a result of his education and work as a catechist he is treated more fairly by townspeople than his fellow campesinos.

Whereas the catechist school and the JARC have been instrumental in fostering a sense of dignity and shared identity among rural parishioners, the parish priest tends to reinforce the traditional pattern of domination over rural communities by town authorities. Rural catechists and JARC leaders complain of the parish priest's treatment toward them.[12] According to Fausto, the catechist from the community of Masra, "since I've been here, the priests never helped us, they never even had thirty, fifteen minutes to spare with us, they never showed any interest in the catechists . . . but whenever any of us made a mistake they were quick to shout at us . . . and we had to put up with it." The rural communities rely on the parish priest to celebrate the central activities of their religious calendars but complain that he is only interested in collecting his fees. Willy, a catechist from the community of Musho, compared the evangelizing work of the catechists to that of the parish priest: "We [the catechists] are in closer contact with the people, we work harder . . . they [the priest and his assistant] say they are doing evangelization, but it's evangelization for pay, because when they come to celebrate Mass, they charge money; in contrast, we commit a lot of our time accompanying the people, but we don't receive any income for it. In this sense I would say that our evangelizing work is closer to that of Jesus: we dedicate our time and receive nothing in return."

Given the presence of divergent pastoral approaches among local church elites, it is not surprising that catechists and JARC leaders enjoy considerable autonomy in their pastoral work. For example, during a celebration of the Word in the community of Rayan Shuyup, José used a passage from Exodus to denounce the injustices of local authorities, especially their failure to support the pastoral work of the catechists. In another community, Panash, the catechist drew on a passage from Matthew to criticize the parish priest: "The Word of God is a gift, it's free. He doesn't charge us anything. Just as we receive the Word of God for free, we must share it with others."

Another example of the large degree of autonomy for local religious expression is the radio program administered by rural catechists. Two catechists from the parish of Yungay and two from neighboring parishes direct a weekly radio program in Quechua. They arrive to the parish on Wednesday evening after a two- to three-hour journey on foot and spend most of the night preparing the program before going on the air at five o'clock the next morning. By 6:15 A.M. they are on their way back to their communities ready for a full day's work on the farm. Although the radio program was initiated by the bishop of Huaraz in 1989 in response to evangelical "incursions" into the airwaves, the catechists are solely responsible for the production and content of the program. They received some initial training and technical support from the Coordinadora Nacional de la Radio (CNR) but no ongoing training other than their participation in the catechist school. The weekly program includes prayer, music (both religious and popular), biblical reflection, local and national news, and community announcements. The catechists believe that the program is an important way to preserve their language and culture and to bring greater unity to the upland communities.

Besides enjoying significant autonomy in their pastoral work, catechists are exposed to a variety of religious and ideological influences outside of the parish context. Isaías, for example, told how his encounters with different evangelical churches enriched his own faith. Although evangelicals represented only 4 percent of the district's population (INEI 1993), in Isaías's community of Musho, approximately one-third of the residents belong to one of the two evangelical churches. Several relatives on his mother's side are active evangelicals, and Isaías has several friends that are evangelicals. Not surprisingly, he often attends services at the evangelical churches: "I've always, always participated, and thanks to them [the evangelicals] I learned to play the guitar and learned some Christian lessons. Because they really love one other, they fulfill their obligation to love their neighbor; when someone goes to them with some need for pastoral service, they help them not just with money, and when they do give financial support they don't expect anything in return."

Similarly, when Isaías was working on a plantation along the coast, he was often visited by Seventh-Day Adventists. He never told them to go away, but he always peppered them with questions about their own religious beliefs. He sees his participation in summer theology courses in Lima as a way to bolster the theological foundations of his faith and better prepare him for his encounters with evangelicals.

Instead of "simply mixing traditional folk beliefs with elements from official Catholic tradition" (Carroll 1996, 242), Isaías draws from a variety of sources to cultivate his own faith. His desire to search beyond the confines of the local parish is rooted in his everyday experiences. Most importantly, his interactions with parish priests left him disillusioned and crushed his dream of one day entering the priesthood: "I watched to see how they (the parish priests) acted in society, to see if they really put into practice their Christian faith, like Christ did by demonstrating his faith with actions. I'll tell you sincerely that the parish priests that came here did not have much love for the people in the countryside, they marginalized them, sometimes they wouldn't celebrate Mass . . . they stole from the people, even people who didn't have anything." Consequently, although Isaías's participation in the JARC has provided opportunities for more positive interactions with pastoral agents, his distrust of church elites leads him to act with a high degree of autonomy in his own religious life.

Religious Pluralism, Conflict, and Community-Building

This discussion of popular religion and community-building in the aftermath of a devastating natural disaster points to the impact of multiple local, national, regional, and global forces on religious expression. At the same time, however, it reminds us that these external forces are mediated by local institutions and the experiences of everyday life. For example, in the context of growing religious pluralism in the wake of the disaster, Yungaínos have been exposed to religious ideas and practices from a variety of sources, including autonomous lay associations and transnational religious movements outside of the parish. But instead of simply reacting to these external influences, Yungaínos have drawn on these additional religious resources to give meaning and form to their own local expressions of Catholicism.

In Yungay, the aluvión entirely destroyed a community, including most of its inhabitants and all of its infrastructure, and severely damaged surrounding communities. In addition to rebuilding the physical community nearby the original site, survivors struggled to preserve community symbols and rituals. The post-disaster reconstruction period opened the way to Catholic reformists and to modernizing elements in the Velasco government to put their new thinking into practice. The religious and military reformers hoped to create a model planned community, one that was more modern and equitable but bore little resemblance to the old Yungay. For survivors, asserting allegiance to the old community became increasingly difficult in the wake of the disaster, as the new Yungay was resettled by migrants from surrounding communities and traditional social, political, and economic hierarchies were overturned. This massive dislocation and internal migration, combined with the reconstruction process, the agrarian reform program in the countryside, and the program to train rural lay leaders, generated conflict along a number of axes.

First, the accelerated pace of change exacerbated traditional tensions between Indians and mestizos as rural communities became more assertive in their relationship with the town. These tensions were especially evident in relations between original Yungaínos and post-disaster settlers, and they also manifested themselves in the religious field. For example, the fiesta of Santo Domingo went into decline as control was wrested away from religious and political authorities in the town. At the same time, original Yungaínos cultivated an alternative popular devotion (Señor de Mayo) to bring greater unity to townspeople. Within the local parish, the penetration of reformist currents contributed to two divergent pastoral orientations, one represented by the parish priest and the other by the JARC and rural catechist movement. The program for rural catechists produced a whole new cadre of self-confident campesino lay leaders who were no longer willing to accept the institutional church's traditional domination of rural communities.

Although the growing religious pluralism generated conflicts that undermined to some extent the local church's ability to contribute to the process of community-building, there were new opportunities for religious innovation from below. The autonomy of popular religious groups was evident in the program for rural catechists. Although the program was a diocesan initiative implemented by a group of Franciscan sisters, our interviews demonstrated the significant level of autonomy enjoyed by catechists. For example, while the catechists and JARC leaders could count on the local church for important organizational and symbolic resources, their participation in religious and secular activities and organizations outside of the parish also enriched their repertoire of religious resources. In addition, despite the decline in some religious fiestas, there were opportunities for new popular devotions to flourish with considerable autonomy from the local church. Although rural communities still relied on the parish priest for key celebrations in their religious calendars, as a result of the catechist program, most rural communities could now count on the presence of catechists in directing some local religious activities.

Whether or not this newfound pluralism will serve as a foundation for the rearticulation of civic life in Yungay is hard to say. Certainly, in the countryside there are signs of this happening. Even in the town, where the sheer magnitude of the disaster and subsequent reconstruction made it difficult to build a shared sense of community, Yungaínos, like María, continue to dream of a Yungay "that is more united, where people can live in community." While up to now the local church has been ineffective in fostering a strong collective identity, at a minimum it has provided laypeople, especially rural parishioners, with important religious resources to develop self-confidence and dignity and become more active participants in the process of building their communities.

Notes

1. All quotations from individuals are taken from personal interviews conducted in Yungay between June and August 1997.
2. Garrard-Burnett (1998a) found that the 1976 earthquake in Guatemala resulted in major social and political changes that facilitated the rapid growth of evangelical churches.
3. On the Velasco regime's developmentalist program, see McClintock and Lowenthal (1983), and Palmer (1980).
4. I am grateful to Tony Oliver-Smith for this observation.
5. Although such claims by the town's survivors are common, they should be viewed with some skepticism.
6. I am indebted to Paul Doughty for his observations of the fiesta during the 1960s.
7. For a good discussion of *fiestas patronales* in another community in the Callejón de Huaylas, see Stein (1961). Also see Ingham (1986) on folk Catholicism in rural Mexico.
8. See Garrard-Burnett's (1998a) similar discussion of the use of catechists in rural Guatemala to combat indigenous *costumbres*.
9. Such rumors of "saint-switching" are common in the Callejón de Huaylas. For example, see Bode's (1989) discussion of a similar conflict over the image of Señor de Soledad in Huaraz following the 1970 earthquake.
10. In some communities, the *doctrineros* felt threatened by the catechists who stressed understanding the Catholic doctrine and the ability to explain biblical passages.
11. The Catholic Action movement originated in Europe during the late 1920s. It channeled peasant, labor, and student groups into church-sponsored organizations, initially as a response to the growing influence of communist movements.
12. In a survey of twenty-five rural catechists, twenty-two claimed that the local parish did not respond to the needs of their community. This contrasted with urban catechists, where nine of fifteen thought that the parish *did* respond to community needs.

Part II

Civil Society, Citizenship, and Democratization

Chapter 4

Hortensia Muñoz

Believers and Neighbors

"Huaycán Is One and No One Shall Divide It"

On July 15, 1984, two thousand families, grouped into twenty-three associations of residents from the eastern edge of Lima, moved onto the land around Huaycán ravine, located off kilometer 16.5 of the nation's central highway, to create the *asentamiento humano* (human settlement) of Huaycán.[1] The occupation had the approval of the Provincial Municipality of Lima, led by Mayor Alfonso Barrantes of the United Left coalition. This was a project of urban joint management, through which the leftist municipal government responded to the demands of the residents of the eastern zone of the city for a place to live.

Moved by the promise of attaining a dignified way of life, thousands of residents, children of migrants born in Lima, embarked on the adventure of building a new community on the periphery of Lima. Among them were evangelical Protestants who, with their Catholic and "nonbelieving" fellow settlers, were willing to work to achieve their dream of owning a home. The new settlers in Huaycán came from popular (working-class) neighborhoods where diverse Christian beliefs had coexisted for the past twenty or thirty years; that is, the residents' "common sense" had allowed for the existence of religious differences.[2] That common sense, however, was far less charitable toward the expansive missionary zeal of the evangelical residents and their criticism of Catholic beliefs and customs.

For the evangelicals, this presented a predicament. To secure their ideological and political space in their new neighborhood, evangelicals had to define themselves against the dominant Catholic culture. They had to go against the common sense that finds it "natural" to set aside sites for Catholic churches among the public institutions when planning a new community. Indeed, Protestants could not request assignment of a public area because they were not considered a neighborhood service, as was the Catholic Church. Today, fifteen years after their arrival, evangelicals have achieved a certain degree of success, founding thirty-five temples throughout Huaycán. But the process has been gradual.

Huaycán developed under precarious social, political, and infrastructural conditions. Those conditions, and the evangelicals' participation in that development, brought them together to negotiate the recognition of their religious differences within the new political-secular community. Yet although they shared common demands and valued collective action, the evangelicals had difficulty consolidating a permanent level of coordination that would allow them to present their claims in a way that would produce lasting results.

This point is important because it sheds light on the process of citizenship-building for evangelicals in Peru. The Peruvian constitution recognizes the right to religious differences, but at the same time it maintains a preferential relationship with the Catholic Church. Although the evangelicals feel comparatively excluded, it is still hard for them to take concrete actions that would turn their experiences of exclusion into a concerted set of demands on the state.

The political participation of evangelicals in Latin America has received much attention lately. As noted in this volume's introduction, earlier studies that emphasized evangelicals' apolitical or conservative nature have given way to more nuanced views. For example, Burdick's (1993a) study of Pentecostals in Brazil has shown that in some settings Pentecostals are just as likely (and perhaps even more likely) to become involved in progressive political movements as are members of Catholic base communities. Similarly, Ireland (1997) argues that different Pentecostal logics can inform at least three types of citizenship, including a "critical citizenship" that encourages civic engagement. Nevertheless, Ireland points to the limitations of such involvement beyond the local level. This study of evangelical politics in Huaycán adopts a similarly nuanced view, demonstrating both the possibilities and the limits of evangelical political participation.

A local pastor estimates that the evangelicals in Huaycán constitute approximately 2 percent of the population. This figure is low, considering that in the entire Ate-Vitarte district, where Huaycán is situated, evangelicals are about 6 percent of the population (INEI 1993). However, the dynamism of evangelicals seeking, in recent years, to legitimate their presence in a mainly Catholic environment makes them seem more numerous to their Huaycán neighbors.

Unlike the Catholic residents, evangelicals have felt the need to reiterate that they are "part of the neighborhood."

A wide spectrum of Protestant churches are represented in the area. Among them, the Assemblies of God of Peru and the Evangelical Church of Peru (Iglesia Evangélica Peruana, IEP) have been prominent for their dynamic outreach and pastoral efforts. The Assemblies of God are a Pentecostal denomination whose first church in Peru was founded in 1922 by a North American missionary. It is the largest Protestant denomination in Peru.[3] In Huaycán the Assemblies of God have five churches.

The second largest Protestant group, the IEP, is a non-Pentecostal denomination organized in Peru in 1922 through the efforts of a foreign missionary group in which Scottish Presbyterians were prominent. From the Presbyterians the IEP derives its doctrinal orientation and organizational structure. In Huaycán four churches have been established.

The social composition of the Assemblies of God and the IEP is similar: they both have a strong national presence, especially among the lower-middle and poorer sectors of the population. During the last two decades, the Assemblies of God have maintained a strong pattern of growth, while IEP has followed a more moderate course.

Huaycán in the Eye of the Storm

During its first years, the Huaycán settlement was the focal point of conflicting expectations and diverse, even antagonistic projects: the political expectations of the first leftist municipal government of Lima, the national capital; the political-military project of Sendero Luminoso (Shining Path), the powerful Maoist guerrilla insurgency that terrorized the country from 1980 until 1992 to occupy the capital; and the demands of an increasingly dissatisfied urban population for land, housing, and amenities.

With Huaycán, the municipal government was realizing a proposal to meet the population's demands through legal means, taking advantage of its authority to administer uncultivated land belonging to the state. By doing this, the municipal government hoped to prove its capabilities to large sectors of the population, demonstrating that it could manage the city and respond to public demands without resorting to illegalities. Expectations were high, particularly in light of the presidential elections of 1985, when the United Left saw the municipal government as a step toward the presidency of the republic.

Because of this context, the occupation of the land in Huaycán was backed by a written agreement between the associations of residents and the municipality (Calderón and Olivera 1989). According to the document, the residents agreed to abide by the urban planning design proposed by the municipality, and in return the municipality agreed to support their settlement legally. To achieve the expected goals, a technical team was put in charge of negotiating the joint management of the project with the residents.

The urban plan for the municipality proposed the active participation of the population, organized in units of sixty families, not only in the planning stage but also in the provision of facilities. As such, the plan required a tight-knit management organization. At the same time, it opened the door for the different political groups in Huaycán to compete for control and management of the project.

The process of establishing the organization, however, was directly affected by Peru's environment of political violence. Situated on the central highway, the route that connects Lima with the Andean regions to the east, Huaycán was strategically important to Sendero Luminoso. This is the route that links Lima with the interior of the country, along which travel most of the food supplies to the capital and the mineral production from the sierra. For Sendero, to control this area meant the possibility of controlling one of the main arteries to the city. Soon after Huaycán's neighborhood organization had been established, Sendero decided to establish a "base of resistance" in Huaycán as part of its strategy to "surround the city."[4] This was among the first sections of Lima that Sendero occupied, with the goal of establishing "support bases" in others.

The expectations of Huaycán residents were also high; their hopes for progress were at stake. Residents of the popular neighborhoods on Lima's eastern edge and children of migrants joined groups of public school teachers and urban employees to fight for their interests. According to a self-conducted census in 1985, the residents were a young population with some urban experience: 48 percent of the heads of household had been born in Lima; 49 percent were younger than eighteen; and 35 percent were between nineteen and thirty-five.

These were mainly poor people who hoped to own a parcel of land. Although they needed housing, they were used to having some of the basic services, such as electricity, water, transportation, schools, and medical clinics, albeit inadequate and insufficient. Having grown up in the city, many of them had political experience and were ready to demand that the municipality fulfill its agreements. The municipal project for Huaycán appeared capable of satisfying these demands; but even though the Lima Municipality planned to carry out the agreements promptly (especially to give title to the lots and provide electricity and water), it took some years to attain its goal, and development was piecemeal.[5]

All these circumstances caused dissatisfaction and uncertainty for Huaycán's residents. The paradoxical combination of dreams of progress, discontent, and uncertainty also reflected the economic and political crisis of the period. The government of President Alan García (1985–1990), which began its tenure with high expectations for more equitable economic development, ended in economic turmoil and an annual inflation rate of more than 2,000 percent. The structural adjustment program implemented by the succeeding government of Alberto Fujimori only aggravated poverty without providing a social compensation plan to make it bearable.

Economic crisis, combined with political violence in the sierra, fueled massive migration to urban areas. Settlements on the periphery of Lima, like Huaycán, experienced explosive growth. Lima's municipal government was ill-prepared to deal with the increasing influx of migrants, which taxed the city's already inadequate infrastructure. Life in the new settlements was characterized by high levels of unemployment, a lack of basic services, housing shortages, violent crime, and infectious diseases. Although community-based movements were instrumental in pressuring the government to improve conditions, the disintegration of the United Left by 1990 deprived them of an important source of support (Stokes 1995).

The established political parties also lost legitimacy, if not collapsing altogether, with the public during the economic crisis.[6] Whereas during the 1980s the traditional parties regularly polled more than 80 percent of the total vote in elections, by 1995 their combined vote had fallen to less than 15 percent. Increasingly, poor Peruvians turned to independent candidates and became less inclined to participate in public demonstrations or state-directed petitions sponsored by political parties or movements (Dietz 1998).

Sendero Luminoso took advantage of the increasing discontent and uncertainty, alternatively challenging and negotiating with leaders of the various leftist groups in communities like Huaycán. Sendero sought confrontation with the government. To accomplish this, it tried simultaneously to convince and intimidate residents. Sendero fueled conflicts and exploited the weaknesses of Huaycán's neighborhood organizations; for example, the struggle between late-arriving settlers, who had to scramble for patches of land, and nonresident builders and cooperatives that had entered during earlier phases (Smith 1992, 137). In response, leftist leaders, competing among themselves, vacillated in their demands on the government, at times publicly demanding the fulfillment of agreements made with the municipality and at other times calling for tight controls over neighborhood activities. This complex power struggle forced residents to align themselves with one or another of the groups. For those who served as community leaders, the political struggle between Sendero and local leftist leaders turned their job into a minefield of countless dangers and difficulties. To make the situation more unsafe, Huaycán was subjected to successive military operations.

Between 1988 and 1990, Sendero concentrated all its efforts toward taking over the central management of Huaycán. It was defeated, however, by the residents, a majority of whom, in the neighborhood elections, backed a conglomerate of the United Left and APRA (the American Popular Revolutionary Alliance). Sendero thereby lost its chance at political hegemony in Huaycán, even though it maintained a presence and some influence in the area.

This is the setting in which the evangelicals had to build a place for themselves in Huaycán, to demonstrate that they were part of the population, and thus to gain the right to have their differences recognized.

Finding Unity in Neighborhood

"Huaycán is one and no one shall divide it!" With this slogan the residents marched through the center of Lima to demand basic services. With the same theme, they remember today the epic of building the neighborhood.

The evangelicals and their neighbors interviewed for this study were convinced that Huaycán, contrary to other similar urban settlements, had "progressed" in only thirteen years. In their opinion, this happened through the unity they all achieved to press for the provision of facilities; this, they believe, is why today they have basic services. They also are convinced that their solidarity was nourished by their own neighborhood efforts and the spirited work of all, even though the right to occupy a lot for residence depended on participation in the assemblies of residents and the public protests—a strategy and duty established by the neighborhood leadership. According to one interview subject, "the [neighborhood] leaders also put pressure on us. Because we did not have a title on which to rely, they would tell us, when we needed to go to a march, 'if you do not go, if you do not protest, tomorrow I will get you out of your lot and you leave.'"[7] This enforced responsibility to participate in a political act is valued today, in hindsight, as necessary to the extent that it was successful. In the words of one evangelical: "We have had to take by force, march so that we are heard . . . a baby cries because he is hungry, if he does not cry and is quiet, the mother does not remember. We have had to employ this tactic so that we are heard."

In their interpretation of their neighborhood participation, evangelicals associate the effectiveness of the political action with the lessons learned in the neighborhood organization. "[The organization] is what has taught us to unite. . . . and that unity also puts pressure on the authorities, that is what it has taught us, what is lacking in other places."

Being regarded as residents of a "red zone" also united evangelicals with their neighbors. Today it reminds them of the injustice of being rejected for jobs or sometimes even detained as presumed terrorists because of where they live. Today, evangelicals associate the red zone with the courage of their neighborhood organization, their leaders' ability to minimize the effective presence of Senderistas, and, once again, the importance of unity as a way to see their demands met. "[W]e were putting pressure on the government in a united way; for this reason we would get results. Then people from the outside would brand us: 'that town is rebellious, that town is red,' [but] thanks to our unity we achieved everything."

A crucial element for the evangelicals was, however, the legal justification of their participation. "Defending a just cause and rights cannot be terrorist, [but] because of that many branded Huaycán as terrorist," said one. The "just cause and rights" were defended, on the one hand, because the settlement of Huaycán "was not like an invasion. Many claim Huaycán residents are squatters, [but] we have occupied this land with the authorization of the municipality." On the other hand, it was established that "we own this place because it has cost us many sacrifices . . . for these reasons we feel the right to protest."

In the tension between the anxiety of being branded as Reds and the certainty of occupying the territory legally, having forged their right to possession through their work, the evangelicals understood their neighborhood participation as Christian testimony.

Obligation to God and Society

"Even though we are evangelicals, we have never been isolated . . . we have always participated," says a leader of the Vaso de Leche (Glass of Milk) program of her evangelical brothers and sisters.[8] It could be argued that they participated solely because they were forced to, but this does not seem to be the case. While evangelicals did not join the various neighborhood organizations under the label of a particular church, their participation had two points of reference: the conviction of their right to be there and their faith. In the words of a former neighborhood leader who today is a pastor, "[W]e also teach our brothers that if there is a job to be done to benefit our organization or the community, we need to participate willingly, because that is the duty of the Christian, to participate for the self-improvement of our community, for the betterment of our people; that is, like a Christian, not as if you are afraid of someone but as if it needs to be done! With pleasure as if for God, that is what is practiced."

These ideas of self-improvement and the Christian duty of service to the community have guided evangelicals in assuming leadership positions in their neighborhood organizations. Some volunteered; others were nominated by their neighbors. Many rose to intermediate-level positions, which required them to assume leadership in tasks involving political negotiations within Huaycán.

This role was not simple for Huaycán's evangelicals. Helping to manage the conflict for control of the neighborhood required them to work with the various political groups, each of which pressured them to support its particular project. On the one hand, the evangelicals risked adopting the positions of the extreme left or even the Senderistas. On the other hand, they were subject to the negative views held by those same groups about religion in general and the evangelicals in particular. Sendero disparaged religion as the proverbial "opiate of the people"; leftist leaders assumed that the evangelical churches taught their followers to abstain from political participation. Both these groups thought, moreover, that the evangelical message could weaken their legitimacy with a sector of the population. Meanwhile, the evangelicals, motivated largely by the need to define themselves, understood their neighborhood participation in terms of a testimony of Christian life, trying to distance themselves from "the political" by means of being "an example." "We do not consider this in a political manner, we do not see it from that point of view, but we understand, on the contrary, that we Christians have to be examples . . . [have to] comply with our [neighborly] duties, we also need to be at the assemblies . . . [to] fulfill our responsibilities to society. God also commands this."

The evangelicals were reticent to participate as political leaders: "the leader has been appointed to serve and assist the people, not for the leader to serve himself and live off the people." Therefore they configured their own neighborhood participation as a service, an "example."

Behaving as an exemplary Christian is a difficult task. An exemplary Christian does not just abide by the leaders' decisions; "to serve the people," an exemplary Christian must discuss the proposals presented by the different political groups, reject "radical" proposals, denounce bad administration, and overcome fear, threats, and criticism. "We need to be an example in the good things but not the negative things. We always had to put a stop to the things we were not in agreement with . . . [to] become strong; just because you are an evangelical you don't have to be subjugated, trampled on."

In their neighborhood participation, the evangelicals tested their traditional public image as good neighbors, moderate and discreet. This image was challenged when they tried to behave in exemplary fashion. "[Just] because we are Christians . . . we don't need to be crouched in a corner, without saying, 'This is my voice!' We are individuals also, and . . . I believe that wherever it is just we always need to say, 'this is my voice' . . . that is the way we have always participated here."

In addition to their belief that they had earned the right to their place in Huaycán, evangelicals also emphasized their conviction of having served the community as neighbor-believers. The feeling of belonging to the Huaycán community was rooted in these two claims. Participation in neighborhood management, moreover, exposed them to arguments (from the left) about equality and the legitimacy of demand and protest; it also taught them that through protest and negotiations it is possible to achieve demands. Consequently, it is worth asking if the experience of exclusion, which they attributed to their status as evangelicals, forced them to develop new methods of coordination that would allow them to solve their own common problems and accomplish medium-term projects.

Exemplary Christians also obey God, however, by building churches and preaching to expand their congregations' influence, thereby gaining recognition through their evangelical identity. Because pastoral work was always plagued with difficulties, it is also worth asking whether their civic experiences had a bearing on the way the evangelicals established their churches in Huaycán.

Evangelical Unity

Initially, in 1984, only one group of the Assemblies of God could negotiate with Huaycán's leaders for a parcel of land for its church (on what is called "the business strip" in the center of Huaycán). It was "the first church, along with the Catholic church," says one of its members. For this reason, it was the meeting place of the first evangelical settlers in Huaycán. Believers from different denominations congregated there because it was practically impossible to travel to their home districts to attend services; the settlement lacked public transportation. "Some brothers came from different churches, Chosica, Vitarte, Naña, Morón; that is, all had their meeting place in this church. But because they came with different points of view, unity was not seen there; they came with their point of view: 'No, I am from the Assemblies [of God],' or another would say, 'I am Pentecostal,' 'I am from the *Peruana* [IEP].'"

These members of disparate Pentecostal churches had to learn to "praise the Lord" in a style that would let all of them feel recognized. Although they accepted each other as evangelicals, they brought with them different denominational experiences. Each group recognized the need to bring new members to its specific church and, to a certain extent, knew the theological and liturgical differences that divided them. Under these circumstances, it was not easy to reconcile all of them in one common service and even more difficult to organize them as a single congregation.

This collective experience lasted a short time, however, true to the sectarian pattern common to evangelicals. As they found each other, believers of the same denomination began to congregate independently, generally at a member's home. All the evangelicals recall this period in positive terms as a common starting point.

If sharing a roof was problematic, preaching and conversion were worse. The neighborhood requirement of carrying out their assigned tasks and attending meetings in the evening and on Sundays left little time for pastoral and ritual activities. There was also the ominous presence of Sendero Luminoso, which disapproved of prayer meetings or Bible study. On various occasions, Sendero threatened evangelicals for congregating during its "armed strikes" *(paros armados)*, but they sought strength in their faith and overcame their fear. "We were threatened with death. Once the pastor was preaching and they [Sendero] left a flyer that said: 'If you quit preaching the gospel nothing will happen to you, but if you continue preaching the gospel and do not move to another place, you will have to face the consequences' . . . but it is there where we can see that God's word says, 'if for my sake you are killed, I will be with you every day until the end and only the brave will inherit the Kingdom of Heaven.'"

The evangelicals learned to defend their theological convictions even in front of leftists and nonbelievers who joined the congregations and participated in the religious meetings. These *agents provocateurs* questioned evangelical beliefs, seeking to discredit them in the eyes of the congregation. "A great part of the settlers who came here were persons who had other ideologies, they were atheists, did not have a god, they denied the existence of God, and we had to struggle against them, well, not through fistfights, but by prayer. We had to fast and pray so that we would have the strength to talk to them. But in spite of this [difficulty], we have always tried to do outreach."

Because of the threat of violence, institutional ties between the churches in Huaycán and their regional counterparts were very weak at the beginning. Today, "the brothers" recall the times they went to churches outside Huaycán to request support for pastoral work. Their efforts were unsuccessful: because the petitioners lived in a red zone, the pastors of those churches, with few exceptions, were unwilling to venture into Huaycán. Other regional churches probably also decided that the effort was worth little because evangelicals in the settlement were few. Thus Huaycán's evangelicals were left to cooperate with each other to fulfill their pastoral requirements and increase their membership. "We mainly have tried to remain with the ones that are here, because I invited a brother from outside to give his support to us and he said, 'No, brother, it is very dangerous.' Then we were with God because whoever is with God fears nothing."

To all of this must be added the difficulty of securing land assigned for the evangelical temples. One pastor also served as neighborhood leader for many years, gaining great acceptance as a civic leader. According to his neighbors and other neighborhood leaders, this pastor had great influence and was capable of controlling meetings even when the Senderistas pushed their proposals. Nevertheless, he had to negotiate for three years to get a parcel of land, during which time his congregation was evicted from two other places. Finally, the congregation acquired a lot through a transfer (paying the owner for the right to occupy it). The pastor declared that his petition had found no support in the neighborhood meetings. "They did not want to have an evangelical church. That was the point: the people did not want it. In the first place, they said that this [lot] was for housing and there cannot be evangelical organizations . . . there was a rejection, they made it known they were Catholics, they made it known they did not want anything to do with things of the [evangelical] church, that it was going to keep them from sleeping, that [the congregants] were going to make too much noise . . . some [leaders] belonged to the Left and [said that they] did not want anything to do with religion."

Huaycán's urban plan did not provide for evangelical churches. Nor was it easy to obtain commercial lots, because these, unlike residential lots, required payment. In addition, the tenants had to demonstrate that the commercial lots would bring financial benefit to a family in need. Their best hope was to negotiate in the neighborhood assemblies for spaces designated for family houses. In all cases, evangelicals needed to procure an "exception" to the urban plan, which was obtainable only through the approval of the neighborhood leaders and their immediate neighbors. This was all the more difficult when the evangelicals were preaching against the Catholic faith of those neighbors. For this reason, most Protestant churches relied on land transfers to acquire lots.

In the face of these difficulties, an agenda of common demands began to take shape as evangelicals began to coordinate their activities. The process resembled that followed by other Protestant groups in Lima, but the singularity of Huaycán is that when remembering and evaluating these activities (in particular those conducted up to the 1990s), evangelicals recognize them as part of a shared history, emphasizing that their true significance lies in how they disregarded the intradenominational boundaries.

Thus a second milestone in the collective memory is the first evangelizing campaign, in 1986. "At the height of terrorism we organized an evangelical campaign," remembers one brother. The campaign included fasting and prayer meetings to gain strength and overcome fear. In that way, and in the dark—Huaycán still had no electricity—they gathered the courage to venture, for the first time, into all populated areas, preaching from house to house, putting themselves at risk to try to convince even "persons who had other beliefs or were atheists." Various denominations participated, "not because they were going to preach their institutional beliefs, but because we were going to preach the gospel. Everyone supported this; they knew that there was going to be a campaign and all would go. No one said: 'I belong to the Assembly [of God],' or 'I am Pentecostal.' No, all were in support. Because of this, I can see the unity there."

United in their evangelizing efforts, residents with different ecclesiastical and social backgrounds identified themselves as part of a common project. Their differences faded, and they shared their demands as evangelicals. In this manner, evangelicals forged their own presence in Huaycán, combining periods of unity and cooperation with periods of competition, centering on the development and consolidation of the various congregations. Through this tense combination of unity and competition the number of evangelicals grew as new temples sprang up (especially those of the Independent Pentecostal Churches). The Assemblies of God and the IEP obtained sites in various parts of the district. Their ties with their regional institutions outside Huaycán also strengthened, partly because of their growth in numbers but mostly because of Sendero Luminoso's loss of hegemony in the area.

In these improving circumstances, in 1992 and 1993, the evangelicals launched a second campaign, this one a daring public effort to pressure Huaycán's local government to recognize them as "neighbor-believers." No longer the timid settlers of 1986, the evangelicals had learned to negotiate amid political conflicts, handle the leftist discourse of equality, and obtain homes and land for their churches.

The local Assemblies of God organized the public campaign in mid-1992, supported by regional churches, IEP congregations, and various independent Pentecostal churches. Coordinating their tasks, the churches carried out myriad initiatives ranging from small campaigns lasting several months in particular locations to evangelization from house-to-house year round to a major public event in the center of Huaycán.

Recognizing the energy and expectations generated by this mobilization, the pastors of eleven participating churches agreed to join together as the United Evangelical Church of Huaycán. The group comprised pastors and members of the IEP and independent Pentecostal churches. The United Church appointed a board of directors. The presidency fell to a member of the IEP, who was also an ex-member of the Central Executive Council of Huaycán's neighborhood government.

According to some "brothers," pastors from the Assemblies of God also participated initially. Even though everyone desired unity in principle, the Assemblies of God churches withdrew from the new association, disapproving of the unified church. Initially, unity was a strategy to sustain and coordinate the campaign the Assemblies of God had convened, but later the initiative became institutionalized in a format that seemed to contradict the Assemblies of God's own interests. The name United Evangelical Church suggested the integration of the various churches into one single "church," all under the control of whoever happened to preside over the directorate. This also privileged the association's leaders, making them seem to represent the evangelical "community" of Huaycán as a whole. In particular, the Assemblies of God pastors did not trust the president of this United Evangelical Church, with his government experience; they feared he would utilize the church as a personal platform.[9]

Despite this setback—or maybe precisely because of it—in mid-1993 the directors of the new evangelical association asked the Huaycán neighborhood government to include evangelicals in the annual July 15 celebration commemorating the settlement of Huaycán. The negotiations required courage, for evangelicals rarely demanded a place beside the Catholic Church in public celebrations. The association president took the initiative: "[I asked] one of the central directors if they practiced democracy, and he said, 'of course.' I said [that] well after the mass, after the religious ceremony of the mass, which was conducted by the Catholic Church, that they should give us an opportunity because we are also part of the town! And he said, 'That is not a problem, we will give you a place.'"

The political significance of demanding participation in this symbolic act is clear, given that in Peru, traditionally, public or state celebrations, such as the commemoration of national independence, always include events organized by the Catholic Church.

To the surprise of many, on July 15, 1993, at center stage, beside district and neighborhood authorities, a pastor addressed the gathering in the name of the United Evangelical Church of Huaycán. Afterward, in the parade, behind groups from the area's social organizations and civic institutions, marched the evangelicals: youth, children, and adults, preceded by a banner that also read "United Evangelical Church of Huaycán." In the words of one interview subject, "all of us singing with our Bibles [held] high arrived at the stage, and to the authorities we presented full Bibles, and we were well received." The Assemblies of God did not participate in this activity as a denomination, but some of its members marched in the parade.

The participants agreed that appearing in the parade was important to show the Huaycán community "the existence of people of God." The evangelicals differed, however, in their interpretation of the parade's deeper meaning. Some emphasized the aspect of conversion: parading was "a manner in which one is making it known that God has acted upon us"; that is, a way of proclaiming that even when "all are created by God, few are God's children." In this sense, they publicly distinguished themselves from their neighbors who had not yet opted to "give themselves to God." Others stressed evangelicals' desire to be included—in their difference—as Huaycán residents, "at least being considered part of the anniversary program," and demonstrating their solidarity.

These different emphases did not automatically correspond to denominational differences, for members of all the churches echoed both responses. The different interpretations do, however, appear to be linked with the experience of neighborhood leadership. This, in turn, corresponds with ways of dealing with exclusion or injustice and living as a Christian example. Those who offered the first interpretation had not occupied leadership positions; for them, evangelicals must denounce *(levantar sus voces)* situations of exclusion and injustice. This denunciation is predicated on the conversion experience and on evangelicals' self-distinction from worldly affairs. The second group believed that evangelicals must act, becoming more directly involved in the secular world. Said one, "The Bible says that if for preaching the Word of God someone slaps my face, I should offer my other cheek, but the Bible says that if there is an injustice, I am not going to offer the other [cheek], I am going to give him a beating, because God is fair and as God's children we are not going to allow injustices."

Participating in the parade and using the banner and the Bible as identifying symbols expressed a deliberate attempt to construct a "community of belonging." As Cohen (1985) observes, the community is a symbolic configuration that selects some common traits with which all members identify to show differences from others while at the same time emphasizing the group's uniqueness. Cohen adds that the effectiveness of the chosen symbols stems from the different ways they can be interpreted; they can evoke the myriad experiences of the participants without dividing the group. In this manner, the community can embrace differences by integrating them through a common reference point. In Huaycán, the notion of a Unified Evangelical Church of Huaycán served all those purposes. The complex combination of unity and difference explains why all the evangelicals interviewed agreed that "when there is unity everything is accomplished." Many can therefore remember the parade as the pinnacle of Huaycán's evangelical unity.

The success of the parade appearance convinced the United Evangelical Church that it was possible to organize evangelicals around a strong idea: from sharing a history, evangelicals could expand their range of influence and thereby strengthen their position to demand recognition in community affairs.

To begin increasing their influence, the church leaders arranged for a donation of Bibles from Gideons and staged a massive distribution campaign. Fifteen thousand New Testaments were distributed in the schools of Huaycán and the adjacent urban settlements of Horacio Zevallos, El Descanso, and Santa Clara. To carry out this undertaking, the congregations in Huaycán coordinated their actions and enlisted the help of evangelical teachers working in the district public schools. The impact of this undertaking must have been unusual, for even people who, as youths during that time, supported the work of the Catholic base communities vividly remember the power of the campaign.

Despite this and other successes, however, the evangelical association had a relatively short life. The United Evangelical Church participated in the July 15 parade for two more years and continued to convene joint services once a month. Attendance at these services declined, however, and the United Church thereby lost strength among its own flock. Eventually, the association also lost its legitimacy as a mediator for negotiating the evangelicals' specific local demands.

Religion and Politics

What lessons about the relationship between religion and politics can we draw from the case of Huaycán? More specifically, what is the impact of affiliation with, and participation in, evangelical Protestantism in settings like Huaycán, characterized by poverty, violence, and fragmentation?

We might argue that what happened in Huaycán fits the tendency among evangelicals to unite in conversion or healing campaigns and to disperse afterward. That is, we can understand the events in purely strategic terms: evangelical Protestants create a sense of unity principally in response not to secular politics but to a dominant Catholic environment (Kamsteeg 1993). This reading makes sense for Huaycán: unity came when the evangelicals needed to put aside their differences at particularly difficult junctures in their struggle to carve out their own legitimate space in the religious environment. Subsequent disunion or dispersion corresponds to periods of "normalcy," moments when members focused on the daily lives of their own congregations.

This interpretation, however, is insufficient for Huaycán (and similar cases in Peru) because it neglects an important dimension: the Catholic Church's privileged place in relation to the Peruvian state and the public sphere. In this context, actions taken to strengthen the evangelical churches' position in the religious field potentially will have political implications affecting the configuration of the local civil society. The United Evangelical Church had a dual purpose: to expand its scope of influence and to negotiate its public recognition. Thus, it was not only a matter of promoting conversions or creating a symbolic community but also of giving a public orientation to that constructed community. Articulating a public orientation, in turn, required evangelicals to develop a voice (or voices). Here a theology built on the certainty of election, on having a duty sanctioned by God, and on moral rectitude plays an important role. In this sense, the evangelical church can potentially play the same role that Catholic base communities have played during the democratic transition: that of forming members confident and capable enough to voice their needs and aspirations (Levine 1992).

To the extent that we can extrapolate from the case of Huaycán, we might say that politics, for evangelicals, is neither a primary concern nor an overarching horizon of praxis. Instead, political mobilization flows from evangelicals' earnest search for salvation and their concern to lead exemplary Christian lives before suspicious neighbors. In this religious framework, the impact of political mobilization will tend to be restricted to the local, to the politics of community and self.

In Huaycán, however, this complex link between religion and politics was further complicated by other factors. First, the Assemblies of God's withdrawal from the United Evangelical Church undermined the symbolic power behind that unified image. Yet that refusal came primarily from the Assemblies of God's leadership. The followers, by contrast, felt free to participate in various events, such as the July 15 parade. Thus the members of the various congregations were able to display their "public orientation."

Second, the insertion of politics into the "evangelical community" was contested, particularly the United Church president's congressional candidacy. He was criticized for "mixing religion with politics"; even some members of his denomination who sympathized with his leftist views criticized his "hastiness." Those who questioned him affirmed, however, that a "Christian can participate in politics"; only people who represent the evangelical community should not participate in politics. Here evangelical perceptions of politics became explicit: because politics is considered a game driven by financial interests or personal benefit, a "representative" of the evangelical community, who by definition must behave like an "exemplary Christian," should avoid the danger of contamination by unwholesome things. (Large sectors of the secular population shared this negative view of politics.)

The social and economic differences among denominations and within congregations were another impediment to effective political action. In the routine activities of the church, evangelicals did not see themselves as sharing the same circumstances. Evangelicals in poorer areas of Huaycán complained of not receiving consideration or good treatment from the more "affluent" brothers of their church; others charged that the competition for conversions by better-equipped churches was unfair. The combination of these problems hindered the attempt to coordinate the interests of evangelical settlers in order to negotiate their recognition.

Cleary claims that Pentecostals participate in politics when they consider that the benefits they will obtain outweigh the costs of political participation (Cleary and Stewart-Gambino 1997, 13). This formula could help explain the experience of the "United Evangelical Church of Huaycán" and its consequences. Simply as settlers, however, Huaycán's evangelicals had simultaneous demands for recognition both of their material needs and their specific faith. For this reason, their claims were at the same time both political and religious. That situation problematized the path from the public sphere to the political arena.

The directors of the United Church were certain that evangelicals shared a history and an agenda for the future. They thought that by basing their proposal on these experiences, they could stabilize coordination among the churches and present medium-term projects. They assumed the epic myth of the unity of Huaycán and thought that to face an adverse, mainly Catholic environment, evangelicals might achieve a similar unity. This has never been accomplished. Organizing around the demand for collective recognition, while at the same time accommodating denominational differences and economic and social disparities, has turned out to be an extremely complex task.

Notes

1. *Asentamiento humano* is the official designation for these *urbanizaciones populares,* or urban mass settlements. The term was part of the neighborhood association's official name until about 1990, when it was changed to Comunidad Autogestionaria de Huaycán (self-managed community of Huaycán) to symbolize both the culmination of a political contest within the neighborhood association and the community's political victory over Sendero Luminoso, which was active in the area. Sendero opposed the change because *autogestionario* implied that the residents were taking charge of their own development (e.g., working with the state to install basic services like electricity and water), thereby removing Sendero as their "instrument" of confrontation with the state.

2. In this regard see Marzal 1989, which studies the evangelical presence in the neighborhood of El Agustino, a ward that forms part of Lima's eastern zone.

3. According to data provided by the National Evangelical Council, the Assemblies of God of Peru represent 19.8 percent of the evangelical population of Lima. They are followed by the Iglesia Alianza Cristiana y Misionera (Christian and Missionary Alliance Church) with 16.8 percent. The same source has the IEP in sixth place, with 4.9 percent of the total evangelicals in Lima. PROMIES 1993.

4. According to the documents of Sendero Luminoso circulating at the time (see Degregori 1991), in 1984 the group began to reorganize and strengthen its Metropolitan Committee in Lima.

5. The original core settlements took five to six years to establish their basic infrastructure, while the most recent settlements were still struggling for basic services
at the time of this study. Despite the municipal government's initial support, successive administrations failed to fulfill the commitment; meanwhile, Huaycán's population grew from 22,000 in 1985 to about 70,000 by 1990. Nevertheless, Smith notes,
"Huaycán consolidated its basic infrastructure almost twice as fast as other spontaneous land seizures and avoided the pitfalls common in shantytowns" (1992, 137).

6. To understand the political complexity of this period, see Cotler (1994) and
Grompone (1991).

7. All quotations from individuals are taken from personal interviews conducted in
Huaycán between August 1997 and February 1998.

8. *El Vaso de Leche* was an organization of poor women that the left promoted in the
Lima municipality. It was one of Peru's strongest female social organizations of the
1980s and early 1990s.

9. While the United Church was being organized, the president agreed to be included
on the list of Izquierda Socialista Party candidates for the October 1992 elections
of the Democratic Constituent Congress (convoked by Fujimori to reform the constitution). During a radio interview, he stated that his candidacy had the support of
the United Evangelical Church of Huaycán. The Assemblies of God pastors criticized this at the time, but the criticism did not prevent the United Church from pursuing its activities or the faithful of the different denominations from participating
in its meetings. This occurred even though the Assemblies of God's criticism was
widely available to the faithful when the United Church leaders presented their goals.

Chapter 5

Rosa Castro Aguilar

Faith and Citizenship

Local Catholic Experiences in Peruvian Communities

Citizenship connects people to a political community and institutions that give them an identity and enable them to assert their fundamental equality (Cortina 1997; Jelín 1996b). People derive this equality not only from sharing the same rights under the law but also from sharing the same opportunities and respecting each other's dignity. In Peru there is no single citizenship but rather many "citizenships" (Heater 1990). Citizenship, in other words, exists at various levels and is lived in different ways, each influenced by multiple social and political processes (S. López 1997). As a consequence of the democratization processes of the 1960s and 1970s, the Peruvian constitution recognized that the state had a fundamental role to play in securing social rights such as health, education, social security, and employment. The constitution recognized that the state must help remove the limits that poverty imposes upon citizenship. Nevertheless, with the implementation of neoliberal economic reforms during the 1990s, the state's social function has been modified in order to increase efficiency instead of equality. Recent changes in Peruvian law have diminished some social rights such as employment, thereby reducing the legal protections for workers.

As in much of Latin America today, Peruvians' identification with the political community is very ambivalent. Although many people try to integrate themselves into politics and to become recognized members of this community, these efforts are frequently rejected. Despite making the transition from military authoritarian rule to a civilian democratic regime in 1980, the political system has not succeeded in equalizing people's access to rights. The Peruvian government shows little respect for political institutions and for the legal system. This weakens trust toward the political institutions among the population. In addition, public offices and the judicial system give differential treatment to different members of society.

A growing number of poor and working-class Peruvians aspire to full citizenship status. Still, they realize the limits that poverty, social exclusion, discrimination, and the political system places on them. They have exerted their right to live in the places of their choice, to have access to public services, and to be educated. They have come to view themselves as subjects with rights and not as objects of favors. However, many Peruvians are unaware of the rights accorded them under the country's constitution, much less of the civil rights that supposedly protect them. Within such a context of "low-intensity citizenship" (O'Donnell 1993), how can religious faith contribute to building what Jelín (1996a, 1996b) calls a "culture of participation and citizenship"?

Peruvian Catholics understand their Christian commitment in ways that foster distinct notions of citizenship. For some, a commitment to "doing God's work" means assuming responsibilities outside of their church. These Catholics are more likely to participate in local organizations struggling to find solutions to community problems. For others, their evolving understanding of their responsibilities as Christians leads them to participate more actively in their parish, to appreciate the dignity and value of those around them, and to provide moral support and consolation for those in need. However, their understanding of social problems as rooted in the "lack of faith in God" sharply limits their willingness to exercise a more active citizenship.

Comas: Identification and Withdrawal

When Comas was established in 1959, settlers struggled to obtain housing, public services, and transportation. Initially, settlers constructed their shacks on barren lots without any infrastructure. As infrastructural improvements were made, more formal urbanization occurred. Comas rapidly evolved from being a large squatter settlement to becoming the second most populated municipal district in Peru. In the past several decades, many of the earlier struggles to establish basic infrastructure in the district have succeeded. However, other goals, such as that of raising household incomes or sustaining the development of the district, have not been achieved. The expectations of the early residents were only partially achieved and at present new dreams are being created. Today, residents face new and old problems. Yet they no longer see themselves as "conquerors of the city" as they once did. Instead, they are struggling to become full citizens. The Catholic parish, Our Lady of Peace, originated in the 1960s with the purpose of accompanying the people who had settled in Comas. The parish worked side by side with residents, helping them celebrate their faith and also participating in their daily struggles. During the 1970s and 1980s, the parish priests and some parishioners believed it was necessary for the church to act in solidarity with the community as it struggled to defend its rights. They saw this as one way of relating their faith to the world, of announcing the scriptures and denouncing injustice. Other parishioners questioned whether they should associate themselves closely with community struggles and organizations. This solidarity, they thought, would require them to intervene in politics and take sides with certain groups. These parishioners thought it best to distance themselves from such actions and instead rely on prayer for community problems to be resolved.

In recent years, parish life has acquired a new dynamism. The population of the district has increased, more people have begun attending church, and there has been a greater demand for church-sponsored services. This has placed greater pressure on both the clergy and laity to perform pastoral work. As the parish, neighborhood, and nation have changed under the weight of economic restructuring and political violence, the relationships between government authorities, district leaders, and members of the parish have also been altered, becoming less personalized and more institutionalized. Despite these changes, the local parish remains an important place where people are able to strengthen their faith and give new meaning to their lives.

The majority of our interviewees migrated to Lima from their place of origin in the late 1950s and 1960s. They moved to the capital for various reasons: to improve their personal and family lives, to increase their income, and to seek new opportunities. Upon arriving in the capital, they followed different paths, converging in Comas. Although most migrants to Lima aspired to work and study, the majority were not able to achieve this. Some only worked and did not finish secondary school because they lacked the income to do so. A few were able to finish their basic studies and even pursue advanced studies over a period of time. The disappointment that Fanny and other parishioners suffered when they came to Lima may be an expression of their frustrations during those first years in the city. "I started to get excited," Fanny explains. "I wanted to get to know Lima . . . [I thought] it would be different there, pretty . . . I thought it would be like my home town . . . [I thought] I would find plants . . . water, little animals . . . But when I arrived in Lima everything was different. I did not like it because the people, the houses, the things, the food were different."[1]

During the 1950s and 1960s, information, communication, and culture were concentrated in the capital, while the provinces and the countryside were deprived of opportunities. For these reasons, our interviewees, despite their frustrations, decided not to return to their place of origin. Fanny explained that after ten years of living in the capital, she moved to her hometown for two years. However, the lack of opportunities there made her return to Lima.

Most people we interviewed in Comas arrived in the district after having lived in Lima for some years. They came to Comas with new dreams and in search of new opportunities, just as they once had done in Lima. They sought a place where they could build a different life than what they had found during their first years in Lima. All of these people asserted their citizenship by recognizing their right to have their own place of residence, to have access to public services, and to educate their children. As time passed, some resigned themselves to these accomplishments and concentrated primarily on their own struggle for survival. However, others found within the Catholic Church the possibility of obtaining a different life, of working in the parish and developing their capabilities. Encouraged by their participation in the church, some people continued searching for better living standards in the district by participating in social organizations and the municipal government.

Lay Catholics have developed different ways of relating their faith to citizenship. Some participated actively in the creation of the district and worked with their neighbors to obtain public services. As time went by, they continued to maintain some level of participation in social and church organizations. However, other parishioners, like the majority of residents in Comas, turned toward the challenges of their private lives, to the everyday struggle for survival, and to the parish's institutional concerns. Although the boundaries are not always clear, for the purposes of this analysis we can distinguish between these two ways of relating faith, everyday life, and rights. The first centers on trust in God. According to this view, God will help them confront the problems and difficulties in their daily lives. Consequently, these parishioners believe that their main responsibility is to communicate and share their faith experience with others. To an extent, this implies evading responsibility to change reality. A second group, acknowledging the presence of God in history, commit themselves to their parish and community and work to change those situations that cause injustice.

For the first group of laypeople, religion provides strength and comfort during difficult moments. Celia, a lay celebrant who migrated to Lima from Piura in 1960, described how prayer gives her consolation and the strength to face daily problems. Celia's abusive husband left her and her ten children to find work in Venezuela in 1977. During critical moments in her life, prayer has enabled her to communicate directly with God and to feel his constant presence. Before becoming involved in the parish, she thought God was distant. "Look, what I like most is to be able to have that freedom of saying, 'God, help me!' . . . just like that, very simply . . . Before, I was not aware that by simply asking God to help me, he was going to be there." For Celia, finding God resulted in a dramatic life change. She felt compelled to show her gratitude through service to the community. Her personal encounter with God also led her to believe that God is present in people and that God acts in the world urging good deeds. "God for me is alive. He is in the world, in me. I think that way. And when one does good deeds, it is because of the Lord and not because of men." For most parishioners in Comas, this Christian commitment entails inviting others to participate in the experience of prayer, helping the afflicted by praying with and for them, and teaching others the power of personal and collective prayer. Faith also requires people to assume an active role in Christian communities. Celia believes it is the duty of all devoted Christians to participate in the community, to attend mass, and to meet and discuss problems with neighbors. Ultimately, an encounter with God through prayer brings these people hope and comfort in their daily lives and encourages them to communicate and share this experience with others. The power of this prayer experience moves them to action. Along the way, people change their lives: they change their attitudes by placing greater trust in the Lord and offering others a community that teaches prayer and gives comfort and support.

Our interviewees realize that there is inequality in Peru, that some people have more than others, that some have a good job while others struggle for a position in a factory or for a stall in the marketplace. They recognize that inequality is also present in the way housing or business loans are distributed by financial institutions. Celia, whose sons operate a small business from their home, noted that although commercial banks offer mortgage loans, these are not accessible to the poor. The difficulty of obtaining a loan or a job or of finishing construction on a house limits poor people's ability to work and have a dignified way of life. Fanny, a single mother and the coordinator of her Christian community, has struggled to provide for her children. After she and her sister lost their jobs in a factory cafeteria in 1991, they began selling prepared lunches to the factory workers on an informal basis. They prepare the meals at home and then travel one and a half to two hours by bus from Comas to San Borja. Fanny defines democracy as equality, whereby everyone enjoys the same rights. She argues that parish and community organizations should encourage the equality of individuals by respecting their opinions and acknowledging their right to participate in these groups, although she believes that this equality does not currently exist.

Hilda, a small shopkeeper and *celebrante* (lay celebrant) in another Christian community, disagrees. She believes that Peruvians have the right to express an opinion and decide how they will live. This, for her, is an indication of the existence of democracy. "No country is free. We always depend on someone. But we have the freedom to speak, to express ourselves. We have the freedom to think. We have the freedom to act. We have the freedom to realize our potentials."

Many parishioners we interviewed value the freedom to express their opinions and to choose where to live, how to act, and what to think. Their views about these rights are linked to their life experiences, especially to their employment, housing, and economic conditions. They are aware that inequalities exist in the country and that this sometimes prevents them from fully exercising their rights. Despite facing the reality of poverty, impediments to socioeconomic improvement, and low self-esteem, faith has given our interviewees a sense of self-worth. It has allowed them to foresee a gleam of light on the horizon of their lives and to affirm their dignity and capabilities. This is a minimum condition of social equality needed in order to talk about citizenship (see Weffort 1992). Although faith provides our interviewees with comfort and hope in their daily lives, it also leads them to believe that problems arise because of a lack of faith in God. They do not see how the roots of their problems lie within society, nor do they commit themselves to working with others to build a society that respects the rights of all. Thus, Celia argues, "The greatest hope we have is in God's help. He comforts us to continue living. That certainly will never end. Many things will happen if we forsake God's love . . . I would not change that for anything."

Similarly, Fanny indicates that in order to perform different duties in social and church organizations and to convene the church members to share the experience of community, one must have a strong faith in God. "There is a lot to be learned. We have a lot to learn about living in hope, waiting for Christ." For Catholics like Fanny and Celia, trust in God provides confidence, and their pastoral experiences contribute to greater self-esteem. However, they do not feel obliged to discover their rights and responsibilities in the world.

In contrast to this approach, other laypeople in Comas emphasize the values of the reign of God: justice, life, and solidarity. According to Inés, a social worker, "The reign of God is in this world . . . [during] moments of joy, moments of happiness, in the solidarity that is shared. When those values are experienced, the reign of God is present."

Solidarity with the needy is a main characteristic of the experience of faith among these parishioners. For Elsa, a *celebrante* and small shopkeeper, it is not possible to preach God's word if it is not accompanied by tangible gestures of support for those in need. "We should not just preach the Word or bring it home and say, 'Thank you very much, Lord. You sent us this message and we offer you nothing.' No, we must help the families in need. If one has a little more, then share with the one who does not have."

Faith also requires the kind of solidarity that is expressed by participation in social organizations. Rita, who became a leader in the *comedor* (communal kitchen) movement through her participation in parish groups, stated, "We experience faith in practice. Through an organization, we share needs and sufferings. For example, in my community, I see the neighbors . . . each one lives his life and that is that . . . In the organization, there is life because while you are there, there is a lot to share with your fellow members, with your friends. We are one." This is what allows parishioners to give a testimony of faith and trust in the Lord to their family, neighbors, and fellow members of the Christian community and social organizations.

In this view, Christians should commit to the reality around them, denouncing corruption and injustice. Miguel, a coordinator of his Christian community, argues that we need to denounce and announce, like all prophets did during their time: "It is part of the Christian commitment . . . denounce injustices, announce justice and denounce what is unjust. We need to be, at least try to be prophets, denounce what is not just. Then, I think, we are doing that, even though there are people who may not agree." Miguel's convictions about denouncing injustice have encouraged him to play an active role in petitioning state officials on behalf of his community's needs. For these parishioners, faith and social reality should be closely intertwined in pastoral work. According to Bruno, a *celebrante* in his Christian community, a lay leader should be someone with whom others can relate. To be a Christian, in his view, implies commitment to the church and social reality, to announce the reign of God and denounce injustices, to meet with neighbors in search of solutions to community problems.

As is common throughout much of Peru, there is very little awareness of citizenship rights among residents in Comas. Consequently, Diego, a *celebrante* and a member of the Comas municipal council, believes that it is necessary to develop an educational program in the country regarding rights, responsibilities, and democracy. Only by doing this can a democratic culture be promoted and practiced. Presently, Diego says, "I do not see democracy anywhere . . . For example, I have gone to exercise my right to vote. I have voted for the legislators, but what member of the legislature feels that he is a representative of his electorate at this moment? No one. Each one does whatever his political group wants, whatever is indicated or ordered of him."

Diego believes that in order for people to exercise their citizenship fully, democratic opportunities should be created in places such as the municipality. People should be allowed to participate, plan actions, and reach agreements to strengthen democratic citizenship at the local level. Laypeople like Diego recognize the need to join with other Peruvians whose rights are limited by authoritarianism, poverty, and inequalities in the country. They realize that the population needs to be informed and educated about their rights and that this awareness will promote citizen participation in politics and thus strengthen their country's democratic culture. For example, Miguel believes every Christian has a political dimension that leads him or her to denounce injustices and to organize to protect rights: "A Christian must denounce, must organize to face all of this. But the Christian should be conscious of his community and should not allow others to say that what he is doing is politics. What is being done is to unite [with others in order] to move ahead." Likewise, for Inés, Christians should participate actively in the life of their community, including politics and local government: "we must also participate in local politics, even pastoral agents . . . to express our point of view, to criticize, to question." Faith and active participation in parish life have helped these parishioners better understand the social reality of their district. Through their involvement in parish and community organizations, they have discovered their rights and capabilities and have become committed to promoting citizen participation and the protection of human rights.

Huaycán: Asserting Dignity

In many respects, the residents of Huaycán have had experiences similar to those of the early residents of Comas. The residents in both districts were searching for housing. Early settlers organized and selected a place to occupy. Later migrants also organized but coordinated with the municipal authorities for the most convenient place to settle. Neighborhood organizations were important in the urban planning of both areas and in helping people obtain public services. In Comas, residents obtained services after years of mobilization and negotiations with leaders and government authorities. In Huaycán, they were obtained sooner because the government had conducted studies and determined what projects were needed for establishing water and sewage services (see chapter 4). Nevertheless, the residents of Huaycán had to mobilize and demand that government agencies in Lima implement the public services they had promised. The dreams and efforts of the population from both of these areas now center on improving incomes and creating new employment opportunities.

Despite the similarities between Comas and Huaycán, there are important differences. While Comas has changed from being a squatter settlement to a bustling commercial district, Huaycán is still in the former state. Poverty and illiteracy are more widespread in Huaycán than in Comas. Despite these problems, or maybe because of them, there is a greater spirit of progress and hope in Huaycán.

Before the parish was officially established in November 1992, a group of Monfortian priests from a nearby parish ministered to the original settlers of Huaycán. They coordinated activities with community leaders for the benefit of the local population, including the construction of chapels, the cemetery, the "sports-cultural complex," and the parish center. As the years passed, the church's relationship with the "central and local administration has become more difficult and conflictive" (Parroquia de San Andrés 1998). However, the church is an important organization for the whole population due to the activities it sponsors to benefit the community, and the parish of San Andrés has tried to be responsive to the needs of the population. It has actively embraced progressive currents of Latin American Catholicism, including the preferential option to the poor. Its pastoral plan has incorporated a series of auxiliary activities aimed at reducing the poverty of the local population.

Parishioners in Huaycán pointed to their faith as a source of hope, encouragement, and comfort. They also explained how it helps them to acknowledge others as fellow human beings and to reach out to their neighbors. Their faith inspires a commitment to both the parish and the neighborhood. Prayer is important in the community life of Huaycán. It brings encouragement to people with family problems and allows them to better understand God. Julia, the coordinator of a Christian community, related that after losing her parents, prayer enabled her to see God as a welcoming and loving being and not simply as a punishing one, as she had previously viewed God. This change now prompts her to communicate her faith to others and to serve her community as president of the local neighborhood association.

Faith in God also helps sustain individuals during difficult moments in their lives. Mario, a schoolteacher and lay leader in the parish, feels the presence of God during those moments. For this reason, he tries to share his experiences with others. The acknowledgment of God's presence in their lives does not prevent the parishioners in Huaycán from getting involved in their community. On the contrary, as Julia explained, although God helps individuals, they also must look for solutions to their problems. In her view, faith is not a passive trust but an active one. For Blanca, participation in the Legion of Mary has allowed her to look at her own life from another standpoint: to trust the Lord and help her brothers and sisters. She serves her community by comforting, praying with, and singing to others.

For many laypeople, religion helps redefine the meaning of their lives. It offers them a guiding principle, as Mario explains: "[Faith] helped me define many things in my life . . . my way of thinking regarding life, regarding responsibility, regarding solidarity, identification with those more in need and a series of things that to me were very valuable." According to Mario, the church promotes the preservation of life through its orientation and encourages all its members to identify with the suffering of others. This leads them to protect different forms of life.

Participation in the parish *comedor* program allowed Martha to collaborate with others in her parish. Before joining the comedor, Martha sold food in the market to supplement her husband's income. However, health problems forced her to seek assistance from the parish comedor. There she learned to help others and to share with neighbors in need. It also made a difference to her family: her husband stopped drinking and she started going out of the house. Martha explains: "now he supports me a lot . . . and doesn't ask me why I have to go to the community meetings or Mass."

Silvia's participation in the parish comedor program and her local Christian community has led to dramatic changes in her life. She came to Huaycán from Cerro de Pasco with her six children after her husband passed away. Struggling to provide for her family, she was constantly overworked and often took out her frustrations on her children. The educational opportunities offered by the church helped Silvia to reflect on her life and to work on improving her relationship with her children. She began to regularly read and reflect on the Bible, to value herself, and to grow in self-esteem. This allowed Silvia to share her discoveries with others: "You start sharing with other people and in dialogue, in a conversation, you start talking, you start mentioning everything you have learned. Sometimes there are women that are too submissive to their husbands. They are mistreated. Then you start talking to [these women and telling them] that they should learn to defend themselves, that women, like men, should be valued equally." Thus, Silvia learned and taught others that women and men are equal, that women should not be submissive, and that both genders should respect each other.

In Huaycán, as in Comas, many Catholics have little awareness of citizenship rights. Some associate citizenship with being a resident in the city. The rights they mention most are the right to life, employment, freedom of expression, and health care. Parishioners recognize the limitations that poverty, discrimination, and the government place on the full exercise of rights. The poor are not aware of their rights because they have very little education. They do not know who to approach with their demands or they are ignored by government authorities.

Julia believes that every person has a right to a dignified way of life. "Well, our rights are ... to demand to be taken into consideration, to be respected and ... to be allowed to participate." However, Julia thinks that these rights are not respected among neighbors because there are people who consider themselves above others. In other words, she believes that discrimination prevents people from securing their rights. She acknowledged that citizens should have a right to life; however, she indicated that this right did not exist in Peru because the government, with its family-planning campaign, works against the life that God has created.

In addition to the government's family-planning policies, there is opposition to the government's labor policies, which have significantly reduced the rights of workers. Given the lack of legal protections that Peruvian workers now face, there is growing awareness about the right to employment. Blanca indicated that the right to employment is not respected either because there is no work or because temporary contract work creates great instability. Similarly, Julia believes that the rights of workers are permanently violated. As president of her local comedor, she sees how people are exploited: "People are taken advantage of because they are poor. These people are hired to work because they are poor; however, they're paid a pittance or not paid at all."

For Peruvians to be able to pressure the government to change its policies, parishioners pointed to the importance of the right of free expression. Silvia, who coordinated the parish's comedor program, believes that the right of free expression is a right not only for the news media but for all individuals. She explains: "The right to free speech is everyone's right. We cannot inhibit ourselves. We are free to communicate or say what we think." At the same time, Silvia acknowledges that this right is not practiced because everyone has to abide by what the president says. In general, parishioners in Huaycán have little experience or awareness of citizenship rights. Few are knowledgeable about the constitution or the channels of legal recourse available to citizens. Nevertheless, despite limited knowledge about existing rights, parishioners recognize the limitations that reality places upon them and struggle to overcome these obstacles.

As a result of their participation in the local parish, many Catholics in Huaycán have developed a better sense of the world around them, their community, and their neighbors. In the process, they have realized that they are individuals with dignity, with special capabilities and qualities. The assertion of their dignity is a minimum requirement for the exercise of citizenship. In their daily lives and in their neighborhood activities, the ethical requirements of their faith orient the ways in which parishioners exercise their leadership roles. Julia explains that before presiding over meetings of her Unidad Comunal de Vivienda (Communal Housing Unit), she tells God: "God, in your name I'm going to start this meeting . . . touch the hearts of my brothers and sisters so that they will understand me and so that I can understand them." The strength she acquires from prayer and participation in her Christian community helps make her a more effective leader.

Within church groups, parishioners find opportunities to express themselves freely and exercise their rights. However, some argue that the acknowledgment and exercise of rights should not be limited to the church: the voices of all must reach the government. An expression of political connection presumes the existence of rights. In this light, religion allows people to assert their dignity, know their rights, and be concerned about the well-being of all. Through the exercise of citizenship, faith is not limited to the parish or diluted in good intentions but can establish roots that will grow with time.

Yungay: Search for Integration

Life in Yungay is very different from that in Comas and Huaycán. Unlike the latter two communities, Yungay is mostly rural. Its residents feel "distant" from the urban, developed world despite being closely connected to it through the road and communication system in the country. The farming communities of Yungay are poorer than the urban areas of Comas and Huaycán. People live differently also: collaboration, cooperation, and solidarity are widespread.

Yungay suffers from endemic poverty and has little history of significant political participation. Some peasants have improved their quality of life by appealing to the state for financial assistance and official recognition. Nevertheless, the exercise of citizenship has been circumscribed here due to people's limited education and the difficulty in communicating in Spanish. The residents of this region share a peasant identity, but they do not possess a Yungaíno identity that would allow them to constitute an effective political community.

The spirit of Vatican II and of the Latin American Episcopal conferences is very tenuous in the ecclesial life of the parish. As discussed in chapter 3, there are two distinct tendencies evident in pastoral work: one that emphasizes administering the sacraments and another that attempts to deepen understanding of the sacraments and promote the active role of laity in evangelization of rural communities. Nevertheless, in the context of widespread poverty, low levels of education and the weak political and cultural identity among the mainly Quechua-speaking population, the Catholic Church occupies an important role in the life of the district. In the absence of strong social organizations, the parish keeps laypeople informed on subjects related to their family and community life, their faith, their religious practice, and the economic, political, and social situation of their department. The church also constitutes a place where residents from different rural communities can meet. Occasionally, the church provides opportunities for catechists to participate in national and regional meetings of *campesino* leaders. In all of these activities, many catechists have learned to assert their dignity, to relate to representatives from the national and local level, and to feel more connected to the urban world. As leaders in their own communities, catechists have come to view themselves differently, as equal to others, especially urban Peruvians.

Faith in a God who encourages, protects, gives hope, and helps during difficult moments is central to the lives of rural catechists. Through prayer, catechists and their families find strength to cope with daily problems. Fausto, a catechist from Masra, moved to Yungay a few years ago to attend the normal school. Before moving to Yungay, Fausto attended high school in the evenings. After working on his *chacra* (farm) all day, Fausto walked one and a half hours each way to school and back, often arriving home at two o'clock in the morning. When an opportunity arose to study at the normal school in Yungay, the family moved to town. In the beginning, they lived in a small kiosk in the market where Fausto repaired shoes. Faced with many hardships, Fausto and his family prayed all the time because "prayer helped a lot." Because of the support he received through prayer, Fausto is more committed than ever to the work of the church.

Others trust that God will always protect those who love the Lord. Isaías, president of the Juventud Agraria Rural Católica (Catholic Rural Agrarian Youth), for example, believes that he who loves God will never be forsaken by God. For this reason, he believes that God was with him during moments of financial crisis: "I always know that the person that always loves God does not suffer as much . . . God always gives me what I ask for. I always have faith." This faith entails a change in personal behavior, which in turn improves relationships with family and neighbors. Isaías explains: "I have always cultivated my own faith. But the most important thing for me as a Christian is the consciousness that you have towards others. Practice with deeds whatever little you may have learned, not just say that one should be like this, because people are always looking at what you are doing."

Catechists perform both a religious and social role in their community. They are in charge of religious celebrations in their community and of preparing children to receive the sacraments. They also are role models in their community, participating actively in community activities. Sebastian, who became a catechist in 1967, believes that catechists are teachers of the faith; they promote love, solidarity, and fraternity. Catechists reach out to people who have problems at home and who develop "undesirable" behavior, since this behavior can affect everyone in the community.

Willy, a catechist from the community of Musho, also commented that catechists participate actively when community tasks are undertaken. They must offer testimony of work, advice, and solidarity. "In our community we work as we are taught in school. First, we have to be in the thick of things . . . working, helping or participating in an activity that authorities may organize. Then, when there is a problem, for example in the family, we reach out even if it is to encourage [people] . . . In this way we think that we may be able to help mold individuals that are conscious of the reality in which we live."

Our interviewees all expressed an awareness of social responsibility as part of their faith. However, the immediate social reality of most campesinos is their rural community. The district, province, and nation seem too distant to them. They feel that their actions would have no effect beyond the local level. Nevertheless, because of their access to news and information through the radio, catechists are aware of events at the national level and recognize themselves as Peruvians.

In rural areas, it is more adequate to speak of rights and duties than of citizenship. Our interviewees from Yungay either did not know what citizenship meant or associated it with reaching eighteen, the age when people can obtain identification documents and participate in elections. Willy, who spent eleven years working in Lima before returning to his community, was unsure whether he was even a Peruvian citizen before turning eighteen years of age. He remarked: "Then I was a citizen, isn't that right? Then I was a citizen."

José, a catechist from the community Rayan-Shuyup, believes rights are the ability to have resources and decide what to do with them without depending on anyone. He thinks that the rights of Peruvians are not respected when resources are privatized: "Now they are thinking about privatizing the water . . . That isn't respecting the rights of the country . . . Peru is a bit marginalized, like an employee . . . Those who come from other countries, they give orders . . . They don't respect [rights]." Others believe that the rights of the poor are not protected because those who have more money and power impose their will upon others. Sebastián, who spent several years working in the harvests on the large coastal estates, commented: "The truth is, those who have more means crush those who are poor and those who are in power are the ones who command everything . . . Our governments want to impose the law upon us. For example, with regards to family planning they are taking away too much life."

The Catholics we interviewed in Yungay always mentioned the right to life, referring both to political violence and government-sponsored family planning. In response to the government's emphasis on sterilization, the Peruvian Catholic Church undertook an extensive pro-life campaign during the 1990s. The rural catechists affirmed the right to life partly in response to this. Nora, one of two female catechists in the parish, commented that the church helps people to protect their lives, to counsel, and to learn: "They help us to educate ourselves . . . They visit us in all the monthly festivities . . . They explain to us. They teach us. Sometimes they advise us." Nora believes that because life is a gift from God and no one has the right to violate it, family planning is against life: "We Peruvians have the right to life. We want to live and we want our life cleansed. With regards to family planning, I think the government has decreed this law so that humanity may decline."

The importance of the right to life was also evident when our interviewees discussed Sendero Luminoso. All were critical of Sendero's violent tactics, especially against innocent civilians. Willy's community of Musho was considered a "red zone" at one time because of the presence of Sendero from 1989 to 1991. While he never witnessed Sendero's presence firsthand, he had heard from others about sympathizers in the community. Although Willy agreed with the need to protest government abuses, he condemned Sendero's tactics: "If someone protests, it's because they see problems in society, it's not for the fun of it. But when they began to kill innocent people, that's something I couldn't accept, Sendero was wrong to act like that . . . Sendero killed campesinos or forced them to join their movement."

In addition to the right to life, one of the rights most valued by parishioners is education. In Peru, education is especially important for the Quechua-speaking population. It allows them to have access to society and to improve their personal and family lives. Education signifies fluency in Spanish and progress. Education is even more fundamental for peasant women, among whom illiteracy rates are highest. Illiteracy often prevents women from assuming leadership positions in their community. Since most rural women cannot read or write, Esther, a catechist from the community of Cajapampa, believes they are not prepared to defend the interests of their community: "Women cannot be authorities because we do not have enough education and without knowing [women] make commitments that cause the town to lose."

Various projects recently submitted to the Peruvian parliament have resulted in national discussions regarding education. One of these projects proposed privatizing secondary-level education. This has created a lot of confusion and uncertainty among the poor in rural areas. Willy said that this project would create more illiterates because campesinos without financial means would not be able to educate their children. "When education is privatized, how are we campesinos going to support our children? How are we going to educate our children? Illiteracy is going to increase." Willy considers education a right which the state should fulfill for the rural poor. He explains: "Just as there are schools for the rich now, there should be state-sponsored schools for the poor also . . . I don't think that everything should be privatized. The state should always watch over those who need the most." Willy believes, in other words, that the state should offer the necessary opportunities to the poor so that they will have access to social rights such as health and education. This, he thinks, will prevent poverty-induced inequality among Peruvians from increasing.

Esther also believes that the right to a free education is fundamental. She thinks that privatization will prevent parents from educating their children because many will not have the necessary financial means to pay for a private education. Esther argues that parents in the countryside are responsible for feeding their children, and the state is responsible for educating them. However, this arrangement will no longer be possible if education is privatized. "If education is free," Esther explains, "[parents] are going to feed their children. But if the government says that everyone has to pay [for an education], how will parents get what they need to survive?"

According to Nora, the other female catechist in the parish, education prevents inequality and helps solve problems. It breeds respect for people. She argues, "Without education, sometimes there is corruption, there is ignorance, there is inequality, there is controversy . . . When there is ignorance, people can fall into all kinds of evil: theft, lies, gossip, everything." In short, the limited opportunities for education and civic involvement in rural areas, as well as the political centralization of the country, hinder the construction of a more genuine citizenship by Yungaínos. Education is the right that allows them to struggle against these limitations.

Faith and the pastoral experiences of rural communities help strengthen individual dignity by offering tools that allow people to develop their capabilities and confront the limitations imposed upon their citizenship. Because of their religious authority, catechists occupy a central role within their community. They are no longer anonymous members of the community but role models for others to follow. They realize they have the capacity to undertake a new way of life, to offer advice to their neighbors, to read and interpret biblical texts in Spanish, and to speak in public. The church organizes meetings that allow catechists to learn and practice Spanish. Similarly, the church offers courses that inform catechists about topics related to religious life and to national and regional developments. They also learn techniques that assist them with their agricultural work. In some cases, the church also helps them implement small projects that create employment opportunities. All of this allows catechists to improve themselves and overcome the limitations that poverty and centralization impose on their citizenship. It enables them to look at themselves differently and to face their national and local reality differently. Along the way, they develop self-esteem and a sense of equal membership in society.

Faith and Citizenship

Citizenship is not homogeneous in Peru. Variations in the level of poverty, degree of education, the history of political and social organization, the accessibility to modern conveniences, and geographical location can all affect the practice of citizenship among and within different districts. The task of achieving a more genuine citizenship for all Peruvians begins by recognizing and acting within the different contexts in which citizenship is exercised.

For migrants struggling to find a place to establish roots and to overcome the challenges of urban life, achieving equal rights is a central demand. They desire to be treated as equals, as individuals with dignity. Likewise, rural populations constantly strive to achieve "modernity," while their children leave in search of new horizons. In this way, rural communities confront the limitations of their ability to live in dignity and to be full members of the national political community. On the other hand, the awareness and exercise of citizenship rights enables people to become protagonists in cultivating a democratic culture in church groups and establishing bridges between their social reality and their faith. They become attentive to the "signs of the times," willing to listen to the will of God and to serve humanity by defending rights.

Church involvement has enabled many Catholics in Comas, Huaycán, and Yungay to discover previously unknown capabilities in themselves. These capabilities have been developed through assuming responsibilities as active members of their parishes. Many have discovered a sense of life different than what they had imagined during their youth, a sense of life they were not able to achieve previously because reality led them along a different path. In their adulthood, where everything revolved around work and family, they discovered the possibility of personal realization. They found an alternative space that enabled them to nurture their family, religious, and community lives.

Faith allows these Catholics to assert themselves as individuals with dignity entitled to equal respect. Their understanding of their Christian commitment results from their awareness of injustice. This leads some to participate actively in church and society, to assume collective responsibilities and work for the common good. Others are moved to participate actively in their parish and to adopt a positive attitude toward life yet refrain from most civic engagements. Even so, this limited way of relating faith and citizenship can contribute indirectly to building a culture of citizenship. Laypeople who believe that God will help them overcome their problems and move forward with their lives are often inspired to comfort those in need. The experience of helping others allows these parishioners to relate to neighbors, friends, family, and those unknown but in need. This caring relationship can be expressed through social assistance activities or through social organizations oriented toward defending rights. These convictions, attitudes, and activities create a sense of belonging, of being part of the larger community. In turn, these ties of solidarity can serve as the building blocks for the exercise of a more effective citizenship.

Note

1. All quotations from individuals are taken from personal interviews conducted in Comas (May–August 1996), Huaycán (October 1996–June 1997), and Yungay (June–August 1997).

Chapter 6

Ileana Gómez

Rebuilding Community in the Wake of War

Churches and Civil Society in Morazán

El Salvador is currently undergoing a promising but precarious process of democratic transition after twelve years of civil war that claimed the lives of more than seventy thousand people and displaced one-fifth of the population. The war ended in 1992 with a negotiated settlement calling for sweeping reforms, including the demobilization of the Frente Farabundo Martí para la Liberación Nacional (Farabundo Martí Front for National Liberation, FMLN) and its transformation into a legal political party, the reduction of the government armed forces, and the redistribution of land. However, the continued weakness of civic institutions and the absence of viable programs to deal with poverty, unemployment, and economic inequalities represent a constant threat to the formation of a stable democratic society. The primary achievement of the peace accords is the creation of opportunities for various sectors to participate in shaping national goals and to enter debates about the future shape of Salvadoran society. This process began "from above" with former President Calderón Sol's creation of a commission of politicians, activists, and intellectuals in May 1997 to draft a document identifying national priorities. The document, titled "Bases para el Plan de Nación" (Bases for the National Plan), proposes measures to eradicate poverty, strengthen the judicial system, stimulate an inclusive and internationally competitive economic system, and ensure law and order.

Initiatives from above help strengthen and legitimize democratic institutions and procedures. However, the real key to successful democratization lies in mobilization at the local level around the search for solutions to problems affecting the everyday lives of citizens. For democracy to put down deep and lasting roots, Salvadoran society must resolve problems connected to health care, environmental degradation, violent crime, the expansion of public services, and the struggles of families to make ends meet. Further, it must resolve these problems in a way that involves citizens, especially marginalized sectors such as peasants, displaced people, women, and youth, in a participatory and open process. Involvement in local projects that practice democratic discourse and organizational styles represents a crucial building block for deepening democracy. Scholars have pointed to grassroots religious and "bread-and-butter" movements as the most promising ways to refranchise all Salvadorans, from the smallest rural village to the thriving immigrant communities in the United States and Canada (Guidos Béjar 1998; Levine 1992; Menjívar Larín 1998). The question remains, however, which organizations and strategies can best serve such mobilization and its twin goals of empowering citizens and achieving concrete improvements in their lives.

Churches did not play a major role in the drafting of the National Plan. This contrasts sharply with the experiences of the 1970s, when progressive Catholics were central actors in opposition social movements, and of the 1980s, when Catholic, Lutheran, and Baptist leaders organized the National Debate for Peace to lobby for a negotiated solution to the war. Since the war's end, many religious activists and organizations have turned their attention away from large structural problems, which dominated the ethical discourse and pastoral orientation in the 1980s, and toward institution-building and personal and spiritual concerns. When they do turn to social issues, both Protestants and Catholics often focus on local quality-of-life issues such as strengthening the family or repairing neighborhood infrastructures. This altered perspective results in part from the severe repression of the 1970s and 1980s, which demoralized and exhausted many religious activists. In addition, the public sphere in El Salvador is becoming increasingly secularized due to the wider political participation made possible by the peace accords and the growing pluralization of the religious field, which diminishes the public impact of any single voice. Further, the New Evangelization, as the present pastoral focus of the Roman Catholic Church, directs resources toward spiritual rather than social concerns. All these factors are helping to redefine the political role of churches in El Salvador.

Although Salvadoran churches presently play a less direct and less obvious role in the construction of democracy than in prior decades, their role may be more foundational than ever. In a society plagued by bureaucratization and authoritarianism, churches can address social problems in a participatory way, responsive to local and personal interests and needs. Congregations and religiously based organizations address issues surrounding self-esteem, sense of belonging, the (re)construction of community life, domestic violence, and the alienation felt by many young people, particularly ex-combatants. A further question, however, concerns the ways and extent to which these personal and local issues are connected, in discourse and practice, to larger questions about the shape, direction, and priority values of Salvadoran society. These issues are critical as Salvadorans rebuild the fabric of a society fractured by war.

This chapter argues that religious participation can contribute to a renewal of individual and collective identities and to the reestablishment of commitment, solidarity, and civic behavior among the most vulnerable and marginalized sectors of Salvadoran society, especially young people. Thus the churches' efforts to inculcate different patterns of behavior, strengthen collective identities, and reintegrate young people into local communities are crucial to the task of rebuilding civil society. (This complements the analysis in chapter 9 of transnational Salvadoran gangs in the United States and El Salvador.) This chapter focuses on three religious communities: the Roman Catholic parish of San Francisco Gotera, the capital of Morazán; an Assemblies of God congregation, also in San Francisco Gotera; and the base Christian communities in Ciudad Segundo Montes, a repopulated community north of Gotera. These communities represent distinctive approaches to the problems of democratic reconstruction in postwar El Salvador, each with particular strengths as well as weaknesses in addressing the complex local, national, and international dimensions of El Salvador's current political situation.

Morazán and the Civil War

Morazán is a primarily rural province, isolated from San Salvador, with extremely high levels of poverty and very low quality-of-life indexes.[1] The region suffers, in more intense form, from the inequitable distribution of land, lack of political openness, and concentration of wealth and power in the hands of a small elite that have characterized El Salvador for most of its history. Because of its geographical isolation and its infertile and rocky land, Morazán was excluded from the export-oriented model of agrarian exploitation that characterized the central and western parts of the country. This exclusion, while contributing to the region's poverty, also helped facilitate the rise of leftist social movements beginning in the late 1960s. Many of these movements were influenced by progressive Catholic pastoral projects, which often allied with peasant organizations for agricultural cooperatives and other self-help initiatives as well more explicitly political projects. In the 1970s, guerrilla organizations, especially the Revolutionary Army of the Poor (Ejercito Revolucionario del Pueblo, or ERP), began establishing strongholds in Morazán as well. Throughout the 1980s, Perquín, in the northern part of the province, served as the ERP's headquarters.

Following the Nicaraguan revolution in July 1979, the Salvadoran army began a counterinsurgency strategy based on intensifying material and strategic support from the United States. In an effort to isolate the Salvadoran guerrillas from their bases of popular support, the army combined political programs with military attacks, including "scorched-earth" campaigns that relied heavily on aerial bombings, helicopters armed with artillery, and army commandos (Gordon 1989). Civilian casualties in these actions were high: a November 1980 operation in Morazán killed at least 3,000 civilians, and the November 1981 massacre in El Mozote killed more than one thousand people, leaving only one survivor (Cagan and Cagan 1991, 16–17; Danner 1993). A permanent state of war began in 1981 when the FMLN launched its first major military offensive as a united guerrilla army. Morazán became the geographical rear guard of the insurgency, with its northern part serving as one of two main guerrilla strongholds or "liberated zones," along with Chalatenango, the headquarters of the Popular Liberation Forces (Fuerzas Populares para la Liberación, or FPL) (Benítez 1988).

The war provoked a massive exodus of peasants from Morazán, Chalatenango, and other areas of guerrilla strength. In one of the first mass migrations, approximately 100,000 refugees from the northern part of Morazán left for neighboring settlements within El Salvador. Later, 10,000 residents of the province took refuge in Honduras, creating the Colomoncagua and San Antonio camps, which received aid from the United Nations High Commissioner of Refugees (Montes 1989). Refugees from other rural areas in El Salvador swelled additional refugee camps in Honduras and San Salvador. In contrast to residents of El Salvador's towns and cities, relatively few peasants moved to the United States; a combination of lack of resources and enduring ties to family and place kept most *campesinos* fairly close to their places of origin, usually with the hope of one day returning. Many peasants from rural areas of Morazán also moved to San Francisco Gotera, which had become the military base of the army.[2]

Throughout the war, some peasants remained in the zones of guerrilla control *(zonas de control)*, concentrated in villages like Perquín in Morazán and Arcatao in Chalatenango, where guerrillas provided some protection from the government army (López Vigil 1987; Pearce 1986). Civilians in the war zones struggled to make a living and to preserve their families, which often included at least one combatant. Their efforts to continue farming and to sustain community life in the zones suffered from frequent aerial bombardments and ground operations, which prompted long marches, called *guindas*, to safer territory. The continuous repression, strife, and forced displacement dismantled most of the local networks that constituted community life, the terrain where daily interactions were sustained. The disintegration of the family groups, due to death, disappearance, combat, and migration, is one of the most significant results of the war. In a number of cases, neighbors and even relatives turned against each other politically, and the political conflict sometimes provided means for the enacting of personal vengeance (for example, through accusations of "subversion" that effectively served as death sentences). Despite the disintegration of local areas and the crisis of family structure, many peasants managed to maintain collective ties, often based on a combination of revolutionary political ideology and an eclectic religiosity that included both progressive Catholic elements and folk traditions.

The capacity to maintain collective solidarities and values even in exile contributed to intense organization among refugees, especially in Honduras. By the mid-1980s, while the war still raged, many displaced people in camps began plans to return to their places of origin and reclaim areas lost due to the war. Their carefully organized collective project represented both a practical decision to build better lives for themselves and their families and an ideological commitment to constructing, at least in microcosm, a new model of society. Progressive Catholic values and organizational styles were central to this effort, as reflected in the name of the group that coordinated most of the resettlements—the Christian Committee for Refugees and the Displaced (CRIPDES), founded in the mid-1980s by residents of a church-run camp in San Salvador. The first repopulation involved the resettlement of the village of Tenancingo, in Cuscatlán province, which had been depopulated two years earlier due to combat in the area. In 1985, 187 Salvadorans who had been living as refugees in San Salvador or smaller cities returned to Tenancingo. Support for this initiative came from the archdiocese of San Salvador (Edwards and Siebentritt 1991, 29–46).

More complex and larger-scale repopulations—which were also repatriations since they involved the return of refugees who had been living outside El Salvador—began in 1985–1986. During that period, thousands of refugees began returning from camps in Honduras and San Salvador with support not only from Salvadoran church and political groups but also from foreign organizations. Most of these early repatriations were in Chalatenango province around the *cantones* (hamlets) of San Antonio Los Ranchos and Guarjila, guerrilla strongholds that had mostly been depopulated during the late 1970s and early

1980s. Throughout the late 1980s, displaced Salvadorans returned to dozens of abandoned villages in Chalatenango, Cabañas, San Vicente, and Usulután provinces. Most of the repopulations took place in areas dominated by the FPL and involved not only intense political organizing by Salvadorans but also large-scale international solidarity, including the involvement of Roman Catholic and Protestant churches from the United States and Europe.

The repopulation of Morazán began later but involved the largest single group of refugees. In May 1989, refugees in United Nations–sponsored camps in San Antonio and Colomoncagua, Honduras, decided to return to El Salvador. Their decision was influenced by the successful repatriations of other regions, by their conviction that their internal organization would enable them to build a new community, and by the intractability of the war, which suggested that waiting for peace to return might mean many more years in exile (Cagan and Cagan 1991, 114–115). A massive FMLN offensive in November 1989 delayed the return, but in January 1990 the repatriation began. In endless lines of buses and trucks, carrying all their worldly goods and closely monitored by the Salvadoran army, the United Nations, and various Salvadoran and foreign organizations, approximately eight thousand refugees crossed the border. They headed for the abandoned village of Meanguera, which they renamed in honor of Segundo Montes, a Jesuit sociologist killed by the army during the November offensive.[3] The return to Meanguera was even more highly organized than previous repopulations, in part because the unprecedented size of the group returning demanded organization and because the Colomoncagua refugees could draw on their own years of organizing in the camps as well as the experiences of earlier repopulations elsewhere in El Salvador (Cagan and Cagan 1991; Macdonald and Gatehouse 1995).

In the refugee camps and in the war zones, a variety of Christian congregations have contributed, in diverse ways, to the rearticulation of broken communities. Religious rituals, narratives, and values have helped people make sense of and respond to political violence, social injustices, and dramatic changes in their lives and communities (Peterson 1997). Religious communities have helped create or re-create collectivities that fill the void left by the still-weak mechanisms of local social representation and have strengthened institutions such as community directorates and peasant associations. In particular, religion provides local networks and effective ties for individuals and groups most affected by the economic crisis and the war. For women, young people, and displaced peasants, other institutions have largely failed, and religious community plays a central and unique role in restructuring both individual identity and collective ties.

Young People, Local Religion, and Civil Society

Many Salvadorans, including young people themselves, cite the plight of young people as the most urgent challenge facing the country today. They view the violence and alienation of youth as both symptoms of spiritual and social malaise and a major cause of the country's inability to recover from the divisions and violence of the war. The alienation, apparent aimlessness, and growing violence among young people reflect their discouraging prospects due to chronic poverty, lack of employment and self-improvement opportunities,[4] and the disintegration of sociocultural institutions, mainly the family (Smutt and Miranda 1997). These problems are especially acute in former war zones such as Morazán, where the more complete destruction of families and local communities, the lingering divisions and resentments of the war, and the greater degree of social dislocation make the problem of youth violence especially acute and the task of rebuilding civil society both more demanding and more urgent. In interviews and surveys, residents of Morazán express consistent concern over the conditions of young people, including the prospects for their own children and the social threat posed by delinquent youth, especially those in gangs. Government programs have been limited to infrastructural and housing projects and efforts to strengthen formal education. A combination of church, community, state, and NGO resources, together with remittances from the United States, has made it possible for the majority of children of displaced families in Gotera to be able to finish their high-school educations.[5] However, this formal education often creates instability, separating young people from the world of their parents and from traditional rural ways of life. Standing at the border of the adult world, they do not know how to break the bonds of family dependence. The immediate working world does not offer clear alternatives for fulfillment, even for survival (Pontes 1994). In Morazán, as in many rural areas, these problems are aggravated by the paucity of recreational opportunities and the persistence of patterns of violent conduct derived from the war. As we discuss in more detail in chapter 9, many young people find in gangs not only diversion but also a sense of purpose, belonging, and community absent from the larger society. I turn now to the ways that three different religious institutions in Morazán are addressing the problems facing young people in their region.

The Catholic Parish of San Francisco Gotera

Like many parishes today, the church in San Francisco Gotera reflects a blend of styles of Catholicism. For more than thirty years the parish has been run by Sisters of St. Clare (Clarisas) and Franciscan priests, who began progressive pastoral projects such as base communities in the early 1970s. Their work had a strong influence throughout the region, but the rise of political violence in the late 1970s sharply decreased church activities. Some pastoral agents remained in Gotera during the war to assist the approximately twelve thousand refugees who came to the city from villages to the north. Many of the parish's present lay leaders moved to Gotera during that period, and today the most active sectors of the parish are in the wards that emerged out of refugee settlements. Today base communities and Bible study groups remain central to the pastoral work of the parish, although the aftereffects of the war and changes in the priorities of the institutional church have transformed the parish's pastoral efforts. The longstanding conservatism of the diocese of San Miguel has been reinforced by the rise of the New Evangelization. Many parishes in El Salvador that have long worked under the CEB model now operate on a dual track of sorts, with influences from both progressive Catholicism and the New Evangelization, sometimes competing, sometimes coexisting peacefully, and sometimes overlapping.

The parish in San Francisco Gotera reflects the occasionally smooth, occasionally uneasy meshing of these two pastoral approaches at the grassroots. Pastoral agents and lay leaders retain a strong commitment to the poor and the sectors affected the most by war. Pastoral programs still depart from and reflect on everyday reality, as in progressive initiatives like CEBs, but their perception of that reality has changed. Participants interpret their life experiences through the Bible and the sacraments but focus on strengthening spiritual values, personal moral discipline, and family solidarity with little explicit reference to larger political and economic issues. The church does not seem to be a connecting point between faith and life. Rather, faith withdraws to the inner world of the self without projecting itself clearly toward the social. Further, the growth of Charismatic groups in the parish has increased divisions as groups now compete to make their symbols, ideals, and methods hegemonic within the parish.

The focus on individual spiritual and moral discipline is especially evident in pastoral work with young people. The Gotera parish has no direct program to counteract the increase in youth gangs, but it has promoted the creation of teen and preteen pastoral groups as a way to channel youth participation in their communities. Programs and sermons are directed toward helping young women and men develop a responsible attitude when making personal decisions daily. This stress on autonomy is very important in Morazán, where young people often must confront daily challenges alone due to the disarticulation of family structures. Walter, a young man from Gotera, explains his own situation: "My mother died about two years ago, not long ago, then. We have two brothers in the United States. My older brother gives [money] for my studies and the other helps my brother who is handicapped. Under these conditions, [I] go to eat at a lady's down there; she gives me food. That is our life. My other brother has to prepare food for himself."[6]

The pastoral emphasis on personal and interpersonal relations allows young people to reach the "maturity" needed to differentiate between the options facing them: joining the gang or a religious youth group, which then becomes a refuge in the midst of all the chaos of local life. This is evident in the reflections of Elisandro, the coordinator of one of the parish's youth groups:

> We formed a youth group with five coordinators; today I am the only one. And I thank God because the group has remained together. On occasions I receive an inspiration that strengthens me, because I have felt that something has been accomplished . . . it has been very important for me because sometimes I say, the *maras* are here! and if we did not have a youth group, many young people would be in that. For this reason we have talked to them [the gangs], we have approached them, even though they think that we are very tough, but I have the feeling that I have helped somewhat. For me the change is that I have matured.

Perhaps unconsciously, pastoral work reinforces the notion that individual autonomy and personal moral choice are the main, perhaps even the only, responses to social and political chaos. Young people seek refuges, and the problem is teaching them how to choose the proper havens and habits—churches rather than gangs, personal discipline rather than violent crime.

The political uncertainty generated by youth gangs and the lack of educational, recreational, and work opportunities are exacerbated by the fact that young people in Morazán mistrust the capacity of state institutions and the political system to resolve the problems of everyday life. In other words, the larger crisis of democratic civil society is felt at the local level, just as local problems deepen the crisis at the national level. The lack of confidence among young people is part of the political parties' lack of credibility among the population. Salvadorans, especially youth, widely perceive that political parties do not represent the interests of the common person and that they are removed from the realities of everyday life. This alienation reduces parties' capacity to provide effective solutions to pressing problems. Young people also tend to blame politics for the war and the loss of their families and communities. For many young people, political life has become synonymous with corruption and greed.

The deep distrust of politics is particularly problematic for young Salvadorans. Previous generations of youth possessed visions of democratic change, which, however repressed and attacked, at least provided a guide for ethical action, an interpretative framework for understanding national politics, and a moral horizon for desired change. The Roman Catholic Church played a crucial role in the articulation of the desired goals and the provision of practical means for pursuing them. However, for various reasons the collective memory of these democratic aspirations has not been fully transferred to the present generation of young people, who are so crucial in the future of Salvadoran civil society. Lacking utopian visions, young people have largely retreated from the public to the private sphere. New generations seem to have forgotten the historical and social background that brought about the conflict. For them social transformations depend more on internal, personal changes than on social struggles. This attitude is reinforced by the New Evangelization, which increasingly shapes young people's opinions about the church's role in social problems. About 55 percent of the young Catholics we surveyed in Gotera believed that prayer is the church's best answer to the social problems. Echoes remain of the church's prophetic stance during Archbishop Romero's time, as seen in the strong desire to intervene in social matters and to build person and community according to the principles of justice, truth, and solidarity. However, this desire has not translated into collective action geared directly toward repairing the badly damaged civil society. The New Evangelization emphasis on personal change appears to fall short in the face of the urgent requirements of the postwar period.

The Assemblies of God

During the 1980s, San Francisco Gotera served as a destination not only for activist Catholics but also for many Pentecostals who fled the political violence in rural areas of Morazán. Juan José, the deacon of the Assemblies of God church in Gotera, explains: "When the people emigrated from their land they would come here, many who in their town had churches and were evangelicals there. When they came here that helped the growth of the church. Those persons would come and would join and that is how the church became bigger." The Assemblies of God church in Gotera has served as a social base for evangelical families dispersed by the violence. However, the support provided by Gotera's Assemblies was basically spiritual, since, unlike the Catholic Church, it did not offer any material assistance for the displaced. Further, it appears that evangelicals did not migrate en masse during the war. Rather, migration was a very gradual process involving individuals supported by family resources.

After the peace accords of 1992, the number of followers increased. In the beginning, thirty or fifty people met. Now the number of members has multiplied, and there are from four hundred to five hundred steady members in the church. This phenomenon stems from the increased freedom since the end of the war. However, we cannot discount the impact of continuous evangelizing work carried out despite the war. While it is true that the members of the Pentecostal churches in El Salvador were not persecuted or intimidated as were Catholic pastoral agents, the war limited aggressive outreach efforts typical of Pentecostals. Despite this limitation, Gotera's Assemblies of God became a safe space where Pentecostals from areas affected by the armed conflict could continue practicing their faith and preaching their message.

Today, the Assemblies church in Gotera is a vibrant center for evangelization and outreach to other parts of the province. The church is supported by the weekly contributions of its members for tithing and specific projects. Besides the traditional focus on personal conversion, the stress has fallen on concrete projects such as the expansion of the temple and the building of the children's church and a clinic. Many of the projects respond to the immediate needs of the population in the areas of health or education; they almost never carry the structural-political vision typical of liberation theology and CEBs. While projects constantly mobilize the community of believers, this is done in an inward-looking fashion. Projects that go beyond serving the internal needs of the congregation are usually geared toward attracting new followers. The constant efforts to build the church and involve all members in reaching goals reinforce evangelical identity and strengthen the congregation's effectiveness.

The success of the Assemblies' various projects is anchored in the social composition of the congregation. Many are small businesspeople, professionals, or artisans with middle-class incomes that allow them to contribute to pastoral work. Possibly because the church is in the capital of the province, the presence of the middle class is more noticeable there.[7] Deacon Juan José describes the mixture: "There are all kinds of people here, such as myself, a humble person who works in a steel shop, but there are also individuals that are engineers, attorneys, all of that, from here downwards. Let's say there are even school teachers, they finish their working hours and from there they come to the church." The members' commitment to the church and support for its various projects are evident in the response that the pastors and deacons receive, Juan José continues: "It is a church that responds. It is a church where if we say, 'Brothers, let's collect 10,000 [colones],' they come one day and they collect it. If we say we want to put together an offering, we would like to have some 6,000 colones [about seven hundred U.S. dollars] on a Sunday it's collected. These are exceptional cases, but the brothers and sisters respond."

As the church meets its objectives—and the members perceive that it does—and establishes a strong local presence, it will likely seek to extend its radius of influence. Nevertheless, although members of the Assemblies are conscious of the major social problems that affect them, such as violence and poverty, they maintain the traditional vision of many Pentecostal churches vis-à-vis society, and they do not link the work of the church with reality beyond their own missionary work. It is not the responsibility of the church to solve problems of a social nature. Social change is valid only if it will contribute to the goal of saving souls. Spiritual transformation implies the acceptance of the divine will, of the human frailty. Conversion and acceptance of divine intervention thus constitute the path to changes at the personal and, perhaps eventually, social levels.

This perspective shapes the Assemblies' approach to youth problems. Like many other Pentecostal congregations, the church in Gotera focuses particularly on the conversion of ex-gang members. In contrast, many Roman Catholic parishes direct attention toward keeping neighborhood young people away from gangs in the first place. As we discuss in chapter 9, this religious mission has an essentially transnational dimension since a large number of gang members have recently been deported from the United States. Pentecostal churches often strive to move troubled young people from "the world of the gang" to "the world of faith" through a renunciation of "the world of sin" and a baptism in the Holy Spirit, which translates into the adoption of a different, more ascetic lifestyle. This understanding of youth problems reflects the dualistic theology of Pentecostal Protestantism, usually phrased in terms of a perceived opposition between the things of God and things of "the world."

The Assemblies of God youth ministries rely heavily on groups like Castillos del Rey (Castles of the King) and the Exploradores del Rey (Explorers of the King), which combine Bible study with recreation and cultural activities in order to motivate group participation. The churches have also gone in search of potential converts in the spaces where gang life unfolds. A case in point is outreach work inside prisons. Former gang members come to preach to incarcerated *mara* members, at times in coordination with sister churches in the United States. The message is one of conversion, spiritual release, and belonging, a counterpoint to the desperation and dislocation experienced by many gang members caught in the transnational cycle of migration and deportation between El Salvador and the United States. The promise of spiritual salvation makes possible a clean break with a past of crime, violence, and existence at the margins. This is evident in the testimonies of young converts, as we explore further in chapter 9.

The spiritual message of transformation and rupture with the past is accompanied by demonstrations of solidarity and support. Church members offer comfort and new alternatives to face crises on a personal level, in the context of a decision for God and against Satan—represented by gangs and the general corruption of "the world." This represents a particular instance of Pentecostalism's larger effort to appeal to people in crisis (Williams 1997). The church provides a supportive, caring, and safe community of faith, with new social bonds that allow for a reworked relationship to the larger society. The church—which stands firmly on the side of God and not the world—mediates the convert's relationship to the outside world during the process of conversion and beyond. This is apparent in the way that Pablo, a former gang member, describes his conversion: "The whole church prayed for my life and interceded on my behalf. As they were doing this, I was building up my soul."

Pablo attests not only to the importance of the church community but also to the theological significance of the Holy Spirit; it is an energy that penetrates the most intimate being of the individual, addressing personal weaknesses and fears and leading to a profound emotional catharsis and moral cleansing. The link that arises with others who have experienced conversion produces a new social connection—in this case based on a charismatic religious congregation. It is the formation of an "us" that revolves around religious commitment and the acceptance of the structures of the church. This "us" is also opposed to, or at least clearly distinguished from, the mundane world. Personal purity and identity come at the cost of a certain alienation from the world.

In El Salvador, youth groups like the Castles and Explorers of the King perform several missions: evangelizing, education, and Bible studies. They also offer opportunities for recreation and camaraderie, turning into a meeting point where young people can ventilate their aspirations, expectations, and needs. Often, leadership roles in youth groups serve as vehicles for the pursuit of a professional religious vocation. The groups become training grounds for budding pastors and missionaries, a kind of alternative space where rural young people can become educated and experience the personal growth that the public educational system fails to provide. Youth groups also provide a commitment to a larger institution, with a distinctive worldview that helps make sense of life experiences and social processes. However, this commitment, and the worldview in which it is embedded, are clearly limited, perhaps even "hermetic," as Rowan Ireland (1991, 222) suggests.[8]

Base Christian Communities in Ciudad Segundo Montes

For both Pentecostals and Catholics in San Francisco Gotera, religion has provided continuity in the face of the fragmentation produced by the civil war and its aftershocks. Religious practice has helped maintain and re-create a background of common experiences and bonds through which the local population, especially young people, can construct personal and collective identities, loyalties, and commitments. For the Catholic parish in San Francisco Gotera and especially for Pentecostals, these collective commitments, and especially their relationship to the larger task of strengthening participatory democracy in El Salvador, remain largely in the background. In contrast, the base Christian communities of Ciudad Segundo Montes present a self-conscious alternative to the other churches, following a vision in which a new sort of church forms a cornerstone in the construction of a transformed nation. The repopulation's motto—"a hope that is born in the east for all of El Salvador" *(una esperanza que nace en el Oriente para todo El Salvador)*—points to the community's conviction that it represents a model for a new kind of society in El Salvador.

This vision has roots in the progressive Catholic pastoral work that began in Morazán in the late 1960s and early 1970s. Morazán's own diocese of San Miguel offered little support, and the region was isolated from the archdiocese of San Salvador (which then included Chalatenango province), the center of progressive pastoral work in El Salvador. Pastoral agents in Morazán thus looked elsewhere for educational materials and support. Their primary resources were progressive pastoral workers in Honduras and, inside El Salvador, the *centro de formación campesina* (peasant training center) in El Castaño, San Miguel province. El Castaño and other centers in El Salvador during the late 1960s and 1970s provided training for laypeople in rural areas, with their main goal "to develop leadership qualities in peasants, with knowledge of the value of mutual help and of cooperative work; to train men for change, ready to form part of a parish and diocesan pastoral work, putting themselves at the service of bishops and priests. Briefly: holistic education for liberation" (CEDES 1975, 7). Beatriz, a native of Morazán, summarizes the ways this vision differed from earlier pastoral models and what those differences meant for her and other campesino participants:

> Before, you went to mass, you didn't understand what the priest said, but not now. Today, those priests that we have now, they say that we have to look after the poor, that you have to be in solidarity with each other, love each other like brothers and sisters. That's what these priests today have shown us. But the ones before didn't understand any of that. Not now, because, you see, if someone's sick, you have to go visit them, if your neighbor is poor and doesn't have anything to eat, you have to share with him ... Now we know that, and before we didn't know all that.

This model of pastoral work and its connections to social projects such as the creation of peasant federations and agricultural cooperatives helped make CEBs central to opposition political organizing in Morazán during the 1970s. Progressive Catholic pastoral work in Morazán offers an example of the strong symbiosis between progressive Catholicism and leftist political movements that characterized El Salvador's *iglesia popular* (popular church). While some sectors of the popular church established direct links to the political opposition,[9] the vast majority of progressive Catholics worked within the parish structure, taking *cursillos* and participating in Bible studies and retreats. Their ideological and practical links to radical social movements were real and substantial but usually remained distinct, conceptually and organizationally, from their religious identities.

In Morazán, the Clarisas and other pastoral agents established a foundation of socially committed pastoral work in the 1970s, which persevered throughout the war and even in refugee camps. The Clarisas themselves remained in Gotera throughout the war, working with residents of San Francisco Gotera (including the waves of refugees from villages to the north) and with surrounding villages. Their efforts received little support from the diocese of San Miguel, but the Clarisas continued with strong backing from their religious superiors in Great Britain. Pastoral work was even more difficult inside the war zones. A few priests, notably the Belgian Rogelio Ponceele (López Vigil 1987), accompanied Catholics to zones under guerrilla control in Morazán, but they did so with material assistance from the lay population and from popular political organizations in the region, rather than from church authorities.

Progressive pastoral work, like everything else in northern Morazán, was transformed by the return of refugees from the Colomoncagua and San Antonio camps. While in exile, the refugees had elaborated a complex and ambitious plan for rebuilding their communities, founded explicitly on the religiously grounded vision of solidarity, justice, and self-sufficiency that took root during the 1970s (Cagan and Cagan 1991; Macdonald and Gatehouse 1995). Many community leaders in the camps, like those throughout rural El Salvador, had first been exposed to progressive ideology and collective action in CEBs, *centros de formación campesina,* or other pastoral projects. Progressive Catholic values, in sum, were the foundational ideology of Ciudad Segundo Montes, as in other repopulated communities.[10] Luisa, a lay activist with Base Ecclesial Communities of El Salvador (CEBES), explains: "People in Morazán have experienced a very deep community life beginning in '75 through '79. This was a persecuted people, with many disappeared. It is a very "martyred" community, with 647 mothers of fallen children. Also a majority of the women are widows, those persons that have lost their dear ones, their sisters, their husbands. This means that it is a community with a lot of experience, and . . . an experience like that is [not] very simple, it is very costly."

The strong collective bonds forged during the war remain part of a common memory that remains potent among many rural residents even in the postwar period. This is particularly true for Salvadorans who lived through the war in refugee camps or in the conflicted zones. Today, collective memories still help unite the community, as Luisa makes clear: "We know that as base Christian communities we continue being the same CEBs as twenty-five years ago, and this year, 1998, we celebrate the twenty-fifth anniversary of the first CEBs, and we're still those same base communities as in '78, '79." In maintaining their identity and unity, progressive Catholics continually refer to the martyrs of the *iglesia popular,* and especially Archbishop Romero. Rosa explains: "Monseñor Romero is like an endless fountain. You never stop discovering, or if you discovered it today, tomorrow it has another meaning, something else you've discovered about his life." Other martyrs also, she says, "motivate you to keep going, because their commitment, their sacrifice, is a commitment for us who live out this model of church."

In this model of church, most pastoral work is undertaken by lay leaders. Ciudad Segundo Montes is divided into five sectors, and each sector has a team of catechists (consisting of three to fifteen members) that coordinates pastoral work. Their efforts include a variety of projects. Every Sunday, pastoral messages are transmitted over the community radio for the entire repopulation, and progressive priests offer masses at different intervals, perhaps every two weeks in the bigger sectors. When there is no mass, Delegates of the Word offer celebrations of word. There are also traditional celebrations of Christ the King (Cristo Rey) and Pentecost, as well as commemorations of the Vía Crucis (Stations of the Cross) and other festivities during Lent and Holy Week. One of the most well-attended religious events in the community is the anniversary of Romero's assassination on March 24.

While these celebrations are important for bringing together larger parts of the community, small groups remain the core of pastoral work, following progressive Catholicism's emphasis on building collective solidarity and empowering individuals. As Luisa explains, "the center of all this is the community, the base Christian communities, which meet to reflect on faith and life." In addition to CEBs, a number of "specialized" pastoral groups operate in Ciudad Segundo Montes. The most important of these are women's groups, including the Mothers of the Fallen, and work with young people, adolescents, and children. The prominence of these programs reflects the fact that a majority of the population in Ciudad Segundo Montes, as in most resettled villages, are women and children.

As a result, women play many leadership roles, which has not only filled the void left by the absence of men but also has brought an increasing appreciation of women's work by the group. This new appreciation is facilitated by the breadth of women's contributions and capacities: they minister to mothers, children, and the public in general, bringing together educational and pastoral approaches. Women in CEBs in Morazán also maintain links with other organizations within the Salvadoran women's movement, entering discussions about the need to address problems specific to gender in the democratic transition. The deeply religious character of the dominant worldview in the repopulations is reflected in the efforts of women to find indications of women's significance in biblical history. Rosa explains: "As women we meet once a month and we have been analyzing topics of women participation in the life and actions of Jesus, and also in Jesus' Passion. It is very interesting to discover that in the Bible there is a full procession of women that accompanied Jesus. Also there is some in the Old Testament, even though very little is mentioned."

The experiences of women in Morazán represent an especially important part of CEBs' larger emphasis on giving voice and raised consciousness to poor people. As Levine (1992) and others have emphasized, CEBs' primary contribution to political democratization in Latin America comes through their capacity to engage people in participatory democratic processes at a local level. These experiences are crucial, Levine argues, to the creation of citizenship values and skills. This is explicit in the CEBs and progressive Catholic discourse, which deliberately connects parish and locally based experiences in democratic decision-making and mobilization to the goal of transforming the larger society. Some scholars (Martin 1990) contend that congregational life in Pentecostal churches also helps create democratic citizens and organizational styles. Others, however, suggest that Pentecostal theology itself, especially its ultimate rejection of "worldly" things, places limits on Pentecostalism's potential contribution to the democratic transformation of national polities (Ireland 1992).

If Pentecostal theology constrains Pentecostalism as a force for democratic change, a variety of factors also weaken the political impact of Catholic initiatives. In El Salvador, as throughout Latin America, an increasingly conservative hierarchy has transformed the sociopolitical role of the church, at both local and national levels. This is evident in El Salvador. Archbishop Rivera died in late 1994, and in April 1995 Pope John Paul II named as his replacement a relatively unknown Spaniard, Fernando Saenz Lacalle, auxiliary bishop of Santa Ana. Saenz, a longtime member of the secretive, highly conservative organization Opus Dei, made it clear in his first days as archbishop that he would guide the Salvadoran church in a very different way than his two predecessors, lowering the church's public political profile in order to concentrate on "spiritual" matters. In his first three years as archbishop, Saenz has supported the Charismatic Renewal and other conservative lay groups and has emphasized the need for obedience to authority and ecclesial unity. While Saenz

Lacalle has not restricted progressive pastoral work in the archdiocese or elsewhere in El Salvador as much as some feared, he has weakened the material and the moral support available to CEBs and other progressive initiatives. He has openly criticized progressive Catholicism, describing the theology of liberation, for example, as "a Marxist re-reading of the Gospel, with a tendency toward violence that no longer has a place in El Salvador" (Rohter 1996, 6).

Throughout El Salvador, base Christian communities increasingly lack institutional support from their diocese. Thus the catechists and other pastoral workers in Ciudad Segundo Montes have virtually no contact with local priests or the bishop of San Miguel. This independence from the institutional church gives lay leaders the freedom to set their own pastoral, theological, and social agendas. However, it also creates problems. On a practical level, their lack of material resources and support for pastoral agents weakens the communities' ability to carry out many of their goals. Their alienation from the institutional church, at both parish and diocese levels, means that CEBs receive pastoral guidance not from parish priests but from groups like CEBES and from members of religious orders, such as the Clarisas. The CEBs in northern Morazán function in many ways as a parallel or, as Luisa puts it, "autonomous" church, with pastoral practices and theological values that differ strikingly from those of the institutional church. Rosa explains: "Here we're trying to respond to the reality of the community. The thing is that with the naming of the new bishop [in San Miguel], we don't know how we're going to keep doing that. First of all, we'd like to talk to the bishop and above all ask him that he respects the experience of the church here *(de esta zona),* above all because we't= a model of church . . . as we say, that began with the Second Vatican Council, and we know that we've revived the values of the first communities."

Despite the strength of that vision, CEB churches in Ciudad Segundo Montes are currently suffering a crisis of participation that is also reflected, on a larger scale, in many progressive organizations, religious and secular, throughout El Salvador. Rosa recalls that in the refugee camps "up to three hundred women would come together, but here we're talking about sixty." Still, she emphasizes:

> People know that we're always there. . . . The number hasn't grown, but we keep the faith and hope, and we keep meeting, even in the midst of this economic crisis, and what's more, the lack of recognition from the institution. I mention this because there's another priest here in this zone who follows a traditional model of church, and so he says that what we do here isn't worth anything. This influences people, and so people begin to say, "Well, and what are we, another church, or what?" So you see a certain division, and the

people who least live the model of the church of the poor, they're happy with sacramentalism, and they're free. So we can't say that we're a big group, and we don't pretend to be, but the groups do keep going, and that's important.

These experiences in Morazán parallel, in some ways, the situation of progressive Catholic pastoral initiatives throughout El Salvador. In many parishes, progressive projects suffer from divisions among both pastoral agents and laypeople about both overall pastoral goals and the best methods for achieving those goals. This was evident in parishes we studied that were divided between progressive and New Evangelization models, most notably in San Francisco Gotera and San Francisco Mejicanos.

Furthermore, CEBs and other local initiatives are subject to the political tensions and the effects of the economic crisis of the larger society. Political parties have suffered strong fragmentation, dividing the population, which while at the refugee camp had maintained ideological unity. Most relevant for residents of Ciudad Segundo Montes and northern Morazán was the ERP's split from the FMLN shortly after the 1992 peace accords.[11] Some people remained with the party as it evolved into a reformist group, while other residents of ERP strongholds and members of ERP-affiliated popular organizations shifted their loyalty to the FMLN, and usually to the FPL as the dominant faction within the umbrella party. Still others rejected organized politics. Luisa perceives "a complete demoralization among the organizations." She continues: "I'd say that the war taught us good things and bad things, and many times the leaders of the organizations or movements, as they say, many times they've lost their way, the solidarity that is so important. And there's a lot of confusion among the people and in the communities, and it's like the leaders of the communities have lost credibility. So in this sense it's very hard to see how they could offer solutions."

The political divisions and confusion created by the changes within the ERP and FMLN more generally weakened progressive work at the grassroots level, including in strongholds like Morazán and Chalatenango, just as it harmed the revolutionary party's ability to win votes nationally. Luisa explains that after the signing of the peace accords, this community was abandoned politically and only showed up for propaganda, as during the current electoral campaigns.

In addition to disillusionment with and isolation from national politics, progressive organizers in Ciudad Segundo Montes face the problem that some community projects that were conceived as alternatives to the dominant neoliberal model did not result in anticipated economic self-sufficiency and prosperity (or at least subsistence). These failures have contributed to disenchantment and political demobilization. Material conditions remain precarious, and there are no alternatives at this moment that would offer rapid solutions to acute problems such as the lack of food, work, and productive alternatives. Even the state, embarked on a process of decentralization as part of economic restructuring, has not been able to foster regional and municipal development projects. In addition, for most people in the CEBs of northern Morazán, migration to the United States is not an option, mainly because of the reluctance to leave their homes behind after a protracted exile and because of the extreme poverty of the residents. The survival alternatives, then, are very limited. Until today, residents have relied on local strategies like informal or casual labor and productive projects financed through international aid. Many people have abandoned political and religious work in their efforts to keep their families afloat, as Luisa points out: "Since the peace accords, many catechists have left their pastoral work and focused on the needs of their own families, but here in the community there are many projects, and that's possible only with the work of the catechists."

In this context, CEBs gain even more importance as one of the few spaces to deploy collective strategies conducive to the improvement of the local quality of life. However, CEBs, especially in rural communities like Ciudad Segundo Montes, are increasingly isolated from both the institutional church and national political actors. Even with the best intentions, ideological clarity, and the tremendous capacity for hard work demonstrated by *repobladores,* local efforts alone cannot solve all the problems they face. Difficulties felt locally, such as the lack of jobs, the failure of land redistribution, and shortages of schools and teachers, have causes and consequences in national and global processes, and purely local mobilizations cannot resolve them.

Local Religion and National Reconstruction

The churches we studied in Morazán, despite their differences, all contribute to civil society through a shared element: the opportunities for participation that open up to members, creating local leaders among traditionally excluded groups. These sectors find means of expression based on religion. Further, the religious group, as a source of mutual encouragement and solidarity, allows members to seek ways to solve their most crucial problems. For spiritual problems, faith gives strength in personal lives and dignifies the groups excluded. Religious organizations have helped meet material needs and strengthened vulnerable groups such as women, the elderly, and youth.

Participation is, undoubtedly, the main political challenge in postwar El Salvador. Until now, political participation has been confined to voting, which is still limited to a restricted number of citizens, since the discourse of enfranchisement still meets considerable resistance. As in other Latin America situations, the democratic transition in El Salvador has excluded many sectors unable to become civic actors because they cannot find their place in the process of political reorganization. This is coupled with the withdrawal and, in some cases, disintegration of the civic organizations that operated during the era of authoritarianism and the war, such as popular movements of workers, peasants, and ex-combatants. Their response to this exclusion may range from social violence to anomie and indifference (Jelín 1994). This is especially true for young people, as we have discussed, and the churches' (and other institutions') efforts to bring youth into local and national dialogues and projects are crucial to building civil society.

While Christian churches as institutions in El Salvador have withdrawn from the political arena due to secularization (that is, autonomization of civil society and the increasing internal differentiation of the religious field), they are playing a critical role in containing anomie, as in the case of the youth; in modifying values regarding gender roles; and in the integration of communities that have been alienated, like refugees, who need to reconnect to productive life and reorient their political participation according to new utopian visions. The churches' role in holding anomie and alienation in check is particularly significant in war-torn areas like Morazán, where the fabric of social existence has been all but destroyed.

In the debate about the future configuration of Salvadoran society ushered by the Plan de Nación, churches can serve as important vehicles to mobilize disfranchised and marginalized social sectors around issues connected with identity (especially for women and young people), quality of life (for example, the environment, poverty, and crime), and the reconstruction and maintenance of self and community. This mobilization is critical in generating a truly inclusive, widespread, and robust democracy. Our study indicates that in postwar El Salvador the solidarity, reciprocity, and efforts to give voice and find consensus in decision making in various churches may lend support to democratic values of citizenship and civic participation. In societies like El Salvador, with so much instability and history of authoritarianism, the question is whether experiences of religious participation can be translated into sustained democratic practices, as opposed to merely attenuating or reproducing exclusionary patterns.

Notes

1. National data indicate that 48 percent of the population lives below the poverty line. In Morazán, the percentage is even higher: 75.3 percent. According to the Ministry of Health data for 1995, Morazán has the highest infant mortality rate in the

country, at 53.4 for every 1,000 live births, compared to a national rate of 40.2 per 1,000 live births.

2. San Francisco Gotera's population grew rapidly during the war years. According to census data between 1971 and 1992, it experienced a growth rate of 3.6 percent each year, while the entire province averaged 0.12 percent during the same period.

3. Montes had conducted important sociological studies about the living conditions of Salvadoran refugees in Colomoncagua and other camps. A repopulated village in Chalatenango was renamed in honor of Ignacio Ellacuría, another of the murdered Jesuits.

4. According to official data, the youth population between the ages of twelve and seventeen represents 13.2 percent of the total population of the country. Of these, 62 percent live in poverty and 27.8 percent are extremely poor (Dirección General de Estadísticas y Censos (DIGESTYC). *Encuesta de Hogares de 1996*).

5. According to the *Encuesta de Hogares de 1996*, 41 percent of the income from remittances is designated for family consumption and 6 percent is used toward education expenses.

6. All quotations from individuals are taken from personal interviews conducted by Lisa Domínguez and Ileana Gómez in Ciudad Segundo Montes and San Francisco Gotera between November 1996 and December 1997.

7. The economic activity of San Francisco Gotera is concentrated in the service sector, with 43 percent of all those employed. One-third participate in the business sector, 17 percent in manufacturing, and only 6 percent in agriculture.

8. It is worth noting that Pentecostal youths are often more critical and more open in their discussions of these problems than the adults of their own congregations. This could be linked to a greater involvement in politics by many Pentecostal churches in El Salvador, a few of which have formed political parties that maintain successful alliances with leftist parties. The Movimiento de Unidad (Unity Movement Party), whose leader, Jorge Martínez, an important Pentecostal leader, formed an electoral alliance with the FMLN and the Convergencia Democrática, both left-leaning parties. This coalition won the municipal elections of 1997 in various cities of the country, including San Salvador.

9. Two such organizations were the National Coordinator of the Popular Church (CONIP), which was affiliated with the FPL, and Base Ecclesial Communities of El Salvador (CEBES), linked to the ERP. CEBES and CONIP were significant because they made explicit the links between radical politics and progressive Catholicism, but they never encompassed more than a small proportion of progressive Catholic leaders and activists.

10. The working area includes the municipalities of Torola, Arambala, Perquín, Meanguera, San Fernando, and Jocoaitique, all of them within the northern area of Morazán, which according to the 1992 census had 16,990 residents. All these municipalities had been repopulated by families that left in the late 1970s and early 1980s.

11. The ERP initially changed its name to the Expresión Renovadora del Pueblo (roughly, the Popular Expression of Renewal), with the same acronym as before but a much less militant meaning. The leadership then transformed the party into the Democratic Party (Partido Demócrata), then into the Social Democrat Party (Partido Social Demócrata).

Part III
Religion, Transnationalism, and Globalization

Chapter 7

Larissa Ruíz Baía

Rethinking Transnationalism

*National Identities among Peruvian
Catholics in New Jersey*

Transnationalism is emerging as one of the central theories in the study of immigration. Increasingly, scholars working on migration, like Linda Basch, Nina Glick Schiller, and Cristina Szanton Blanc, argue that unlike earlier migrants, contemporary immigrants "forge and sustain simultaneous multi-stranded social relations that link together their societies of origin and settlement" (1994, 48). However, a close inspection of the definition of transnationalism reveals that it has not fully taken into account recent work on the formation of ethnic identity and on multiculturalism. The concept is still caught in the dichotomies of the receiving and sending countries. I argue that there is a need to add another dimension to transnationalism, one that is not bound by the territoriality of national borders. In doing so, we are able to capture the complexities of maintaining and readjusting national identities within the multicultural context of the host society. Transnationalism needs to recognize this constant multilevel and multipolar bargaining of identities as globalization pushes the boundaries of our contemporary notions of citizenship and community. As an emerging theory, transnationalism must respond to the challenges of understanding identity formation from a perspective that is not bounded by space or time but that instead appreciates the fluidity and the dialectical character of the process of identity construction (Nagel 1994, 154).

This study of two Peruvian *hermandades* (religious brotherhoods) presents two distinct models of transnationalism. The first case follows more closely the traditional notion of the paradigm, in which constant exchanges are maintained through vertical linkages between sending and receiving countries. The second case illustrates how the multicultural context of the host country has played a role in the emergence of a Pan-Latino identity challenging the static reading of transnationalism. Quotations from members of both communities will be used to highlight how the process of identity construction is mediated by religion and how it is influenced by the generational and ideological views of the brotherhoods' leadership.

Peruvian Migration to Paterson

In order to understand these cases, it is important to have a brief background of the migratory pattern of Peruvians in Paterson, New Jersey. At the turn of the twentieth century, Paterson was one of the most prosperous industrial cities in the Northeast. Textile industries based in New Jersey expanded their production to Lima, Peru, through subsidiary plants, which became the catalysts for the arrival of the first Peruvian immigrants to the city. Teófilo Altamirano, a scholar of Peruvian migration, estimated that between the decades of the 1930s and 1950s approximately 100 Peruvian families resided in Paterson, among a majority population of Italian and Irish Americans and a minority of African Americans. This initial migration was followed by a much larger flow, which began in the late 1950s and has continued through the 1990s (Altamirano 1992).

By the 1990s, Paterson had been greatly transformed. During the postwar period, Paterson's economic decline began, resulting in a large exodus of the city's population of European descent. They were replaced by Latin American immigrants and African Americans. The 1990 census identified Puerto Ricans and Dominicans as the city's two largest ethnic groups. Peruvian immigrants and first-generation children made up approximately 21 percent of the population. A majority of Peruvians can still be found working in factories and in the service sector, although there are growing numbers of professionals and entrepreneurs. The concentration of Peruvians in this area enabled a substantial degree of social organization, largely centered around religious brotherhoods and social clubs.

Paterson's Peruvian population brought with it a devotion to El Señor de los Milagros, the Lord of Miracles. El Señor de los Milagros is an image of Christ dating back to Peru's colonial period, painted by an African slave who was a member of one of the religious brotherhoods (hermandades or *cofradías*) that worshiped Christ or different saints. The image survived a devastating earthquake in Lima to become a national symbol of the reconstruction of the city and the miraculous power of Christ. The devotees' most important event is the annual procession, celebrated in Lima every October 18, which lasts three days and involves hundreds of hermandades. Among Peruvians living in the United States, El Señor de los Milagros has become the center of social and religious organization. Altamirano notes that masses in honor of El Señor de los Milagros began as early as 1965, but it was not until 1976 that the parish of Our Lady of Lourdes, home of the first Hermandad del Señor de los Milagros (HSM), held the first of its annual processions in Paterson. Other hermandades soon followed, including the Hermandad de San Martín de Porres (HSMP). Today, there are numerous brotherhoods and processions throughout the New York and New Jersey area and in cities such as Toronto, Washington, Atlanta, and Miami. These hermandades have become major vehicles for maintaining Peruvian culture and religiosity in the United States. Furthermore, as this analysis illustrates, brotherhoods such as HSM and HSMP also provide a space in which Peruvian immigrants negotiate and reconstruct their identity.

Transnationalism

Before proposing an expansion in the definition of transnationalism, it is important to clarify how transnationalism is currently understood in the literature. As early as the 1950s, scholars like Mitchell (1956) and Epstein (1958) began documenting the experiences of migrants whose entry into different social environment did not represent a break in the ties with their societies of origin. However, until recently, the dominance of the assimilation model resulted in an intellectual environment that viewed these patterns of cultural retention as temporary phases in the long-term process of incorporation into the host society. For scholars like Robert E. Park and Milton Gordon, the goal was assimilation. They focused in their now classic studies *Race and Culture* (1950) and *Assimilation in American Life* (1964) on the stages of this process. The question was not whether assimilation had occurred, but instead how it occurred. The underlying notion here was that migration was a more or less linear process that pushed and pulled people, causing them to abandon one society and immerse themselves fully in another. This bipolar and mechanistic view of migration left little room for cultural retention, which was seen as at best a temporary phase and at worst a social pathology. As such, the implications of maintaining these ties were left largely unexplored (Basch, Glick Schiller, and Szanton Blanc 1994, 30, 33).

Since the 1960s, the changing character of U.S. immigration has led scholars to question the validity of the assimilation paradigm. Among other things, the shift in the migration profile away from Europe toward the developing world (particularly Latin America), changes in communication and transportation technologies (including fax machines, the Internet, and jet planes), and the persistence of racial segregation and economic segmentation in the United States have made it possible and necessary for recent immigrants to maintain strong linkages with their sending societies. It is in this new context that by the late 1980s academics had begun to talk about transnational migration as part of a larger and complex process of globalization. In their article "From Immigrant to Transmigrant," Basch, Glick Schiller, and Szanton Blanc, for example, describe post–World War II migratory patterns as being characterized by migrants who can no longer be considered "uprooted." The authors state that many immigrants are now transmigrants or individuals "whose daily lives depend on multiple and constant interconnections across international borders and whose public identities are configured in relationship to more than one nation-state" (1995, 48). Immigrants become transnational when they do not cut off ties to their countries of origin or fully absorb the new culture offered to them by the host nation.

Transnationalism suggests that ties to the home country are maintained and encouraged from the host country. Immigrants foster these ties with frequent travel, transfers of funds (that is, remittances and investments), goods, and resources. Studying Brazilian immigrants in New York City, Maxine Margolis (1995, 29) adds to Basch, Glick Schiller, and Szanton Blanc's definition by noting that immigrants "establish and maintain familial, economic, political and cultural ties across international borders, in effect, making the home and the host society a single arena of social action."

Thus far, research on transnationalism has focused on documenting evidence of material exchanges between the sending and receiving communities (Grasmuck and Pessar 1991; Massey, Goldring, and Durand 1994). Though earlier studies collected data on the transfers of money, goods, and resources, scholars like Peggy Levitt are moving beyond this more tangible traffic to uncover ties based on ideas, beliefs, and values. In her work on what she calls "social remittances," Levitt takes transnationalism a step further by recognizing that the concept need not be limited to palpable exchanges but also include ideational and attitudinal linkages (1998b). Similarly, Alejandro Portes has added that transnational communities' " assets consist chiefly of shared information, trust and contacts. As members of these communities travel back and forth, they carry cultural and political currents in both directions" (1996, 74). Therefore, the impact of transnationalism may be much more widespread than originally thought, as communities' values and belief systems, including religion, change based on their interconnections across national boundaries. This is evident in Portes's discussion of anthropologist David Kyle's work among Otavalans from the Ecuadoran highlands in the United States and Europe.

As money and goods flow through transnational communities, so do cultural influences and even politics. . . . [Otavalans] have discovered the commercial value of their folklore, and groups of performers have fanned through the streets of cities in Europe and the United States. . . . The Otavalans have brought home a wealth of novelties and many have taken European or North American wives. In the streets of Otavalo, it is not uncommon to meet these white women attired in traditional indigenous garb. The transnational community has shaken up the Otavalan social hierarchy. The sale of colorful ponchos and other woolens accompanied by the plaintive notes of the *quena* (flute) have been so profitable that Otavalo's native entrepreneurs and returned migrants comprise much of the town's economic elite. (Portes 1996, 75)

Transnationalism, thus, has proven to be an extremely valuable tool. In particular, the concept transcends the limitations of more simplistic models, like the push/pull theory. However, the case of Peruvians in Paterson suggests that the way we understand transnationalism needs to be reexamined. Ties are maintained through participation in brotherhoods, for example. Yet, the evidence presented here illustrates that some immigrants are pushing the boundaries of the pattern identified by Margolis, Levitt, and Basch et al.

Although the case of the HSMP at the Cathedral of St. John the Baptist approximates the more traditional conception of transnationalism, the construction of identities can no longer be understood as solely occurring across international borders. Instead, as the case of the HSM at Our Lady of Lourdes demonstrates, identities are shaped not only by the ties between home and host country but also by the larger social environment of immigrants' experiences. Relating Chinese transnationalism to the process of identity construction, Ong and Nonini (1997) write: "'Chineseness' is no longer, if it ever was, a property or essence of a person calculated by that person's having more or fewer 'Chinese' values or norms, but instead, can be understood only in terms of the multiplicity of ways in which 'being Chinese' is an inscribed relation of persons and groups to forces and processes associated with global capitalism and its modernities" (3–4).

Along these lines, I argue that transnational connections render the process of collective identity formation more complex, requiring us to move beyond dichotomies such as host/home country, center/periphery, and North/South, which have typified traditional approaches to immigration (see Rouse 1991). The dislocation and fragmentation produced by globalization forces us to move "from a vertical and bipolar conception of the socio-political relations to one that is decentered and multidetermined" (García Canclini 1995, 258). Indeed, it is no longer possible to understand what goes on in a receiving society without a careful study of social reality in the sending country. Both sending and receiving societies are more and more embedded in a global system of economic, political, and cultural relations.

A decentered and multidetermined approach to social relations compels us to recognize not just the vertical links established across sending and receiving societies, but also the multiple "horizontal" linkages that immigrants of various nationalities and social conditions sustain among each other and with nonimmigrants in increasingly multicultural host societies. My aim in this chapter is to illustrate, through two case studies, how these horizontal linkages are crucial in the formation of collective identity among immigrants and thus to encourage scholars of transnationalism to take these linkages more seriously. As Nagel (1994, 154) reminds us: "Ethnic identity is the result of a dialogical process involving internal and external opinions and processes, as well as the individual's self-identification and outsider's ethnic designations—i.e., what you think your ethnicity is, versus what they think your ethnicity is." If this is true, then, understanding how immigrants construct national identities in a transnational setting requires us to study how they negotiate relations and ethnic labels within the host society. Thus far, while scholars of transnationalism have argued that conceptions of nationhood and nationality are changing with the new patterns of migration, they have ignored this important dimension.

The role of horizontal relations in identity formation will be most clear in the second case study (HSM at Our Lady of Lourdes), where the leadership of a North American priest has been key in the development of a Pan-Latino identity. Broadening its scope to include cases like the ones presented here will enable transnationalism to address more adequately the nonmaterial, social, political, and cultural exchanges that also form part of transnational communities.

Exchange through Vertical Linkages: HSMP at the Cathedral of St. John the Baptist

Before proceeding with the case of the HSMP, it will be useful to characterize briefly religious brotherhoods and their functions. Historically, hermandades are associations constituted by lay Catholics for the purpose of worshiping a patron saint. Although both men and women can be members, brotherhoods have continued to be male-dominated institutions, restricting women's participation to secondary roles such as *cantoras* (singers) and *sahumadoras* (incense carriers). Brotherhoods emerged in Latin America during the colonial period largely in response to the scarcity of priests, particularly in rural areas. Due to the absence of priests, hermandades were often responsible for the religious functions usually performed by the clergy. Discussing brotherhoods in Brazil, Marjo De Theije (1990, 190) writes: "Their main goal is worshipping the patron saint or, in general, promoting public worship through organizing Masses, processions or novenas in a church or chapel of their own. Apart from that, the brotherhoods look after their members' funerals and the consequent rituals and Masses. . . . Sometimes they also perform social duties [which] may vary from mutual help in the case of illness or poverty to setting up orphans' homes and hospitals, depending on the means available to the brotherhood."

Given this background, it is not surprising that for much of their history, brotherhoods have been largely independent of the Catholic Church. This independence has allowed hermandades to remain virtually unchanged today. Therefore, in essence, they are still colonial institutions that continue to exist largely outside of the church's structure. Particularly in the post–Vatican II period, brotherhoods have been seen as remnants of old Catholicism, only loosely connected to a new, more modern church. Their practices and autonomy have been criticized by those who feel that they are not following the path of the new church (De Theije 1990, 195–201). This complex relationship between old and new Catholicism has been a central element in the development of the brotherhoods in Paterson, including the HSMP.

The HSMP was founded at the Cathedral of Saint John the Baptist in 1975 by two Peruvians, one of whom was a member of the HSMP of Sandia in Lima, Peru. Similarly to most brotherhoods, the hermandad was organized around *cuadrillas* (male legions who carry the saint during the processions). Paterson's HSMP not only retained the structure of Peruvian brotherhoods but also reproduced the rituals and religious symbolism of the processions in Peru. In addition to ensuring the authenticity of the processions, the HSMP has also maintained the historical autonomy of hermandades in the home country.

The size of the cathedral and its community and the philosophy of its priests have played a significant role in enabling the HSMP to retain its autonomy. The parish is headed by an Italian American, Monsignor Mark Giordani, and has two Colombians serving as assistant pastors, Father Luis Rendón and Father Gilberto Gutiérrez. Both Colombian priests follow a post–Vatican II philosophy, emphasizing a "renewed interest in missionizing activity . . . and lay participation" (Levine and Stoll 1997, 69). They believe that communities like the neo-catechumenal and Charismatic groups constitute the new church, to which they are fully committed, and the hermandades are part of the old church. Monsignor Giordani is the spiritual leader of the HSMP, but his administrative responsibilities do not allow him to work directly with the brotherhood. Father Luis Rendón of St. John the Baptist in Paterson, who has more contact with the hermandades, describes the brotherhoods by stating: "I don't feel comfortable calling it a Christian faith. It is closer to the phenomenon of natural religiosity. . . . I can't say that it is a true faith, a confessed faith." The size of the parish and the priests' focus on the new church's evangelization efforts afford the hermandades at the cathedral the historical autonomy of brotherhoods in Peru. The priests provide their services when they are needed, but as we shall see, unlike the Lourdes case, the brotherhoods at the cathedral maintain their financial, administrative, and spiritual autonomy.

For the HSMP, this autonomy results in the ability to pursue goals virtually independently of the church. This is evident in their charitable work. St. Martín de Porres was born in Lima, Peru, from the union of a Spanish nobleman and a freed black slave. Due to his parents' social and racial differences, St. Martín de Porres was raised by his mother in a very humble environment. He entered the Convent of Santo Domingo in Lima and is said to have performed the most menial and arduous tasks. It is for that reason that the saint is often pictured carrying a broom. Accounts afford him supernatural gifts and powers, yet St. Martín de Porres is most remembered and honored for his work with the poor, the sick, and the needy, and for his constant willingness to give of himself for the service of the people. It is this model that his devotees aim to follow. The hermandades of St. Martín de Porres, both in Lima and in the United States, understand service as an important way of honoring the saint's life work.

The Casa Hogar is the childhood home of St. Martín de Porres in Lima. The Casa Hogar enables these hermandades to follow the model of St. Martín de Porres. It houses a small chapel, a bookstore, and a pharmacy. The Casa Hogar provides daily meals for poor children and the elderly, low-cost medical care, and various classes ranging from literacy to sewing. According to the leadership of the HSMP in Paterson, their organization sends approximately two hundred dollars a month to the administrators of the Casa Hogar, as well as medicine and clothes collected from the Peruvian community. Interviews with the leaders of the HSMP in Sandia and Santo Domingo, both in Lima, and with the administrator of the Casa Hogar, Father Villena, did not confirm the figures offered by the membership of the brotherhood in Paterson. However, Villena and the leaders of the two hermandades in Lima did recognize that the HSMP in Paterson did provide some financial help. Further, the HSMP in Paterson also contributed to other needs, such as medicines and toys for needy children.

The HSMP's independence from the parish also enables it to have institutional relationships with other brotherhoods in Peru. Many of the members of the hermandad in Paterson travel to Peru in November to attend the annual procession there. Their attendance at the procession and their financial support of both the Casa Hogar and the St. Martín de Porres brotherhoods in Lima have resulted in direct linkages with hermandades in the home country. When asked about these linkages, Pedro, the president of HSMP in Paterson, answered: "Our cuadrillas, for example, sponsor other cuadrillas in Peru. We are honorary members. . . . When they need something, an economic need, we send a gift. We are in continuous contact with them. They give us . . . the opportunity [of carrying rights] with a cuadrilla they endorse. . . . There are two hermandades in Peru with which we have a close relationship. . . . There isn't just a direct link like that from institution to institution, instead personal friendships."[1]

The members of HSMP in Paterson note that the frequent travel and financial assistance provided are largely funded by individuals. In particular, costs from their participation in the November procession must be covered by individual members. However, it is clear that the organization's charitable work in Peru would be hindered if the HSMP had constant financial responsibilities to the cathedral.

The HSMP's members see themselves as pioneers within the Peruvian community of Paterson. They are the only hermandad in Paterson providing a more formal charitable service in Peru. Aside from charity, the HSMP has also been a leader in the participation of women. The brotherhood was the first to endorse the creation of a women's cuadrilla. Historically, women in the hermandades have been responsible for singing and carrying incense during the processions. Women had never been allowed to form their own cuadrilla to carry the image until the 1995 procession in Paterson, which commemorated the twentieth anniversary of the founding of the HSMP. Juan, a former president, recounts:

> The desire came from the women themselves. They began discussing and asked the hermandad for permission to see if it was possible. . . . Until now Peru has not had one.
>
> There is no tradition for this, because they say that the image is too heavy for them to carry. . . . Today, Washington also has two women's cuadrillas. New York just created a women's cuadrilla. Connecticut is also establishing one. . . . The most beautiful thing of all this is that it has not ended here, it is continuing. In Lima, they are giving us the news that in Sandia, one of the largest brotherhoods in Peru, and one of the oldest, they are also creating a cuadrilla. This is how it is evolving. . . . Naturally there is a great satisfaction.

The creation of a women's cuadrilla provides further evidence of transnationalism. Not only are the expected exchanges of resources and travel occurring, but also the HSMP in Paterson is fostering institutional changes in Peru.

Unlike the HSMP in Paterson, its Sandia counterpart does not have a women's cuadrilla. Instead, women belong to the more traditional women's committee, which serves as a support organization for the brotherhood but is not considered part of the hermandad's structure. The women's committee is largely responsible for the social activities of the brotherhood and volunteers its time at the Casa Hogar, helping with the preparation of meals and other activities. Although the women of the HSMP in Sandia do not have their own cuadrilla, recently, due to the effort of the women from Paterson, they have gained the right to carry the image during the procession. Marcos, the president of the HSMP of Sandia, recounts how the women in their brotherhood achieved this privilege:

> The sisters [female devotees] of St. Martín de Porres never carried. The sisters from Paterson arrived; they arrived for the first time approximately five or six years ago. . . . During one of moments when our brothers from Paterson were allowed to carry, the women who were accompanying them, from the women's delegation, requested the right to carry. We were a bit skeptical, since the image and its stand weigh approximately 1,200 kilos. . . . We wondered if, as brothers carrying the image, we feel its weight, we thought it would be difficult for women to carry it. The sisters carried the image and invited the sisters of Sandia to do the same. They said, "Why don't you carry the image? How is it possible that you don't? So they carried it. For the last four or five years, the sisters [of Sandia] have also requested carrying. . . . This was a result of the experience with the sisters from Paterson. It was something very beautiful; it was a joy.

As Marcos states, it was the desire of the women cuadrilla members from Paterson, who encouraged their fellow sisters in Peru to participate more fully and directly in the procession. However, the impact of the Paterson women's cuadrilla has not been limited to the right to carry the image. It appears that the nontraditional participation of the Sandia women in the procession has resulted in debates within the hermandad concerning the future roles of women. Again, Marcos states:

> Currently, women cannot assume the post of president. We would have to revise our statutes. They constitute a committee, a support group for the hermandad, they have their own decision-making body, they hold their own activities and let us know, but they do not form part of our membership according to our statutes. [Thus] they cannot be part of our decision-making

body. We wanted them to be part of it, actually we have already requested for them to be allowed to participate in our meetings. And we are going to do it, because they are some of the members who have contributed the most. A large part of what you see today is largely their work. So we proposed, being that the sisters have contributed so much, how is it possible that they do not participate in our discussions? We have spoken to the priest and he has accepted the idea that they participate in our meetings, particularly those of the decision-making body.

Marcos allows us to see that transnational ties have gone beyond the issue of carrying rights. His discussion suggests that the women in Paterson were a catalyst for reexamining the roles of women within the structure of the hermandad in Sandia.

This is of great significance for women's participation in brotherhoods. Having the opportunity to carry the saint during the procession is the highest honor that a member of the brotherhood can achieve. As was mentioned earlier, this honor has been denied to women for centuries. Allowing women to have their own cuadrillas affords them equal status within the organizational structure of the hermandad. In other words, it provides women with voice and vote in what has been historically a male-dominated institution. Women are no longer confined to the traditional positions of cantoras, sahumadoras, or social activities' organizers. Instead, women cuadrilla members can now represent themselves in the decision-making processes of the hermandad. Although this movement is still in its initial stages, it holds enormous potential for transforming the institutional structure of hermandades in the United States and Peru.

So far, this analysis of the HSMP in Paterson has provided us with a model that follows closely the traditional definition of transnationalism. The independence of the brotherhood has enabled it to become a vehicle for maintaining clear exchanges between home and host country. Their active involvement in activities like the annual Peruvian parade places them at the center of the Peruvian-American community's efforts to maintain national identity. While their multiple involvements in Peru solidifies their ties to the home country, it is increasingly evident that HSMP's new leadership is expanding the scope of the hermandad, fostering not just North-South linkages but also horizontal linkages in each home and host country.

Evidence of such horizontal linkages are manifested in both the leadership's role in the participation of women and its charitable work. First, the creation of a women's cuadrilla has sparked discussion about women's roles in the Sandia brotherhood. This relationship can be understood as a North-South linkage. Yet by taking the analysis one step further, one can see that full membership for the women in Sandia could potentially be an impetus for other such groups within Peru, which would no longer constitute just a vertical linkage but also a horizontal one. In addition, the women's cuadrilla in Paterson has led to the creation of counterparts in brotherhoods in the United States. Again, this example demonstrates that exchanges are occurring at both the inter-country and intra-country levels.

Second, the community service provided by the HSMP in Paterson is no longer just centered around providing assistance to the needy in the home country. Pedro, as president, has introduced a new project to begin aiding the elderly in Paterson. Pedro comments: "All of this is something new. The truth has been that we have never done it [charitable work] in Paterson. But now we have decided to do the same. Previously the idea was basically to help the elderly in Peru, but we believe that we have been here in Paterson so many years, that we should also provide help to the sick in hospitals in Paterson. . . . I have always had a desire to help my fellow man. . . . And it is the reason why I am in the hermandad, trying to gain support to continue helping people."

Two trends are evident in Pedro's statement. The first is that the HSMP is moving toward forging closer ties with the communities of the host country. The home country is no longer their only focus. This trend might be aided by generational changes within the brotherhood as Pedro seeks younger members. While older members like Juan focus on maintaining relations with the home country, younger members stress linkages with the host country with which they are more familiar.

Given the apparent transformation occurring within the HSMP, we may ask how it has affected identity construction. Juan, part of the older leadership, identifies himself as "American-Peruvian," since he has been in Paterson for more than twenty-eight years. He sees the brotherhood as a means for maintaining Peruvian traditions. Pedro, representing the new leadership, identifies himself as Hispanic and, as the above quote suggests, for him the hermandad is a vehicle for community service. Finally, María, a member of the women's cuadrilla, sees herself as "American, but not North-American." She understands the hermandad as a religious institution attempting to provide help to Peru. Yet, she adds that "Recently, nationalism is being erased within the hermandad. The idea of internationalism, of Hispanicity, is growing. The hermandad is in the process of becoming a Hispanic institution." The case of the HSMP closely fits the transnationalism model; however, if what María suggests is true, then the HSMP may be moving beyond traditional transnationalism.

To summarize, in the case of the HSMP transnationalism is reaffirmed. The exchanges of travel, resources, and funds are all present. The hermandad is a symbol of Peruvian identity and has served to foster vertical linkages between home and host countries. Yet this analysis has uncovered what appear to be hints that the leadership is carving out a new path for the hermandad that emphasizes horizontal linkages both in the home and host countries. What will become obvious in case number two is that these hints have become realities in the HSM at Our Lady of Lourdes. The latter case provides evidence that raises questions about the definition of transnationalism as it now stands.

Pan-Latino Identity: Horizontal Linkages at Our Lady of Lourdes's HSM

Like the HSMP, the HSM at Lourdes made all efforts to emulate the procession and the brotherhoods in Lima. In addition, like in the case of the HSMP, the relationship between old and new Catholicism has been a significant factor in the development of the hermandad. Tensions between these two perspectives came to a head with the arrival of Father Peter Napoli in 1982. As head of the parish, Father Napoli has been instrumental in the transformation of the hermandad and in the process of identity construction among Peruvian parishioners.

Aware of the changing composition of his parish and of the fervent beliefs and practices of the Latin American population, Father Napoli welcomed the use of culture and nationality within the church. However, he also challenges the autonomy of the brotherhood and the divisiveness of focusing on national identity. The parish priest states that "the hermandad is a link to their home [but] . . . they are members of the parish and so they have an allegiance to the parish." In essence, Peruvians, like other national groups, such as Dominicans, Costa Ricans, and Salvadorans, are encouraged to retain their ties to home, but within the context of the larger Pan-Latino church community. The emphasis on allegiance to the parish and on recognizing the larger parish community has had three major outcomes. First, it has transformed the relationship between the brotherhood and the parish. Second, it has shaped the functions of the hermandad. Finally, it has influenced how Peruvians collectively and individually construct their own identities.

Father Napoli's emphasis on allegiance resulted in serious limits on the autonomy of the HSM. In 1982 he requested that the HSM hand over their bank account and contribute their resources to the church. This request tore the HSM into two factions. One group sided with Father Napoli, and the other (including Miguel, the president at the time) refused to comply with Napoli and left Our Lady of Lourdes. As a result of this rupture, another HSM was established in Paterson, at the Cathedral of St. John the Baptist. Despite the split, or even because of it, the HSM sector that remained at Lourdes has developed close ties to the parish. Ramón, the current president of HSM, explains that "we work for the church, aside from being representatives of the HSM, we also collaborate with the church . . . thanks to the support of Father Peter we can carry out activities that fund the procession. . . . We also help the church. Not everything is for the group. Everything that is raised is not for the group. We share a larger quantity [of the funds] with the church than for the group." As Ramón suggests, the HSM at Our Lady of Lourdes has become a group within the church, virtually erasing its historical autonomy.

The second outcome of Father Napoli's pastoral vision can be seen in the differences in the way the HSM understands its functions versus those of other brotherhoods in Paterson. Other hermandades, including the HSMP and the larger HSM at the cathedral have nonprofit organization status. This status allows the brotherhoods to seek sponsorships both in the United States and in Peru to fund their activities. Personal and institutional networks have resulted from these relationships, and the hermandades' visibility has afforded them a civic, and some would argue a political, role within the community. For example, members of the HSMP play important roles in the organization of the activities commemorating Peruvian Independence day, including the Peruvian Parade, which are attended by the Peruvian consul and representatives of City Hall. Unlike the HSMP, the HSM at Lourdes strongly rejects any such involvement. Again, Ramón notes: "We are completely independent. Because we are apolitical. The other hermandades are incorporated to certain groups. They want to make a national group. They are confusing religion with politics." Isabel, secretary of the HSM, adds, "we are just people of faith and devotion to El Señor de los Milagros."

Finally, there is the impact of Father Napoli's teaching on collective and individual identity amongst Peruvians. As Ramón mentioned, members of the HSM also participate in other parish groups, one of which is the Cursillos de Cristiandad. The cursillo movement, as it is known in the United States, began in Spain in the 1950s and spread quickly throughout Latin America. Daniel Levine and David Stoll describe the cursillos as part of a larger effort by the Catholic Church, "designed to insulate the faithful from ideological and political contamination. . . . [Cursillos] combined intense religious experience with affirmation of hierarchy and loyalty to the Church" (Levine and Stoll 1997, 69). At Our Lady of Lourdes, the cursillo movement (along with the weekly *Ultreya* meeting) is one of the most active groups within the parish, integrating members of all nationalities, genders, and age groups. Napoli uses his position as the group's spiritual guide to impart upon them the importance of their shared experiences as Christians and as Latin Americans living in the United States. The personal relationships emphasized in the cursillo movement attempt to erase the divisions of nationality, race, and ethnicity. What has emerged is a Pan-Latino identity.

This Pan-Latino identity permeates all aspects of the parish, including the HSM. Ramón understands the brotherhood as a symbol of Peruvian nationality but points out that Puerto Rican and Colombian members "are also Peruvian, because their devotion cannot be denied." Each nationality represented in the parish celebrates the day of their patron saint as a symbol of national identity. However, those celebrations are not solely attended by individuals from that particular country. The entire parish, irrespective of nationality, participates in the celebrations for the Virgin of Guadalupe (Mexico's patron saint) or the Virgin of Altagracia (the Dominican patron saint), as well as those for El Señor de los Milagros. Thus, at Our Lady of Lourdes, vivid symbols of national identity exist side by side within a larger context of a Pan-Latino identity. The result is that symbols like El Señor de los Milagros serve to maintain Peruvian identity, but that identity is also extended to non-Peruvian individuals.

When asked how they identify themselves, Ramón and Isabel reply "100 percent Peruvian," even though they have been in the United States for twenty-eight and seventeen years respectively. However, other participants of the HSM illustrate how the Pan-Latino identity has permeated the brotherhood and the larger Peruvian community. René and Carmen are a married Peruvian couple active in the cursillo movement. Both identify themselves as Hispanic Americans. Carmen states that the reason for her self-identification is "the contact I have had with people of other countries within the church community." René adds that if asked in 1970 (when he arrived) "I would have answered Peruvian. When we arrived, we made Peruvian friends, but today we don't have much contact with them. [The reason] for the change is our increased participation in the church."

Like René and Carmen, Nancy too shares a Pan-Latino identity. Nancy and her husband, Enrique, were part of the early membership of HSM. Nancy considers herself Latin American, and both identify the church as their community. Antonia, a young Peruvian woman who has recently joined the parish, captures the dynamics of identity construction. She states: "I am 100 percent Peruvian, always Peruvian. [But] Father Peter identifies us as Latinos, as one country. Our differences should not matter."

In all of these cases, the ties to the country of origin are not those expected of the transnationalism model. These individuals do not travel frequently. Most have been in the United States for at least fifteen years, and in that time they have traveled once or at most twice to Peru. They maintain contacts with Peru through letters and phone calls to family members. Remittances and other exchanges are uncommon. In addition, due to the HSM's unincorporated status,

the brotherhood has no institutional or organizational ties to other hermandades in Peru. Thus, what is evident from this case is that it does not fit the
standard definition of transnationalism. At Lourdes, the key point of reference is
not Peru but the local multinational Latino parish community. It is within this
community that Peruvians negotiate their individual and collective identities.

Conclusion

Push/pull theory has largely dominated migration studies. It provides
a model that focuses on the economic motivations behind individuals' decisions
to migrate. Though useful, push/pull theory does not go beyond the initial decision to migrate. It is here that transnationalism has proven to be particularly
valuable. Better wages and employment opportunities may be part of the reasons why individuals choose to migrate, but when, where, and how they do so
are also significant factors in understanding migratory patterns. Transnationalism uncovers the complex networks that have been established by immigrants who have not broken ties to their countries of origin. These networks
continue the flow of immigrants, serve as a support system for new migrants,
and aid immigrants in maintaining national identity. In addition, these links between home and host country help fuel economies both in the sending and
receiving countries. Not only do the home countries often desperately need
remittances, but enclave economies also add to economic growth in the host
societies. By bringing attention to these networks and how they affect identity construction, transnationalism has greatly contributed to how we understand migratory patterns. In particular, transnationalism brings with it a
dynamic character, largely absent from other models. This dynamism now
needs to incorporate the trends highlighted in this chapter.

The case of Peruvians in Paterson does not invalidate transnationalism. On
the contrary, the example of the HSMP in Paterson reaffirms the model. However, what is evident in the case of the HSM at Lourdes is that the concept of
transnationalism, as it is currently understood, needs to be enriched by taking into account the complex ways through which immigrants construct collective and individual identities. In other words, theories of transnationalism
need to capture the impact of the fluid, multicultural character of the host society on identity construction amongst immigrants. If transnationalism is to
move beyond the mechanistic reductionism of early approaches to immigration, it must abandon all vestiges of bipolar verticalism—that is, the narrow,
exclusive focus on the linkages between sending and receiving societies, as if
they formed an isolated, self-contained unit. In a context of increasing globalization, both sending and receiving societies stand not only in relation to each
other but also to myriad international, regional, and global processes that pro-

duce effects at the local, and even personal, level. Thus, for transnationalism to develop a more nuanced and fluid understanding of culture and identity in a globalized age, it needs to adopt a truly multipolar view that recognizes differences and tensions not only among countries but also within countries. This inter- and intra-society complexity is the direct result of the "unbounding" of concepts like nation, culture, identity, and citizenship. Drawing from the work of historian Eric Wolf (1988), Basch et al. put matters in the following way:

> Bounded concepts of culture, whether signaled by the rubric of tribe, ethnic group, race or nation, are social constructions. They are reflective not of the stable boundaries of cultural difference but of the relations of culture and power. Moreover, while at one time, culturally constructed boundaries—be they those of nations, ethnicities, or races—may seem fixed, timeless, or primordial, dynamic processes of reformulation underlie the apparent fixity. The current conflations of time and space brought about by global communications and transnational social relations only serve to highlight more deepseated contradictions in the way in which we think about culture and society. (32)

In this context, the process of identity construction in the host country may produce what Nestor García Canclini calls "hybrid cultures." In his discussion of hybridity, the author refers to the blending of practices and discourses from the First and Third Worlds or between industrialized and developing countries (García Canclini 1995, 258–262). However, this concept of hybridity may be used to describe how Peruvian immigrants draw from their religious traditions to negotiate collective and individual identity. Instead of blending Peruvian identity with the dominant Anglo-American identity, they may be combining Peruvian identity with fragments appropriated from other immigrant (Latino) groups represented in the parish. Once articulated, these hybrid cultures are shared across national boundaries, affecting settled patterns both in the sending and receiving countries.

In the HSMP one can see all of the expected elements of transnationalism. The members have frequent exchanges with Peru in the form of travel, funds, community service, and the like. In addition, the brotherhood has institutional linkages with other hermandades in Peru. The result is that the brotherhood retains a clearer sense of national identity. However, in the case of the HSM at Lourdes these examples of transnationalism, as it is classically defined, are largely absent. Instead, the multinational and multiethnic character of the Catholic community in Paterson leads to a different kind of transnationalism, one that transgresses notions of Peruvian nationality based on birth in a bounded geographical space. As Lourdes shows, Peruvians are redefining their nationality in at least four forms. First, it may lead to the formation (as García Canclini describes it) of a hybrid, Pan-Latino, transnational Catholic culture that syncretizes national discourses and practices. The second option would generate the juxtaposition of various national identities, so as to produce a menu of identities from which immigrants pick and choose in response to particular needs and ritual contexts. In this model, Peruvians would be fluent in the rituals and beliefs of other groups, such as Dominicans, Colombians, or Puerto Ricans, being able to deploy these practices without acquiring an overarching hybrid Latino identity. Third, Peruvians may retain their national identity and simply extend it to other groups who demonstrate allegiance to their national saints. In this model, Dominican or Colombian members of the hermandades, for example, become honorary Peruvians, as it were. Finally, Peruvians might be mixing all the options above.

Determining how these options play themselves out in the Peruvian case—whether one will finally become hegemonic or whether all will coexist, establishing relations of mutual determination—requires further study and is beyond the scope of this chapter. However, what is clear is that these complex processes occurring in the host country affect identity construction. These processes involve not only the immigrants themselves (or the transnational community), but also outsiders with their own designations and categorizations. Moreover, advances in communications technologies, such as the Internet, further complicate identity formation by enabling groups like hermandades to defy strict notions of bipolar, home/host country relations. Understanding the role of transnationalism in identity construction requires that we broaden the concept of the single arena of social action. This arena contains several sub-levels or multiple localities affecting how transnationalism is experienced by the immigrant. A more nuanced understanding of this social arena and, in particular, of religion's role in it, will move transnationalism away from a strict bipolarity and closer to a more complex notion of multipolarity.

Note

1. All quotations from individuals in Paterson, New Jersey, are taken from interviews conducted by the author between June and August 1997. Interviews in Peru were conducted by Philip Williams during the summers of 1997 and 1998.

Chapter 8

Ileana Gómez and Manuel Vásquez

Youth Gangs and Religion among Salvadorans in Washington and El Salvador

To claim that adolescence is a period fraught with conflicts and identity crises is hardly novel. Erik Erickson (1968), for example, saw adolescence as a perilous liminal period involving the simultaneous articulation of a strong, autonomous self and the formation of stable social ties ensuring successful integration into community life. What if we add poverty, violence, disintegration of community life, and anomie as a result of a protracted civil war to adolescence's normal growing pains? What happens when young people are subjected to "multiple marginalities" (Vigil 1988), as in the case of postwar El Salvador?[1] Is this condition of multiple marginality aggravated by global processes like economic restructuring or democratic transition? If so, will it result in increased antisocial behavior at a time when El Salvador is struggling to reweave its torn social fabric and create democratic subjects? Can religion play a role in addressing the outward expressions and root causes of multiple marginality in a globalized setting?

In this chapter, we explore the ways in which Christian churches are responding to problems faced by young people in postwar El Salvador. After a brief review of recent social changes in El Salvador, with special reference to the evolving situation of young people, we turn to the issue of youth gangs, which, according to a study sponsored by UNICEF, are the "most important and complex cultural-generational problem in the country in the 1990s. The high number of young people involved in this form of youth organization and socialization and the presence [of gangs] throughout the national territory have made this phenomenon, and its accompanying forms of violence, an integral part of quotidian life among Salvadorans." Since Salvadoran gangs had their origins in the United States and now operate transnationally, we will be drawing from fieldwork in Morazán, an area deeply affected by the war, and in Washington, D.C., where many Salvadorans fled during the conflict.

To explore how gangs and churches operate transnationally, bridging the local and the global, we draw from Manuel Castells's recent trilogy on the network society. This approach has already been used by Berryman (1999) and Vásquez (1999) to help make sense of religious pluralism, identity, and globalization in the Americas. In our reading, gangs offer disenfranchised and dislocated Salvadoran youths discourses, practices, and forms of organization that allow them to reassert the local against global forces that have disarticulated their communities and families. Gangs also provide a context where the self can be recentered in an intimate setting, where loyalty and collective identity are central. We argue, however, that the localizing and reordering resources provided by gangs are themselves shot through with conflict and implicated in some of the same global processes they seek to address. In light of these contradictions, religion, particularly evangelical Christianity, has emerged as an alternative space, where the synthesis between self and community that Erickson saw as key to the successful negotiation of adolescence can take place. We conclude by arguing that in helping to form ethical and peaceful young subjects, Christian churches are playing an important, if ambiguous, role in strengthening the still-fragile Salvadoran civil society and in negotiating transnationalism for Salvadoran immigrants in the United States.

El Salvador and Salvadoran Youth in the Postwar Period

As Gómez notes in chapter 6, the Salvadoran civil war had enormous costs. Besides the eighty thousand Salvadorans killed, the conflict brought widespread dislocation, uprooting to about one-fifth of the country's population. Dislocation took the form of mass migration from the countryside, particularly from the combat zones in the northern and eastern part of the country, to San Salvador, neighboring countries like Guatemala and Honduras, and to the United States and Canada. Gómez documents how in zones like Morazán, mass migration, in turn, meant the breakdown not only of communities, as entire towns fled the violence, but also of families. Often men were the first to migrate, especially to the United States, escaping random violence, severe government repression, and forced conscription into both the army and the guerrillas. The death, migration, or conscription of men left behind female-headed households struggling to survive. The corollary of all this was that a whole generation has grown up in broken families, surrounded not by tightly knit nurturing communities but by a daily reality of uncertainty, violence, and death. The case of Agustín, a former gang member from Morazán and now a theology student at the Assemblies of God, is typical.

> I began my life in the *maras* when I was twelve. I was looking for something that would fill the void left in my heart . . . you see, I come from a family that has experienced a lot of hardship. My father died when I was seven years old, when the war started. He was a soldier in the army and was killed just like one of my older brothers. Then, there was a void in my life, and knowing that my father could not fill it, I tried to look for friends. I began to drink with them, to do drugs, and to look for the money I needed to satisfy my cravings.[2]

In this context, youth gang violence can be seen as the reproduction of antisocial and violent patterns internalized during the civil war. These patterns are now displaced from the combat zones to every street and neighborhood in the country, serving as the only vehicle to resolve any type of conflict. The pervasiveness of a culture of violence helps us understand why El Salvador has the highest annual per capita rate of homicide in the Americas (150 per 100,000), even exceeding those of Colombia and Haiti. Taking this rate as a yardstick, DeCesare (1998, 23) observes that violence in El Salvador is now greater "than during the 1980s, when the civil war grabbed international headlines and hundreds of thousands of peasant refugees escaping mayhem and economic collapse sought sanctuary in the crowded slums of Los Angeles."

On the surface, by putting an end to the armed conflict and creating the conditions for reconciliation and reconstruction, the peace accords of 1992 would seem to address the problems of violence. Indeed, a central part of the accords is the demilitarization of Salvadoran society, with a drastic reduction in the size of the army, the disarming and incorporation of the guerrillas into the competitive electoral system, and the creation of an independent, civilian police mindful of human rights. Moreover, following investigations by special commissions, the military has been "cleansed" of those in leadership positions who committed egregious human rights violations. Other important provisions of the accords include measures like the transfer of land to ensure the productive reinsertion of ex-combatants.

Despite significant advances, the impact of the peace accords in creating a truly peaceful and democratic El Salvador have been limited, first by endless delays in the implementation of land transfer provisions and second by the failure of the accords to deal with the underlying causes of the conflict—that is, the concentration of economic power in the hands of few. Neoliberal reforms introduced by ARENA, the rightist party in power since 1989, have contributed to overall economic growth. However, the benefits of this growth are yet to trickle down to the most vulnerable sectors of Salvadoran society. As in other Latin American economies that have become globalized, the brunt of the social cost of economic restructuring in El Salvador has been borne by poor families, particularly by women and children. For one, the Salvadoran economy is not generating enough jobs to employ a growing, young population (44 percent of the population is under seventeen). Further, new jobs tend to be in the service and construction sectors, which are characterized by long hours, low wages, and instability. Maquilas, which have been one of the government's key strategies to link the Salvadoran economy to the global market, also employ many Salvadorans, especially women and sometimes minors, in similar harsh conditions. Many maquilas and export-trade zones are located in areas like San Marcos, Soyapango, Apopa, and San Martín, where the gang problem is particularly acute. The scarcity of secure, well-paying jobs with full benefits has dovetailed with a drastic downsizing of the welfare state, leaving many poor families in precarious circumstances.

Like families, young people face economic insecurity. A recent survey of 1,025 gang members by the Public Opinion Institute at the Central American University (IUDOP 1997) in the greater metropolitan area of San Salvador found that 75 percent of the respondents were unemployed. Of those employed, only 52 percent had stable jobs, with women more likely than men to have stable employment. Only 41 percent of those employed held "specialized occupations," as shoemakers, bakers, mechanics, and seamstresses. The rest worked either as errand boys, maids, drivers, and street vendors, all unskilled jobs with relatively low pay. And while the mean for gang members was 8.4 years of schooling (as opposed to 4 years for the entire nation), only 32.5 percent finished high school. About 76 percent of those surveyed had dropped out of school. In other words, this is a population with enough education to understand the contradictions in Salvadoran society but not enough skills to enter the labor force in the narrow high-paying end of the employment structure. This is a recipe for a crisis in expectation among Salvadoran youths, which often generates antisocial behavior.

In addition to the landscape of broken families and communities, drastic economic change, and educational crisis, there are other factors that shape the life of young Salvadorans. Among them are the availability of weapons left behind by the war (and now part of a complex network of international trafficking), a still-weak civil police and judicial system, the formation of shadowy crime syndicates by former ex-military men now turned businessmen, and finally the presence of another global dimension, transnational youth gangs founded by Salvadoran immigrants in the United States, which are now operating not only in the capital but also in cities in the interior such as San Miguel and San Francisco Gotera.

Salvadoran Youth in the United States

For many Salvadorans migration to the United States has not resulted in the fulfillment of the American dream. Sarah Mahler (1995) confirms our discussion, in the introductory chapter, about the subordinate insertion of Latino immigrants in the growing service sector. She offers many poignant stories of many undocumented Salvadorans migrants caught in "niches of low-paying jobs," with little security and hope for mobility—a sort of parallel world of disillusionment and alienation at the margins of mainstream society. Some have been able to bring their families to the United States after saving some money by working two or more jobs and rooming with several other immigrants in small apartments. However, even they have experienced considerable turmoil in the form of family and intergenerational conflicts. In addition to parental absence due to the demands of the labor market, many immigrant men became involved with women in the United States, forming new families. This set the stage for transnational, intergenerational problems, as families vied for limited resources. In many cases, men abandoned their families in El Salvador or brought only the children to live in their new U.S. households, generating conflicts among half brothers and half sisters and between children and their new stepparents. The story of David, a Salvadoran gang member in Los Angeles who came to the United States when he was seven years old, serves to illustrate our foregoing discussion.

> David was initially excited about coming to the United States. He remembered thinking that "Everyone in the United States had a big car, fancy house, and lots of money." But when he arrived in Los Angeles, he and his mother lived in a tiny apartment in a small building that itself was incredibly overcrowded, with 10 to 15 people sometimes living in one apartment. His neighborhood, in the middle of Los Angeles, was teeming with other recent Salvadoran immigrants. Despite the presence of other Salvadorans, however, he felt incredibly homesick, as he was separated from his extended family and even from his mother. To support their new life in the United States, she cleaned houses 7 days a week, 10 to 14 hours a day. His mother remarried, and David transferred all his anger and disappointment with his biological father to his stepfather. Consequently, David refused to obey his stepfather, and his mother who was often absent. (Vigil and Yun 1996, 150–151)

Added to this complex set of problems are the general crisis in urban public schools and conflicting views on parenting. According to Carmen Sosa, a counselor at Comité Hispano de Virginia,

> One of the main problems in the Latino community is how to discipline kids. The parents usually are first-generation immigrants, the majority coming from the countryside, where they are used to clearly defined roles and authority structures. The kids, on the other hand, either came to the United States very young or were born here. They are more used to American mores. However, their parents want them to be like they were when they grew up in El Salvador or Colombia and this leads to conflict. Parents don't know how to deal with all the freedoms and options their kids have here. They often resort to violence to discipline their kids, which in my view, leads to violence at home and in the streets. Or they ignore what's going on, because they really don't understand this society or because they don't have the time to be with their kids.

Salvadoran youths thus suffer "multiple marginality," a complex host of economic, social, cultural, and geographic factors that place them at the margins of society, that push them to find alternatives sources of "attachment, commitment, involvement, and belief" (Vigil 1988). For Salvadoran youths, multiple marginality occurs transnationally: they do not find conventional vehicles for identity construction and empowerment in El Salvador or in the United States. In fact, their "bi-focality," the fact that they have to straddle two cultures, that they are sent back and forth, from parents to grandparents or aunts and uncles, across national borders, is part of the problem, adding to the fragmentation and dislocation they feel. Trapped in a transnational cycle of marginalization, Salvadoran youths, like other Latino and African American gangs, develop their own unconventional subculture, social structures, and localities. This represents an attempt to cut social problems down to size and to deal with the structural and systemic forces that have wreaked havoc with their families and lives. Before we explore in more detail what gangs do for youths in El Salvador and the United States, we need to provide more information on the history of Salvadoran gangs as well as on their configuration and modus operandi.

Transnational Salvadoran Youth Gangs

According to Smutt and Miranda (1998, 30), the origins of Salvadoran youth gangs can be traced to the late 1950s, among students in elite high schools in San Salvador. As Salvadoran society began to slide into chaos and civil war in the 1970s, *maras* became more violent and organized, establishing bases in various city neighborhoods and zones. Although it is difficult to establish precise dates, organized Salvadoran gangs like the Mara Salvatrucha

(MS) and Los de la 18 (the Eighteenth Street gang) emerged in full force in the 1980s, when, as a result of the civil war, large numbers of Salvadorans and other Central Americans migrated to cities like Los Angeles, Houston, and Washington, D.C., settling in poor neighborhoods previously occupied by older, more established Latino groups such as Mexican Americans and Puerto Ricans. Particularly in Los Angeles, young Salvadoran immigrants felt the need to carve out their own space at schools and in the streets vis-à-vis Chicano gangs, which have been active in the city since the 1920s (Mazón 1985). This led to the creation of "self-defense" groups structured around national identity. Because Salvadoran youth have created a subculture in the context of a dominant Chicano culture, they have adopted a lifestyle, speech, and dress similar to that of *cholos* and *cholas* (gang members). Vigil characterizes the "choloization" of first- and second-generation Latino youth as the process of developing a hybrid culture that blends elements of both the sending and receiving societies. "Although cholos are Americanized, either by accident or by design, they refuse or are unable to be totally assimilated" (Vigil 1988, 7).

Smutt and Miranda (1998, 35) estimate that the MS has 3,500 members in Los Angeles County alone, with possibly as many as 8,000 members in the state of California. The Eighteenth Street gang, on the other hand, is considered the largest gang in Los Angeles, with more than 10,000 members. In contrast to the MS, the Eighteenth Street gang has a reputation for being pan-ethnic. The Eighteenth Street gang has moved from its Chicano origins in the Pico Union District of Los Angeles and is now dominated by Salvadorans. Nevertheless, the gang has members of other Latin American nationalities and even includes Asian Americans and some African Americans. Both the MS and the Eighteenth Street Gang have established chapters virtually everywhere there are Salvadorans, especially in Long Island; Fairfax and Alexandria, Virginia; and Langley Park, Maryland (Welsh 1995).

The formation in 1992 of a special anti-gang unit at the INS, together with changes in immigration laws that have made it easier to deport aliens who have committed crimes, has ironically added a transnational dimension to Salvadoran gangs. In 1993, seventy gang members were deported to El Salvador. One year later, six hundred Salvadorans with criminal records, including gang activity, were sent back. By 1996 more than twelve hundred Salvadorans involved in crimes had been deported, more than half of them with connections to gangs. Because of their hybrid, cholo identity, many of the deported find themselves alienated from Salvadoran culture. In a context of high unemployment, social breakdown, and violence, deported gang members have been able to form Salvadoran chapters of their gangs quickly. In the metropolitan area of San Salvador alone, the National Civilian Police have identified fifty-four "clicas" (cliques) connected with the largest Salvadoran *maras* in the United States. Smutt and Miranda (1998, 38) have found that the connection between Salvadoran and U.S. groups is so tight that local actions, like the peace accords between the MS and the Eighteenth Street gang in San Martín and El Congo, small towns in the western part of the country, are not considered valid without approval from Los Angeles (Mahler 1998). In the IUDOP survey of gang members in San Salvador, close to 20 percent of those interviewed indicated that they had entered the gangs in the United States. The great majority of them (99 out of 111) had joined gangs in Los Angeles.

Despite the close links between U.S.- and Salvadoran-based gangs, DeCesare has shown that transnational relations are not without conflict. On the one hand, *maras* in El Salvador respect those who have been gang members in the United States. They are considered older brothers, wiser and closer to the originative gang experience. Nevertheless, many gang leaders in Los Angeles and Washington, D.C., criticize those in El Salvador for being "wild," "reckless," interested only in "el vacil" (the fun and games associated with gang life) and not concerned about *la raza* and the neighborhood. This critique has filtered down to El Salvador through the transnational networks. Smutt and Miranda (1998, 38) quote Julio, a gang member in El Salvador:

> There are many *vatos* [guys, gang members] from Los Angeles who don't like what goes on here *[el rollo aquí]*. When they return to Los Angeles they say that here [El Salvador] we rape, kill children, and that is not approved of. There they respect children, being Salvadoran, you respect your partner. So the styles are different, because those who come to form the MS are those who have had problems there [Los Angeles] with the *vatos* in the *mara*. They are kind of mercenaries, they kill for enjoyment and because of that the MS doesn't want to see them. And because they can't find refuge there they come here.

Julio's declaration provides clear evidence of transnationalism among Salvadoran gang members. To borrow from Basch, Glick Schiller, and Szanton Blanc (1994, 7), gang members "forge and sustain multi-stranded social relations that link together their societies of origin and settlement." Gang members, like other transmigrants, "take actions, make decisions, and develop subjectivities and identities embedded in networks of relationships that connect them simultaneously to two or more nation-states."

Reaffirming the Local: Gangs and the Network Society

Now that we have enough elements to understand the history, composition, and field of activity of Salvadoran gangs, we can ask why Salvadoran youths join these groups. What do they find in these groups? As Jankowski (1991, 313) reminds us, "it is a gross oversimplification to attribute all gang members' reasons for joining a gang to any one motive, such as the lack of a father figure, the desire to have fun, or submission to intimidation. Gangs are composed of individuals who join for a wide variety of reasons." Nevertheless, we can discern some patterns among Salvadorans. For example, Larry Carrasco, a twenty-year-old leader in Barrios Unidos, a group of former gang members that works to promote social awareness, explains the appeal of youth gangs in the following terms:

> There ain't nothing here for us young Latinos. No jobs, no rec-places, you know, like places to play soccer or basketball. The schools stink and the police is racist. Our parents ain't there or just want us to be like them. But you have your homies who help and take care of you. You have your barrio where you live *la vida loca con tu raza* [to live a crazy life with your people]. And that crazy life is worth it, you know, because you're saying that you're somebody to be respected. It is a way of telling your parents, teachers, the police to go to hell.

Along the same lines, Dimas, an eighteen-year-old Salvadoran who recently left the MS, reflects on his experience with gangs: "Gang life is crazy but it has some good things about it: if you live by the rules you are somebody, somebody for your brothers. They respect you and are loyal to you. You belong to some place, your barrio, with your homeboys, which you defend from outsiders, even they are just other Latinos."

Larry and Dimas demonstrate that gangs contribute to the simultaneous reaffirmation of self, family (as an extended community), and place. In the face of dislocation, transnational movement, and multiple marginalities, gangs allow young Salvadorans to construct strong individual and collective identities on the basis of a radical, sometimes violent, affirmation of territory. Through lifestyles and turf battles centered around the neighborhood, gangs reconstruct local, embodied geographies in response to the deterritorializing processes they confront.

To understand the full localizing thrust behind youth gangs, we can draw from Manuel Castells's discussion of the network society and informational capitalism that characterize contemporary society. According to Castells (1996, 469), because of recent changes in information technology, "networks constitute the new social morphology of our society." For example, "capitalism itself has undergone a process of profound restructuring, characterized by greater flexibility in management; decentralization and networking of firms both internally and in their relationships to other firms; considerable empowering of capital vis-à-vis labor" (1). In this "society of the Net," those social actors organized as flexible, decentralized, and open-ended interconnected networks of local nodes thrive, while traditional corporate actors such as unions and political parties suffer. Working under the shape of global capitalism, the Net creates "a sharp divide between valuable and non-valuable people and locales. Globalization proceeds selectively, including and excluding segments of economies and societies in and out of the networks of information, wealth, and power, that characterize the new dominant system" (1998, 161–162). Castells calls those social segments excluded by the new economy "the black holes of informational capitalism," which together form a Fourth World of often territorially confined and "systemically worthless populations, disconnected from networks of valuable functions and people." People within these black holes, in turn, form "defensive" identities, "trenches of resistance and survival on the basis of principles different from, or opposed to those permeating the institutions of society" (1997, 8). People within these trenches seek to find value in the identities denigrated by the system and in the locality shut off by globalization. Those in the trenches operate according to the principle of "the exclusion of the excluders by the excluded. That is, the building of defensive identity in the terms of dominant institutions/ideologies, reversing the value judgement while reinforcing the boundary." Thus, facing a condition of multiple, recalcitrant exclusion, young Salvadorans in El Salvador and the United States

> may then refuse to accept the rules of the democratic game, or accept them only partially. Their response may then become social violence. The economically excluded do not become individual or collective subjects in the newly emerging public and political sphere: They may resist and protest, living under different rules, the rules of violence. Their (limited) energies and resources are not geared to integration, "acting out" instead of participating; at times, this is manifest in forms of communitarian resistance. (Jelín 1998b, 408)

The preceding discussion would seem to imply that gangs provide transnational spaces for the articulation of local oppositional practices. While this indubitably carries an element of truth, Castells's and Jelín's own assertions indicate that reality is more contradictory: gangs may oppose the systems that have marginalized them, but they do so by recognizing and reproducing the exclusion, by failing to produce subjects empowered to participate in the system in order to transform it. Salvadoran gangs reveal that transnationalism does not always result in the formation of transgressive, counter-hegemonic subjects (Guarnizo and Smith 1998). Building further on Castells's work, we might even say that the construction of a rebellious identity through *la vida loca* is "a twisted mirror of informational culture," defined by a "culture of urgency... a culture of the end of life, not of its negation, but of its celebration. Thus everything has to be tried, felt, experimented, accomplished, before it's too late, since there is no tomorrow." Gang identity would be a type of "communal hyper-individualism," or as Jankowski (1991, 28–31) puts it, "organized defiant individualism." Such an individualism combines a radical Hobbesian emphasis on the self and the immediate gratification of its needs—be it respect, catharsis, or the latest brand of sneakers—with a reactive defense of immediate networks and localities. Indeed, in the IUDOP survey of gang members in San Salvador, 46 percent of the respondents affirmed that they joined gangs because *"les gustó el vacil"* [they liked the gang's carefree lifestyle]. This percentage is substantially higher than those for "problems with parents" (12.3 percent), "lack of understanding" (10.3 percent), and "searching for protection" (5.8 percent), the other significant responses offered. In addition, slightly more than 60 percent indicated that what they liked the most about gang life was "el vacil" and "llevarse bien con los homeboys" [getting along well with your fellow gang members], demonstrating again the tense simultaneous affirmation of self, family, and locality enshrined in "communal hyper-individualism."

While Castells is right in seeing gangs as local, highly territorialized cultures of urgency that are "the reverse expression of global timelessness," we would like to take his argument further and propose that gangs are not only defensive reactions to contemporary social change, particularly globalization as expressed by transnational migration. Gangs do not just oppose globalization (in ways that reproduce its exclusionary effects) but also may participate actively in global processes. Recent newspaper articles (Alder 1994; Farah and Robberson 1995; O'Connor 1994) have uncovered how organized crime, including the Colombian drug cartels, the Mexican Mafia, and other U.S. gangs, has taken advantage of the neoliberal push to open markets to set up "branches in countries such as El Salvador and [recruit] new foot soldiers from among the poor and veterans of the region's recently ended civil wars" (Farah and Robberson 1995, A01). Transnational gangs like the MS and the Eighteenth Street gang are now becoming part of a "growing array of organized crime rings that specialize in cross-border trafficking and have turned Central America and Mexico into a hemispheric clearinghouse for drugs, contraband and stolen property." Castells himself discusses how transnationalism allows for the formation of networks in the informal economy (particularly that sector connected to criminal activities) that mimic the modus operandi of global capitalism. According to Castells (1998, 179), "The key to the success and expansion of global crime in the 1990s is the flexibility and versatility of their organization. Networking is their form of operation, both internally, in each criminal organization . . . and in relation to other criminal organizations. Distribution networks operate on the basis of autonomous local gangs, to which they supply goods and services, and from which they receive cash." In this sense, youth gangs such as the MS and the Eighteenth Street gang are part of a "perverse connection" in which crime takes advantage of "desperate attempts" to affirm identity, community, and place to "foster the development of a global criminal economy" (337).

If young gangs betray the desires of their members for self-recognition and for solidarity and intimacy in the face of globalization by reinscribing global processes at the heart of *la vida loca,* what options are left? In the next section, we will argue that churches, particularly evangelical churches, offer an alternative, though not unproblematic, way for Salvadoran youth to negotiate the tensions between the local and the global.

Saving Pablo

Despite their cynicism toward and rejection of mainstream culture and their reassertion of self and community at the margins, Salvadoran gangs reproduce, and even magnify, some of the most deleterious aspects of globalization. To illustrate how churches provide alternative ways for young Salvadorans to negotiate dislocation and multiple marginality, we will focus on the testimony of Pablo, a twenty-four-year-old former gang member who is now a minister in training in the Assemblies of God in San Francisco Gotera, Morazán. Pablo started his involvement in gangs in El Salvador when he was fourteen and was recruited during his frequent visits to San Miguel, the most populous city in the area, as he sought to escape "the boredom of Gotera." After years of petty criminal activity in high school, he left for Maryland (Langley Park) to join his mother and "to get away from it all." There he entered a drug gang and eventually became the leader of 144 youths. Pablo characterizes his life as a gang member before his religious conversion in the following terms:

> My life was real garbage because I lived in the streets. When I worked I used the money to buy drugs. I felt strong; I felt that I was on top of the world, that I was handsome, and a superman. And yet, to the contrary, I was getting thinner and thinner. People would tell me that in the United States you are supposed to get strong because of the food. "Why don't you get vitamins?" I would respond: "yes," but in my mind I was thinking of buying marijuana, that will make me strong. Eventually I didn't just buy the drug, I also sold it with my gang. I also started ingesting drugs, I snorted coke, drank alcohol, and smoked crack.

One day, some of his friends disappeared. After asking around, he learned that a mysterious van, which he thought was associated with the INS, had taken them. Later on he learned that his friends had been taken to a church for rehabilitation.

> And from then on I also wanted to look for God, so I started to search for the address of the church, calling numbers in the phone directory. I told all the pastors: "I want to change my life. I don't want to be what I am anymore. I am trapped by drugs and alcohol. I need somebody to help me." But I couldn't find the right phone number, because the church had just set up the house, a home, especially for young people trying to get away from the drug. Finally, the van arrived again. I saw some policemen get out of the van; for a moment, I thought that they were immigration agents because they were wearing suits and ties; their hair was short and prim; they had shaved and were wearing nice shoes. I didn't recognize them. But then I looked at them more closely and they were my friends. And they told me: "Hey Flaco, get up and let's go. We are taking you to the church." And I went. It was a wonderful experience to arrive at my new home. In two days I received the fullness of the Holy Spirit and I began to pray for my family, my family who were the guys in my new home.

For all its intensity, the conversion proved to be short-lived. Within a week of his conversion Pablo returned to the streets and drug addiction. The police arrested him, took him to jail, and eventually transferred him to an INS detention center.

> Then I humbled myself before God. I asked Him for forgiveness for everything I had done. I told him I wanted to be a clean person. I told him that if he got me out of jail that I would never turn my back on him. And God helped me grow spiritually in jail. In jail I taught the Bible, prayers, and hymns to young people. One day American *hermanos* [missionaries from the Assemblies] came to preach and I accepted God again. I didn't care that they spoke English. God was building up my soul. My heart was joyous; I didn't feel sad or frustrated because I was in jail. Then I was sent back here [El Salvador]. And I came directly to this church [the Assemblies of God in Gotera, Morazán]. You see, the hermanos here knew about me; they prayed every day for me. They came looking for me once they knew I had arrived in Morazán after eight months in the INS detention center in the United States.

After joining the church in Morazán, Pablo started working with youth ministry. "I'm the commander of the Explorers of the Kingdom," he states with great pride. The Explorers, which include about fifteen former gang members, are youths who are training to stay away from the contaminating power of the street vices. These young men, many of whom have recently returned from the United States, "are learning how to control themselves. They are taking control of their lives not through drugs but through the spirit of God. You see, a Christian person must live in brotherhood. That is what I preach to young people; they must walk in brotherly love. Just as Christ loved us so we must walk. A Christian home must persevere in love. Today when we get home we behave more like wolves." Speaking of the most pressing problems faced by Salvadoran youths today, Pablo states: "Young people need clubs or houses where they can learn an occupation. They need jobs and education. Instead of building more prisons, they [the government] could build spaces for recreation far away from the city and its contamination; spaces where one can teach young people how to conduct their lives without vices, without drugs, alcohol, and cigarettes."

Gangs and Transnational Armies of God

Pablo's case raises several important points in relation to the roles religion plays vis-à-vis transnational Salvadoran gangs. First, Pentecostal churches are operating transnationally. Why? The reasons stem from a mixture of theological and sociological variables. In Pentecostalism, conversion marks a radical transformation, an experience of being born again in Jesus Christ. It follows, then, that the greater the sin, the greater the glory to God, who has redeemed an utterly depraved sinner. And who is a greater sinner than a gang member who has rejected all societal conventions to live a life of crime and drug addiction? This logic, in effect, turns conversions of gang members into a symbol of status, a sign that the churches who achieve this are filled with the spirit and thus should be taken seriously in the fierce competition for souls that now characterizes the Salvadoran religious field. The problem is that gangs are transnational. Churches then must follow their potential converts, tracking them, as in the case of Pablo, across national borders. This is not difficult for a global organization like the Assemblies of God, which can mobilize its network of local congregations to deal with the challenges posed by transnational migration. Pablo, who has experienced a transnational conversion, now becomes the anchor for local efforts to convert other transnational gang members. Pablo's case supports Berryman's (1999) contention that Pentecostalism has grown rapidly throughout the Americas largely because Pentecostal churches function as Castells's network society—that is, as decentralized, flexible yet integrated networks providing customized services and goods to individuals and communities (compare with Garrard-Burnett 1998b). The second important point is Pablo's identification of the church with his "new home," his "new family." The solidarity and intimacy he found in the gang gives way to new intense and close ties within the safe environment of the congregation, where he can learn to control himself through "the spirit of God." This rearticulation of self, family, and a place called home is so central in Pablo's new worldview that he sees it as the main challenge that young Salvadorans face today as they struggle against multiple marginalities and social fragmentation represented most dramatically in his eyes by city life. Amid the dislocation and inequity that characterize Latin America, evangelical Christianity represents a "migration of the spirit" that helps poor people break the ties that bind them to their precarious condition.

> Pentecostalism in particular renews these ties in an atmosphere of hope and anticipation rather than despair. It provides a new cell taking over from the scarred and broken tissue. Above all it renews the innermost cell of the family, and protects the woman from the ravages of male desertion and violence. A new faith is able to implant new disciplines, re-order priorities, counter corruption and destructive machismo, and reverse the indifferent and injurious hierarchies of the outside world. Within the enclosed haven of faith a fraternity can be instituted under firm leadership, which provides for release, for mutuality and warmth, and for the practice of new roles. (Martin 1990, 284)

This insight can be applied to our case: Pentecostalism allows gang members like Pablo to break with their "communal hyper-individualism" and to articulate a new form of relational self. Pablo breaks from his previous ties (that is, the gang with all its notions of loyalty and honor) and rebuilds new strong ties within the "enclosed haven of faith." There he learns about "mutuality and warmth" ("brotherhood and love," in his own words) as well as about discipline ("control," as he puts it). It is interesting to note, however, that the language of control and brotherly love occurs side by side with vivid war imagery. This is the third important dimension of Pablo's testimony. The struggle to build a new self and community takes on the trappings of a cosmic war against evil, a Manichean conflagration that pits God and his armies (with a battalion under Pablo's command) against Satan and his minions. Recognition of the centrality of war metaphors in certain strands of evangelical Christianity is not new. Diamond (1989) has shown how these metaphors have been deployed by the Christian right in the United States to advance its dominion theology worldwide. In El Salvador, however, the rhetoric of spiritual warfare fulfills another, more local function: it effectively displaces to the symbolic field the remnants of the civil war (crime and the culture of violence). Put in another way, all the real, physical violence that pervades everyday life in El Salvador as a result of sociopolitical changes now finds a safe outlet in the struggle to produce controlled, disciplined subjects of a sovereign God. Through Pentecostalism, young people, the segment of the population with the greatest potential for violent, destructive behavior, can redirect all their energy to the spiritual struggle of staying clean and of a cleansing society. Like the rhetoric of fraternity and love, the substitution of "Holy warriors" defending God's turf for gangbangers has definite implications for the precarious processes of democratization in El Salvador. We will come back to the tension between the discourses of love and war and its implication for the Salvadoran democratic transition in our conclusion.

Before closing this section, we would like to touch briefly on the strategies used by other, non-Pentecostal churches to deal with transnational youth gangs. As these strategies are evolving and have not proven as successful as those of Pentecostal churches, the discussion will necessarily be limited. Among the historical Protestant churches we studied, the Lutheran church has one of the most visible pastoral initiatives toward youth. The Lutheran Church La Resurrección in San Salvador, for example, has a longstanding youth group, which was founded around 1985. According to the coordinator, the group, which presently has fifteen members, seeks to address "the socio-moral problems of young Salvadorans, helping them recover their moral values so that they can be less disoriented." The group undertakes educational, cultural, and religious activities, including arts and crafts, soccer games, Bible study sessions, retreats, and talks by sociologists and environmentalists. Often members of the MS are invited to the activities. So far no gang member has joined the church, but leaders of the youth group feel that they have established a good communication with the MS and that, as a result, they have learned a great deal about gang life and more generally about the challenges faced by poor and working-class Salvadoran youth.

La Resurrección's emphasis on "instilling Christian ethics" through an "integral" pastoral outreach is in line with the Lutheran Church's evolution in El Salvador. In the face of the Catholic Church's present retrenchment from the social activism of the 1970s and 1980s, the Lutherans have filled the void, taking an increasingly liberationist approach. However, this pastoral approach goes beyond El Salvador. Augustana Lutheran Church in Washington, located near Adams Morgan, operates in a similar fashion. Assistant pastor Lino Cardona, a Salvadoran and former Catholic priest who came of age in the years of the base Christian communities, oversees a ministry to Latinos that focuses on education and social empowerment. For Pastor Cardona the main objective of his Latino congregation is "to form an independent church, with its own name and funds. A church that, following a cooperativist model, can deal with illiteracy, unemployment, and the lack of affordable housing and health care in our community." In a step toward this goal, "We have organized a tenants' association in a building nearby, on T Street. It's mostly Latinos. You see, when people take charge of their own homes, they will be less likely to get involved in destructive behavior, including gang stuff." Pastor Cardona is aware of the importance of the transnational dimension. "We are beginning to establish contacts with La Resurrección in San Salvador. We know that several of our church members came here because they belonged to that church in San Salvador. And also some of our people go to Resurrección when they go back. We also have common problems. But we are in the beginning stages still with so much going on here."

Other Protestant churches in Washington, such as the Methodist and Unitarian congregations in Columbia Heights, have active youth outreach programs. They have worked with Barrios Unidos to set up events that stress ethnic pride and cultural identity. Often these events are cosponsored by secular organizations like CARECEN (Central American Refugee Center), which provides legal counseling and lobbies on behalf of Central American immigrants. According to Larry Carrasco,

> We feel accepted among the Methodist and the Unitarians. They are open-minded enough to welcome us to their churches to do our events. The Catholic Church, on the other hand, won't allow us to hold our meeting there. Maybe they are afraid that we will mess things up or steal things. The other thing is that we want to recover our roots, the teachings of our ancestors, the *indios* who lived here before all the drugs and corruption happened. They are the real *raza,* the real warriors, who we should be following, not the gangbangers. But [Catholic] priests get freaked out when we do sweatlodges and the like.

Here Carrasco articulates "la raza spirituality," which blends elements of an imagined Aztec culture and religion with strong ethnic pride and what Robert Bellah and his colleagues (1985) call "expressive individualism," built on the notion of self-actualization. A key element in this spirituality is the story of Aztlán, the primordial homeland somewhere in the U.S. Southwest. The Aztecs supposedly left Aztlán under the guidance of Huitzilopochtli, a god of war, in order to found Tenochtitlan near present-day Mexico City. This story allows Chicanos and other Latinos to affirm their proper place in the United States as one of the original peoples. In a sense, Aztlán allows Latinos to reclaim a homeland in the United States against persistent marginalization and anti-immigrant feelings and against the constant dislocations they suffer through migration and globalization (Anzaldúa 1987).

The Catholic Church's reluctance to deal with youth gangs stems from several factors, ranging from a renewed concern with orthodoxy to the fear of "politicization" of faith, both of which are connected with a conservative resto-ration. In the parish of the Sacred Heart, where we conducted our study, the pastoral agents focus on the demands of life in the United States, as a way to avoid getting caught up in the divisive sociopolitical struggles the immigrants left behind in El Salvador (Menjívar 1999). While the Catholic Church is a glo-bal institution that increasingly relies on international movements such as the Charismatic Renewal, it remains very much rooted in the parish, which is predi-cated on the notion of a unified, stable, geographically bounded community. Because of their fluidity and transgressive activity, transnational gangs repre-sent perhaps the sharpest challenge to this rigid structural setting. When the need to safeguard the parish against globalizing dynamics is juxtaposed with the Catholic conservative restoration, the result is a general disregard for the multiple marginalities involved in gang life. As a Latino priest at Sacred Heart told his congregants, "I am not a social worker. I cannot be involved in every aspect of your life. I am here to take care of the spiritual side mainly."

Some words of caution are in order here. The situation of Sacred Heart might not tell the whole story vis-à-vis the Catholic Church's response to gangs. Williams and Peterson (1996) have shown how in working-class neighborhoods like San Antonio Abad and Mejicanos in San Salvador, parishes have made pas-toral work with youth and gangs a priority. Berryman (1996) also documents genuine efforts by the Catholic Church to deal with the problems of street chil-dren and youth violence in Brazil. Even at Sacred Heart there are initiatives that seek to specifically target youths "who have strayed from the right path," as a young leader in the Sacred Heart's Charismatic group puts it. "We have an active ministry to prisons. We visit places like Lorton, where many Latinos, Salvadorans and other Central Americans are languishing. There we pray with them and many are awakened in the spirit of the Lord. We follow them wher-ever they go, even after they are released. Jesus saves one soul at the time, one household at the time. Sometimes we are rebuked. But we have the weapon of the Bible because we are part of God's army."

With Catholic Charismatics we have come full circle to the pastoral approach deployed by Pentecostalism, an approach that seems particularly successful because of its ability to link personal redemption and community-building with flexible operation, even in transnational circuits. We conclude this chapter by focusing on the implications of conversions to evangelical Christianity by transnational gang members. Can the new subjects, communities, and locali-ties created by Pentecostal churches contribute to the strengthening of a na-scent civil society in El Salvador? In what sense are these new identities and places different from those constructed by gang members in response to the social dislocation produced by globalization?

Conclusion: Havens or Heavens?

In *Tongues of Fire,* David Martin (1990, 44) argues that in Latin America evangelical Christianity, particularly Pentecostalism, is contributing to, among other things, a "feminization of the male psyche." With its fierce moral asceticism, Pentecostalism is transforming the Hispanic-Catholic culture of machismo by helping to create peaceable subjects who find the violence of the state or guerillas, the right and the left, "deeply repugnant" (267). The free, voluntaristic nature of evangelical Christian congregations represents a direct challenge to the monopolistic and hierarchical politico-cultural environment supported by Catholicism. Can we extend this hypothesis to our case study? Is it possible that in converting to Pentecostalism, Salvadoran youths are breaking with the cycle of violence and power that has defined Salvadoran history from the conquest and that finds its latest manifestation in *maras*? Are Pentecostal churches addressing the social dislocation produced by globalization and transnationalism and producing ethical subjects, who have internalized values like solidarity, fraternity, and reciprocity? If this is so, the implications for the democratic transition, while still difficult to detect, might be significant. As stated in the introduction to this volume, democracy is built not just on free elections and a competitive party system. The foundations of democracy go beyond institutions like parliaments and court systems to articulation of a "culture of citizenship," where all social actors, institutions, movements, and individuals share a civic intersubjective world.

From Pablo's testimony, it would seem that Pentecostalism is indeed "domesticating" Salvadoran youths' most destructive behaviors in response to the multiple, transnational marginalities they experience. This would certainly be a major contribution to the chaos of posttransition Salvadoran society. Angel Reyes, a deacon at Prince of Peace, a Salvadoran Pentecostal church in Hyattsville, Maryland, puts it bluntly: "We started in an apartment in Virginia, and we were evicted after two services for singing and praying. It made no sense, because the building was full of people who drank and fought. The authorities should be grateful because we rescue so many people they can't control. In those two services, we saved five people" (Constable 1995, B07). However, what kind of alternative subject and community is Pentecostalism constructing? Does Pentecostalism's emphasis on discipline and control produce docile subjects, ready to plug into any hegemonic project from above (by state)? After all, Jelín argues that the construction of citizenship also requires a critique of the "culture of domination-subordination" that is the legacy of authoritarian regimes and the violent movements that opposed them. While evangelical Christianity might be producing "peaceable," disciplined subjects, it may be less successful at eroding the larger culture of domination and subordination. Bastian (1993, 39, 50–51) argues that while historic Protestant churches in Latin America in the nineteenth century "arose from the political culture of radical-liberal minorities and questioned the corporatist order and mentality," contemporary Latin American Protestant movements "are no longer vehicles for a democratic religious and political culture. On the contrary, they have adopted the authoritarian religious and political culture and are developing themselves within the logic of corporatist negotiation."

Bastian's point echoes the common assertion in scholarly literature that Pentecostalism does not carry a critique of the political status quo and is, at best, apolitical. For example, when asked about the role of the church in politics, Juan José, an eighteen-year-old former gang member in Morazán, answered: "No, the commitment of the church is to take the message, that is the one and only goal, to take the message of salvation and the rest must be left alone. The world of corruption is something that must be forgotten. The world and people are going to stay just as they are now. It is their choice." Eladio, another former gang member in the Assemblies of God in Morazán, stated: "I lived in the world *[anduve por el mundo]*, but God rescued me. I saw the things of the world and they were a hell, they were rotten to the core. The world is the path of death."

Again, while the Manichean tendency in Pentecostalism is very evident in these declarations, we need to be cautious. Martin, for example, has argued that because the impact of evangelical Christianity is at the cultural level, its role in transforming Latin America's civil society is likely to take time. Because the new selves and communities produced by evangelical Christianity are still precarious, they are likely to be "circumscribed against the intrusive and hostile 'world'" (107). "Once we take into account the coiled up resistance of the social mechanism in Latin American society to any moral initiatives, it is not surprising that Pentecostals erect a dualistic wall between the safe enclosure of faith and the dangerous wilderness of the world. For them that wilderness is occupied by a 'satanic' violence from all sides which will seize upon and destroy those who stray carelessly into it" (266). In addition, because the world is hostile and chaotic, Pentecostal churches must rely on a protective, firm leadership. This will eventually give way to the principle of priesthood of all believers, which is central to Protestantism and is demanded by the antistructural work of the Holy Spirit. In Martin's estimation, Pentecostal congregations represent "experimental capsules or cells in the interstices of culture." They are "anticipations of liberty, initially realized in the religious sphere and stored there until either a shift in cultural underpinnings actually undermined the structural barriers, or protest moved from a cultural to a structural expression" (44).

Martin's hypothesis is helpful to avoid an uncritical stereotyping of Pentecostals as purely conservative, or even reactionary. Nevertheless, Martin's concept of "experimental capsules" is problematic because it assumes that conversion and participation in church life create hermetically sealed enclosures. Even the most committed church members who spend ten to fifteen hours per week at church activities must lead lives in the outside world, at school, work, and the street. There they are exposed to myriad alternative messages and lifestyles, some of which may challenge their faith. Thus, it is not surprising that many Pentecostals are constantly falling out of grace, an experience which they describe as *"volver al mundo."* We saw how this was the case with Pablo; his first conversion, though powerful, did not last long. Perhaps, then, it is more accurate to say that what Pentecostalism offers is not encapsulated, protective spaces but resources—practices, discourses, and forms of organization—to fashion alternative (moral) selves and communities.

More problematic still for Martin's argument is Pentecostalism's rhetoric of war. Is this discourse a displacement, and thus a defusing, of the violent patterns that have characterized Salvadoran life, including its transnational elements such as gangs? Or is it just a reproduction and reinforcement of discourses of domination and exclusion? By displacing the war from the social to the spiritual, does Pentecostalism turn social conflict into a religious sectarianism that finds divine legitimation for exclusionary, dualistic worldviews and practices? Neighboring Guatemala can give us an indication. Under Gen. Efraín Rios-Montt, the "trinity of essential principles: morality, order, and discipline" became intertwined with nationalism and geopolitics to produce a brutal "New Guatemala." In the construction of new Guatemala the struggle for "one soul at a time" and for a clean, redeemed society became "a divinely sanctioned 'final battle against subversion'" (Garrard-Burnett 1998a).

Perhaps Rios-Montt's case is unique, although the same yearning for order, discipline, and stability among ordinary Guatemalans (in the face of a post–civil war wave of crime not unlike that experienced in El Salvador) has recently resulted in the election of a new president with close ties to the general. In Castells's eyes, however, evangelical Christianity in Guatemala and among Salvadoran gang members could be seen as part of a larger trend. Discussing fundamentalist Christianity in the United States, Castells argues that it is a "reactive movement," "an attempt to reassert control over life, and over the country, in direct response to uncontrollable processes of globalization that are increasingly sensed in the economy and in the media." Can Pentecostalism among Salvadoran youth be also an attempt to form a "defensive identity, an identity of retrenchment" that seeks to assert self, community, and locality against the "global whirlwind"? If so, Castells is not very hopeful about the prospect for this new identity to give rise to what he calls "project identities" that can "redefine their position in society, and by doing so . . . [transform] the over-all social structure" (1997, 8). Rather than being the "embryos of a new soci-ety" that transcends the globalizations' exclusionary logics, defensive identities fall back on themselves or seek transformation at the end of times or in the spiritual plane. This inward or otherworldly focus, in fact, reproduces the ex-clusion, the multiple marginalities, brought by recent social changes, further limiting the horizons of praxis for those in the fourth world. "When the Net switches off the Self, the Self, individual or collective, constructs its meaning without global, instrumental reference: the process of disconnection becomes reciprocal, after the refusal by the excluded of the one-side logic of structural domination and social exclusion" (Castells 1996, 25). In this sense, movements like Pentecostalism "build havens but not heavens," as progressive Catholicism sought to do in the 1970s and 1980s. As the pastor of Prince of Peace in Mary-land puts it: "We isolate ourselves from sin, but we welcome anyone who wants to be in the spirit with us. Many of our countrymen get lost in the United States and fall into vices. We try to offer them a spiritual home. We are like a beauti-ful pasture with a fence around it. We want everyone to leave here filled with joy."

It is too early to assess the full impact on Salvadoran civil society of Pente-costal churches' work among transnational youth gangs. However, two things are clear. First, churches often play key roles in transnational and globalizing processes. This is possible because churches can link the local and the global in ways that respond to current individual and collective predicaments. More specifically, churches offer resources through which Latin American and Latino youths can construct alternative identities to the gangs' destructive commu-nal hyper-individualism, which, as we saw, is deeply implicated with globaliza-tion, particularly with posttransition social dislocation, transnational migration, and the global drug trade. As such, while Pentecostalism might have ambigu-ous long-term effects in the Salvadoran democratic transition, its role in re-constructing shattered selves, families, and communities cannot be denied.

Second, even if Pentecostalism offers contradictory strategies to deal with globalization, in linking the global and the local, religion need not necessarily produce a single kind of identity, mostly reactive or defensive, to use Castells's terms. Rather, if we take seriously the example of Barrios Unidos, the Meth-odists, and Unitarians in Washington, religion might produce potential projec-tive identities. Could the emphasis on *la raza* spirituality contribute to the emergence of Pan-Latino identities? In her chapter on the Catholic brother-hoods among Peruvians, Ruíz Baía finds some evidence of a movement toward panethnicity. The larger unresolved question concerns the impact of religiously based panethnicity in civil societies not in the United States and in Latin America.

Notes

1. The term refers to the "stresses and ambiguities" generated by social, economic, and cultural factors at the group, family, and personal levels, which lead to multiple forms of exclusion (Vigil 1988, 11).
2. All quotations from individuals in El Salvador are taken from personal interviews conducted by Lisa Domínguez and Ileana Gómez between November 1996 and December 1997. Interviews in the United States were conducted by Manuel Vásquez in June and July 1996 and June and July 1997.

Chapter 9

Anna Peterson and Manuel Vásquez

"Upwards, Never Down"

The Catholic Charismatic Renewal in Transnational Perspective

The Catholic Charismatic Renewal (CCR) lies at the heart of Roman Catholic pastoral work in the Americas today. Like Protestant Pentecostalism, to which it is often compared, the CCR has been described in varied and often contradictory ways. Some observers portray the movement as a conservative effort to bring lay people into the institutional church and strengthen ecclesial structures without the social concern or democratizing impulse of progressive pastoral initiatives (Lernoux 1989). Initially, scholars often described the CCR as "Catholic Pentecostalism" (Csordas 1980; McGuire 1982; O'Connor 1971), perhaps even an attempt by church leaders to diversify "their product to meet the diverse tastes of their 'customers' and thus stem the exodus of Catholics to Evangelical Protestant churches" (Gill 1999a, 35). Still others have described the movement as irrational, individualistic, and perhaps even heretical (Santagada 1975).

While each of these descriptions may contain partial truths, none offers a full portrait of the CCR today. Protestant Pentecostalism in Latin America, initially derided by many scholars as simplistic, reactionary, and apolitical, has been described more recently as much more complex in its internal structures, theology, and social roles than early critiques suggested. The Catholic Charismatic Renewal is similarly multifaceted and characterized by local variation while remaining within the hierarchical structure of the Roman Catholic Church. By comparing and contrasting the beliefs, practices, and organizational dynamics of Salvadoran Charismatics in El Salvador and Washington, we hope to illustrate some of the tensions involved in embodying a global institution in the local. We suggest that unlike many Pentecostal churches, the CCR is not truly transnational, at least organizationally. Neither is the Charismatic movement fully embedded in local communities, unlike Catholic *comunidades de base*. Borrowing a term from sociologist Roland Robertson, we characterize the CCR as *glocal*, an international phenomenon that thrives by stressing myriad local and personal expressions. This enables the CCR, despite similarities in theology and worship style to Pentecostalism, to remain distinctively Catholic.

History and Background of the Catholic Charismatic Renewal

The Catholic Charismatic movement forms part of what some have called a global neo-Pentecostalism (Quebedeaux 1976) or Charismatic Christianity, which encompasses "present-day Pentecostalism, the charismatic renewal, and third wave movements, African Independent Churches (AICs), independent Pentecostal churches, and the New Independent Churches (NICs) or ministries worldwide" (Poewe 1994, 2). Calling these movements neo-Pentecostal emphasizes their ties to Protestant Pentecostalism, which began with a revival in 1906 on Azusa Street in Los Angeles (Dayton 1987). Like Protestant Pentecostalism, the CCR originated in the Americas, at Duquesne University in Pittsburgh. During a retreat in 1966, "a group of students and young faculty members experienced the spiritual awakening of Baptism in the Holy Spirit through the influence of Protestant Pentecostals" (Csordas 1997, 4). The movement spread rapidly, first among Catholic students and faculty at other universities and later outside the academic community. By October 1970, some ten thousand Catholics participated in Charismatic prayer groups throughout the United States, and the movement had also spread to Canada, England, New Zealand, Australia, and parts of Latin America (Quebedeaux 1976, 67). Most of these early participants were from the middle and upper classes, as Quebedeaux (158–159) points out.

The evolution of the CCR reveals both strong historical ties to Protestant Pentecostalism and significant differences between the two movements. The earliest participants in the Catholic Pentecostal movement were strongly influenced by Pentecostal Protestantism, and many laypeople left the Catholic Church at the urging of Protestant mentors. However, the influence of Protestant Pentecostals diminished during the 1970s. The early Catholic Charismatics developed a number of distinctive features, notably the formation of small, dedicated "covenant communities." These groups share some similarities with CEBs, insofar as both provide intense interactions in small groups, in contrast to the relatively impersonal character of the traditional Roman Catholic parish structure. The distinctive feature of the Charismatic movement, however, is its emphasis on "a born-again spirituality of 'personal relationship' with Jesus and direct access to divine power and inspiration through a variety of 'spiritual gifts' or 'charisms'" (Csordas 1997, 4). Early Charismatic covenant communities met for regular prayer sessions and also joined in larger, often ecumenical, healing services, but most seemed to have relatively little contact with or guidance from the church hierarchy.

Catholic leaders paid increasing attention to the Charismatic movement as it gained numbers in the United States and other countries. As early as 1971, Pope Paul VI took note of the movement's existence, and he publicly addressed its 1975 annual conference in Rome. During the 1980s, the movement gained status as a distinctive movement with a clearly Catholic identity and growing approval from within the international Catholic Church. Pope John Paul II has been especially supportive and has encouraged the group's generally conservative political orientation and its focus on individual spiritual growth. Over the 1980s and 1990s, the movement became more closely linked to the institutional church. Catholic leaders both recognize the strength of the movement and judge that it does not pose a fundamental challenge to church structures or doctrine. The Charismatic movement has thus received very different treatment than progressive Catholicism, which John Paul has perceived as a threat to the hierarchal authority of the church and has sought to limit or even to crush. In contrast, the Charismatic movement has been successfully incorporated into the institutional church and in fact has become central to recent efforts to revitalize the church. Danièle Hervieu-Léger attributes "the remarkable institutional acclimatization of the Charismatic renewal within the Church" to "a successful compromise between the interests of the movement (that attracts, in the context where it develops, only fervent Catholics in quest of a more intense spiritual life and allergic to any sectarian dissidence) and the interests of the religious institution" (1997, 31). Increasingly, boundaries between Charismatics and conventional Catholics became more ambiguous, Csordas notes, "as many who no longer attended regular [Charismatic] prayer meetings remained active in their parishes and as many Catholics with no other Charismatic involvement became attracted to large public healing services conducted by Charismatics" (Csordas 1997, 6). Increasingly, the CCR is not just a movement but a style that penetrates a wide spectrum of Catholic ritual and pastoral models.

The rise of the Charismatic style or movement within Catholicism coincides with the growth of Pentecostal Protestantism, particularly in Latin America and among U.S. Latinos. This parallel growth generates a number of paradoxes. On the one hand, ties between Catholic Charismatics and Protestant Pentecostals have diminished, so it is misleading to speak of a global Charismatic Christianity as a somehow united movement. However, the simultaneous growth of various versions of Charismatic Christianity, particularly in the Third World and among minority and immigrant groups in First World nations, does point to an international trend. Here Poewe offers a helpful definition of *global* as "the unbound spatial, temporal, institutional, and linguistic reach of Charismatic Christianity. The latter has become a global culture or way of life based on perceptions and identities that are transmitted worldwide through high-tech media; international conferences, fellowships, and prayer links; and mega-churches" (Poewe 1994, xi). Charismatic Christian groups may not maintain or seek out links with each other, and in fact the global movement may consist largely of locally based groups that take little notice of each other. By exploring the CCR in relation to Pentecostal Protestantism and to other Catholic lay initiatives in El Salvador, we hope to clarify the distinctive global and local contributions and tensions of the Charismatic Renewal.

The Charismatic Renewal in El Salvador: Community, Movement, and Parish

The Catholic Charismatic Renewal reached Latin America in the early 1970s, often at the initiative of U.S. missionary priests or as a result of a Latin American priest's exposure to the movement in the United States. The movement came to El Salvador in 1983, when a Costa Rican priest, Miguel Angel Zamora, began forming Charismatic groups at the Iglesia El Carmen, in a middle-class neighborhood in the western part of San Salvador. In 1984 Zamora and a group of Charismatic laypeople from El Carmen traveled to Los Angeles, where they met with a former Assemblies of God pastor who had converted to Catholicism and was prominent in the Charismatic movement. They returned to El Salvador committed to making the movement grow. According to Zamora, the lack of support from the parish priest in El Carmen prevented the movement from flourishing initially. Only after Zamora himself became parish priest in 1987 did the movement grow. This underlines the fact that the Charismatic Renewal, like progressive Catholic projects, cannot thrive without clerical support.

Because of the strength of the Charismatic movement at El Carmen, many people came from other parishes to participate in retreats and assemblies. In response to this interest, leaders of the movement developed a strategy of *campos de misión,* or mission fields. After receiving training at El Carmen, new converts formed dozens of Charismatic groups in their communities. Even today many laypeople in parishes with little clerical support for the movement solicit support from El Carmen. According to Zamora, El Carmen has brought about twelve thousand Salvadorans to the CCR.[1] Charismatic evangelization programs in El Carmen include outreach in a poor neighborhood, Colonia Fortaleza, near the church. Zamora argues that the evangelizing activities of the CCR have stopped, or even reversed, the growth of Pentecostal churches in the neighborhood.

El Carmen was crucial to the origins of the Charismatic movement at the parish of María Auxiliadora (Don Rúa). Many participants in Charismatic activities in Don Rúa first encountered the movement in El Carmen and then moved to Don Rúa for its more accessible location and also, perhaps, for its less upscale membership. There appears to be little competition between the two Charismatic centers, however, and a number of people participate in activities in both parishes. Several smaller Charismatic programs exist at other parishes in and around San Salvador, often initiated by laypeople who have participated in El Carmen or Don Rúa. These experiences reflect the strong emphasis on growth and evangelization that is part of the overall strategy of the Nueva Evangelización.

The close relationship between the CCR and the institutional church in El Salvador contrasts with the common perception of similarities between the Charismatic Renewal and Pentecostalism. While the similarities between Pentecostal Protestantism and Charismatic Catholicism are real and substantial, the CCR has transformed and reinterpreted a number of Pentecostal themes to incorporate them within an enduring Catholic theological and institutional framework. This is evident in the Charismatic approach to personal transformation and salvation. Much of Protestant Pentecostal theology is captured in the refrain "I was lost, now I am saved." Pentecostals typically describe their conversions as life-changing moments in which Jesus rescued them from lives of unrelenting sin and misery, or at least from immersion in a worldly realm in which sin and misery reign. Charismatics, however, speak of their past failings in less foreboding terms. They describe themselves as having been overly arrogant or impatient but not as entirely lost to God and goodness. What marks their personal lives and their ritual activities is a celebration of continual moral and spiritual improvement rather than an all-or-nothing leap from sin to salvation.

This notion of continual progress is captured in the concept of *crecimiento,* which represents a Charismatic modification of the model of *cursillos* (short courses) used in Catholic Action groups and CEBs. In cursillos, believers move through a series of stages, each of which involves study and ritual participation. The Charismatic crecimiento program is more elaborate than progressive cursillos, which usually involve eight to twelve weekly classes and a culminating weekend retreat. (Interestingly, progressives usually call their retreat an *encuentro,* or get-together, while Charismatics use the term *retiro,* which suggests literally retreating or retiring from something.) Many of the CCR participants we interviewed spent years passing through the stages of growth, which involve elaborate programs of Bible study, prayer, and small-group participation, all supervised by pastoral agents. The successful completion of each step is a cause for celebration and for increased responsibility in the movement. The crecimientos provide multiple moments of transformation and rites of passage, marked by increasing self-control and knowledge of the tradition and rewarded by expanded opportunities to serve within the church. People in higher crecimientos, for example, sometimes assist those in the earlier stages or coordinate a biblical circle or outreach project.

Both the cursillo and crecimiento models assume that personal change is gradual and ought to occur within a controlled and hierarchical setting. This contrasts with the typical Evangelical conversion, a dramatic moment in which the believer is born again into a radically different reality. The convert may slip, which demands another dramatic moment. Charismatic and progressive Catholic pastoral programs also seek rupture with the bad habits of the past, but this break typically occurs in carefully modulated stages. This structure is also evident in Charismatic celebrations, where participants become emotional but rarely lose control of themselves, in contrast to the weeping, convulsions, fainting, glossolalia, faith healing, and sudden conversions common at Pentecostal services. Within the Catholic Charismatic movement, practices such as glossolalia and spontaneous scripture readings have undergone what Hervieu-Léger (1997, 35) calls a "controlled socialization," which "allows the limited incorporation of some of the trends of the modern culture of the individual within Catholic culture." In other words, Charismatic celebrations allow for diverse forms of spiritual expression while preserving crucial institutional interests.

Catholic leaders are not alone in striving for continuity between Charismatic practices and the official church. Participants in the CCR consistently emphasize their Catholic identity, which is often intimately tied to family loyalties and local traditions, and at the same time work to achieve changes in important areas of their lives, especially the conflicted domestic sphere. In this sense, the Catholic Charismatic movement challenges the sharp distinction Burdick (1993a) makes between "cults of continuity," exemplified by progressive Catholicism, and "cults of affliction," such as Pentecostalism, in which participants experience sharp breaks with their troubled pasts through healing-based conversion experiences. Defying Burdick's dualistic approach, the CCR and many progressive Catholic programs combine continuity in some areas with ruptures in others. Healing, in the personal or social realms, need not require a complete break with tradition but can be effected by a strategic transformation and re-interpretation of parts of that tradition, combined with the opening of new possibilities and experiences.

This is evident in the testimonies of many Catholic laypeople. Participants in CEBs often speak of their experiences as "waking up" or "opening their eyes" while also emphasizing that the process of illumination is ongoing. Israel, a resident of San Francisco Mejicanos, explains that before joining the CEB, he and his wife "only lived to live our lives and sleep, work, and not have to think about others. And now . . . all that has changed." However, he insists, "You can't change overnight, but rather it is an effort that you make every day because the defects that one has, as a human being, are difficult to uproot, to get rid of, so it's an [ongoing] process of change."[2] Progressive Catholicism combines religious education, social engagement, and collective solidarity to facilitate personal changes which, in turn, can inspire people to struggle for social and political transformation. To call CEBs simply "cults of continuity" is thus to miss their transformative capacity at both personal and societal levels.

Although the CCR does not lead to the sort of political conversions that sometimes resulted from participation in the *iglesia popular,* it does provide for rupture as well as continuity in various ways. The capacity of Charismatic pastoral programs to balance change and stability, in fact, seems to be a major reason for its appeal to young people and especially to women. In the CCR, participants can experience personal transformation, including emotional release and healing, in a structured and safe context that does not require a complete rejection of all their previous experience and established identity. Their process of change, like that described by Israel, is "an effort that you make every day." While Catholics, in CEBs or the CCR, rarely change overnight, neither do they need to reject their own histories and the world itself as the price of experiencing profound personal renewal.

This is important for many Salvadoran Charismatics we interviewed, who often emphasized their Catholic identity, even though many explained that before their initiation into the CCR they were Catholics only nominally. Many say their encounter with the CCR deepened their faith, as Julia Guerrero expresses:

> [It's been] marvelous, because you feel . . . conscious of what Jesus wants of you, what he has given us as a rule for our lives, to achieve this change. And so this makes you feel such tranquility, such peace, that all the problems that may come up with the family, all that seems to recede, because you remember and say: "This is mine, God help me," right?—and one picks up the Bible and begins to read it and to analyze it, right, and you say, "Okay, what I'm going through is nothing compared with the life of Jesus and the life of the martyrs that have been in the church."

While the themes of change and personal ties to God and Jesus echo Protestant Pentecostal testimonies, Julia expresses a distinctively Catholic sensibility in her conviction that her faith and ability to analyze the Bible prepare her to handle anything. The sins of her past pale in relation to the faith and confidence with which she faces the future. Her comparison between the experiences of contemporary believers and the lives of Jesus and the martyrs also reflects a confidence that Christians today can know and achieve what God wants of them. This contrasts with the Pentecostal insistence on complete reliance upon God, made more urgent by the believers' past sins and inherent human weakness. Charismatics operate with a typically Catholic nondualism: since we are all created in God's image, we are capable of goodness, even of perfecting ourselves gradually as we seek salvation. The chorus of a song popular in Charismatic celebrations captures the optimistic sense of progress driven by faith: *"Para arriba, arriba, nunca para abajo, mi alma volará"* [upwards, upwards, never down, my soul will soar].

Personal transformations in the CCR occur in the context of an intensely personal relationship with God and Jesus. The Charismatic focus on Jesus reflects a broader post–Vatican II moderation of the traditional emphasis on Mary and the saints. For Charismatic Catholics, as Raquel explains, the saints serve as models for Christian living but not as mediators between believers and God. "We Charismatics have access to the father through the lord Jesus Christ. Now we are not going to go to a church and touch the images [of the saints] and all. Those images remind us of those people, human like us, who had a holiness and honor that is agreeable to God. But if I directly ask Jesus Christ, the son of God, I don't have to ask Saint Martin of Porres, for example. They are valuable because they are saints and are in the presence of God, but we go directly to Jesus, the son of God."

Eva makes a similar point: "The saints are like someone who was close to God and lived an exemplary life," but "the saints do not work miracles. I have to tell you that, and they have even told us that the mother of God does not work miracles, but rather intercedes." The saints and Mary continue to serve as intermediaries between ordinary mortals and God, but they are no longer seen, at least officially, as possessing divine power in their own right. (Eva's comments convey the novel, even shocking implications of the claim that Mary, in particular, cannot effect miracles.)

Many Charismatics express a strong sense of Jesus or God as a close companion, present in believers' everyday lives. Julia explains: "I always give myself over to God before I begin [my housework], for example when I go shopping, taking my little bit of money in my purse, I put myself in God's hands, Lord, deliver from all danger, you know, from all evil." This echoes the words of many Pentecostals, especially women, who describe Jesus as intimately involved in the most mundane details of their lives. Both Charismatic and Protestant believers feel intensely connected to Jesus, who hears their stories, takes on their burdens, and changes their lives for the better.

Echoing progressive Catholics, some Charismatics insist that a "faith without works is dead," as Raquel puts it. In addition to praying and praising God, she explains, "We also need to help the persons who need it, beginning with the home, here [in] the community, helping the brothers and sisters who need it." This reflects the Catholic insistence that the mundane and the divine are integrally connected and that works on earth are tied to one's spiritual status. Further, some of the projects that Charismatics support in Don Rúa resemble those undertaken by CEBs, including a soup kitchen and educational and health services. What differs is the larger framework in which believers place these projects. Progressive Catholics see social projects as part of an effort to transform social, political, and economic structures so that they fulfill God's desire for humans to live in justice, cooperation, and abundance. In contrast, most Charismatics view their social participation as not only beginning but also ending with charity for people in need. This attitude shapes evangelizing efforts in poor areas, where pastoral attention has been minimal and people often feel alienated from the institutional church. Middle-class laypeople from Don Rúa and El Carmen often go door to door in these neighborhoods, publicizing both charitable projects and pastoral programs of their churches. The attitude of middle-class Catholics in these circumstances often blends evangelizing fervor, condescension, and sincere interest in the lives of their compatriots with "scarce resources" (*escasos recursos,* the common euphemism for poverty among middle-class Salvadorans).

Despite their sincere interest in the problems of the poor, few Charismatic Catholics analyze poverty in light of social structures. Rather, they usually interpret problems such as violence, poverty, and unemployment in vague terms and as amenable mostly to prayer and personal effort. For example, many Charismatics attribute the growth in delinquency to "rebellion," as Julia puts it. The problem can be solved, she argues, if young people can only be convinced "to come to church, to seek out the Lord, because the Lord is marvelous and is capable of healing all these problems." This echoes Pentecostal approaches to youth violence and delinquency and contrasts sharply with the progressive interpretation of such problems as the consequences of poverty and unemployment, which require structural as well as religious solutions.

In contrast to progressive Catholics, who see involvement in secular, sociopolitical groups as a key part of their Catholic identity, Charismatics feel that their Catholicism calls them above all to evangelize. This is why door-to-

door missions, among the most recognizable traits of Pentecostal Protestantism in Latin America, have been adopted by some Charismatic Catholics, occasionally to confusing effect. Julia explains that when she has gone door to
door evangelizing for the CCR in poorer sections of her parish, Don Rúa, she
has sometimes been mistaken for a Pentecostal missionary and thus had doors
closed on her. In such circumstances, she says, instead of giving up, she persists until the door is opened and explains that she is indeed a Catholic—at
which point previously reluctant neighbors are willing to talk to her. She wears
a medal of the Virgin on her evangelizing walks to highlight her Catholic identity. (Julia's assumption that Pentecostal missionaries always meet with closed
doors is revealing, if not completely accurate.) Tomasa, also from Don Rúa,
points out that Catholics must be careful to distinguish their evangelizing efforts from those of Pentecostals. It is necessary, she says, to debunk the ste-
reotype, often reinforced by evangelical Protestants, that Catholics tolerate any
level of degenerate behavior. Tomasa explains that sometimes people tell her,
"'I was Catholic before. I drank, I danced, I smoked.' So you have to make
people realize that being Catholic doesn't mean being liberal . . . [and] that just
because we stop drinking doesn't mean we stop being part of this church. Being Catholic means moving ahead, being good, not having vices. Not only
evangelicals should stop drinking. Neither Catholics nor Protestants should
drink in excess."

Personal transformation revitalizes the institutional church by changing the
quality of participation. Increased participation is an explicit goal of the New
Evangelization, which represents a "call to conversion" for all Catholics, especially "baptized men and women whose Christianity is devoid of vitality," as
the bishops proclaimed at Santo Domingo (Hennelly 1993, 81, 82, 100). This
highlights the important fact that despite the conservative aspects of the New
Evangelization in general and the CCR in particular, contemporary pastoral
approaches do not simply return to the preconciliar model. Many of the
changes wrought by the Second Vatican Council are irreversible, and the New
Evangelization accepts and builds on this fact. Thus the Charismatic Renewal
combines the postconciliar encouragement of informed and enthusiastic lay
participation with a longer-standing tradition of deference to clerical authority. Some early observers (Santagada 1975) accused Charismatic Catholics of
minimizing the role of the institutional church, but these fears do not seem
realized in the movement today. The CCR represents, at least in theory, the
best of both worlds for church leaders: laypeople commit to the church without seeking real authority within it. This model reflects John Paul II's paradoxical combination of personal religious fervor and pastoral populism with a
rigid insistence upon hierarchical authority.

Salvadoran laypeople seem to accept this reaffirmation of the authority and sacrality of the church hierarchy, from the local priest to Rome. In response to an interviewer's question about which pastoral programs or reforms she thought were best, Raquel responds, "Well, maybe that isn't up to us laypeople to say, because the reforms come from the Vatican. . . . We obey those orders, because that's where authority comes from. So . . . the pope orders the bishops of different countries to follow his reforms and here . . . we depend on the archbishop of San Salvador . . . the archbishop calls the parish priests and gives them his directions and we as laypeople obey." For the word *obey,* Raquel uses the Spanish term *acatar,* suggesting military-style obedience, rather than the more common *obedecer.* This highlights the hierarchical authority of the priests, who, in Don Rúa, carefully guide and delimit lay participation in Charismatic events. Like most participants in the CCR, Raquel experiences clerical guidance as flattering rather than oppressive. "We work in coordination with the parish. We are the universal church because we are under the authority of the parish priest, and we follow the hierarchy and we respect everything that is related to the hierarchy, beginning with the pope, following with the bishops and the parish priests. We are in a line of obedience to the hierarchy, and I like that a lot."

In contrast, progressive Catholics often insist that the laity should not simply carry out pastoral or social programs imposed from above but rather ought to be active agents in determining both a parish's priorities and the methods it will use to achieve its goals, pastoral or otherwise. Of course, in many concrete instances progressive priests have proved authoritarian and laypeople submissive, due in part to the difficulty, for both clergy and laity, of breaking with traditional roles, rather than deliberate efforts to reinforce clerical authority. Despite the concrete limitations of progressive efforts to democratize parish structures, the public commitment to democratization was significant, and the disavowal of democratization and lay empowerment as goals, even in principle, is also significant.

The emphasis on clerical and episcopal authority in the CCR means that while lay participation is emphasized, it is also carefully guided by priests. Charismatic celebrations illustrate what Hervieu-Léger terms a "dialectic between spontaneity and regulation." Charismatic groups, she argues, "do not want to drop out from their common Catholic home. Instead, they try to negotiate the conditions of a relative autonomy within the Catholic system" (Hervieu-Léger 1997, 37). In this light, we can compare Charismatic services with celebrations of the word, a central ritual of progressive Catholicism in Central America. In the celebrations, specially-trained lay leaders, called "delegates of the word of God" *(delegados de la palabra de Dios),* usually but not always male, gave sermons and actually led the Eucharist, with wafers previously blessed by a priest. Celebrations of the word developed because of practical considerations, especially the shortage of priests, and also because many priests hoped to increase the authority and responsibility of laypeople within the church. The CCR does not seek this radical democratization of power or transformation of the institutional church but rather aims to increase room for individual expression, to strengthen lay participation, and at the same time to reinforce established structures and rules, including those which restrict ultimate material and sacramental power to celibate male priests.

The tension between spontaneity and regulation characterizes other Charismatic events and pastoral programs. In many parishes, CCR leaders have established biblical circles and similar small groups in which laypeople meet regularly to read and reflect collectively on the Bible or other religious texts. In important respects these groups resemble progressive base communities, reflecting the postconciliar emphases on making the Bible more central to faith, on involving laypeople in the church through small units within the larger parish structure, and especially on linking faith and life. Some Charismatic circles are led by laypeople, at least in their everyday operation, thus suggesting a certain degree of practical autonomy that CEBs sometimes lacked. However, most Charismatic groups remain more inward-looking than CEBs, emphasizing personal and private experiences.

These programs reflect the CCR's larger capacity to maintain a productive tension between change and continuity. Charismatic leaders recognize that affirmations of clerical authority can, and even must, coexist with pastoral and ecclesial changes. Most significantly, the CCR, along with the Neocatechumenate and other programs encouraged in the New Evangelization, is transforming the place of the parish in Catholic pastoral work. This transformation began when post-Medellín progressive initiatives crossed parish boundaries, especially in rural areas where many parishes lacked permanent priests. However, the Charismatic movement decentralizes the church in a different manner. On the one hand, participation and leadership are decentralized, as local groups organize their own prayer groups and charitable activities. In Don Rúa, for example, the parish has become structured around movements, notably but not only the CCR. In this light, the parish becomes a flexible center for the meeting of people in diverse areas, transcending both the parish as the place church members live and also the parish as the place people meet. This highlights the way the CCR departs from both the traditional parish model and also from the community model elaborated in CEBs.

While it decentralizes in this sense, the CCR also recentralizes the church by affirming and reproducing the power of the church hierarchy. Charismatic programs reach out to people far beyond parish boundaries, drawing them together under the hierarchical umbrella of the mega-parish. Don Rúa exemplifies this process. The church's central location near downtown San Salvador means that parish residents have easy access to the several churches in the city center, including the newly refurbished cathedral. On the other hand, Don Rúa itself is easily accessible to people who live in other parishes but prefer the pastoral approach, the sermons, or just the feel of events at Don Rúa. Its location thus provides an initial reason for pastoral programs at Don Rúa to challenge the traditional parish-based approach: unlike more isolated parishes, it cannot count on the attendance of all the local Catholics, but it can reach out to residents of other parishes. It has done this by strengthening certain programs that are not available, at least not with the same scope or intensity, in all other parishes. Don Rúa has thus become a magnet church for people interested in the Charismatic Renewal and the Neocatechumenate.

Don Rúa has not rejected the parish model entirely. The decision to pursue certain pastoral approaches stems from the character of the parish, which is mostly lower middle-class, with few residents who are either very wealthy or very poor by Salvadoran standards. The neighborhoods that compose the parish are well-established, without either the shanties inhabited by recent migrants to the city or the housing developments occupied by San Salvador's nouveau riche. Thus pastoral work in the parish of María Auxiliadora can count on a core of local residents who represent the chief constituency of the Charismatic Renewal. The Salesian priests in charge of the parish have built upon this core, possibly excluding some local residents but also inviting many outsiders to become honorary parishioners. By both building on and transcending the parish model, the CCR renews church structures, combining stability and innovation.

The strength of the CCR in Don Rúa depends on the pastoral workers' ability to recognize and adapt to local particularities. This capacity to inculturate has also been essential to the success of progressive pastoral initiatives. Even though the CCR and CEBs have both been influenced by broad trends within the Roman Catholic Church, both are also strongly shaped by local realities, especially the priest. This means that progressive and conservative movements within the church are not always as disparate as they might appear, at least when we look at the local level. As Marjo De Theije has found in Brazil, the CCR takes different forms in different settings, due not only to national differences in political, cultural, and socioeconomic factors but especially to the particularities of parishes. Local Charismatic groups, much like CEBs, often differ considerably from the generalized portrait. Further, De Theije adds, at the local level the CCR and CEBs may not differ from each other as much as some observers assume. "The typical image of the CCR can be attributed to the fact that observers usually emphasize the meaning of the movement in a national and international context, overlooking the peculiarities and distinctive traits of local elaborations of Charismatic teachings. Just as the base communities are not simply liberation theology writ small, local prayer groups are not necessarily the direct expression of ideology of the national and international Charismatic movement" (De Theije 1999, 112). Charismatic and progressive groups in the same parish may not differ from each other or resemble parallel groups in other sites nearly as much as generalized portraits of either movement suggest. This is true in El Salvador also, we found, although clear structural and theological differences distinguish the CCR from progressive lay initiatives taken as a whole.

Charismatic Salvadorans in the United States: Global Institution and Transnational Reality

Very little is written on the history of the CCR among U.S. Latinos. From its largely middle-class and white origins in the United States, the CCR fairly quickly became ethnically diverse. Latino participation in the Charismatic movement began growing in the 1970s , and U.S. Latino Charismatic leaders had their first national meeting in 1977. The growing Latino presence in the Charismatic Renewal has led to official recognition and has contributed to the movement's growth in Latin America. In 1982 the CCR's National Service Committee added its first Latino member and gave funds to Misiones Hispanas, a Charismatic missionary movement active in both U.S. Latino and Latin American communities (Csordas 1997, 20). The dual focus of Misiones Hispanas reflects the close ties between Latino and Latin American Charismatics. This is evident as well in the movement's history among Puerto Ricans in the United States and Puerto Rico. As Csordas (1997, 21) reports, the movement was introduced to Puerto Rico in 1971 by Redemptorist missionaries from the United States, then reintroduced to U.S. Puerto Rican communities by members of the island's Charismatic movement. This represents an instructive example of transnational evangelizing and "reverse missions," in which populations that are usually the target of evangelizing—in this case Puerto Ricans in their homeland—become missionaries to the "dominant" culture. The phenomenon of reverse missions is also strong among Pentecostals in Latin America and U.S. Latino communities (Garrard-Burnett 1998b). Ties between Latino and Latin American Charismatics received official recognition in 1988, when Latinos first participated in the conference of Catholic Charismatic leaders in Latin America.

The movement continues to be particularly strong among Puerto Ricans. According to Father Gilberto in Paterson,

It might well be that there is something in Charismatic style that appeals especially to Caribbeans, to Puerto Ricans and Dominicans, with their more festive, emotive cultures. Peruvians and other Andeans tend to be more reserved, to be used to a more penitential Catholicism. They are kind of put off by all the celebration. The thing is that, at least, in this area, most of the leaders of the Charismatic groups are Puerto Rican. There are some Colombians and Central Americans, but Puerto Ricans still dominate. It may be because the CCR has a longer history in Puerto Rico or because of the special link that I just mentioned.[3]

These comments are echoed by Father John Brogan, who oversees Hispanic ministry in Brooklyn and Queens: "Puerto Ricans and Dominicans have a strong presence among Charismatics. Cubans, who are an increasingly aging population, are more linked to cursillos. I have found that Mexicans, whose numbers in the area are growing very rapidly, are at first reluctant to get involved with Charismatics, but once they do, they can be really committed."[4]

Given the numerical dominance of Central Americans among Latino immigrants in the Washington area, it is not surprising to find that many leaders in the Charismatic movement hail from Guatemala and El Salvador. In both Sacred Heart and Our Lady of Sorrows, the two Catholic parishes we studied, Charismatic groups are overwhelmingly Salvadoran. While both groups are growing, the one at Sacred Heart is much larger. According to some lay leaders, the movement has 150 to 200 members. Their Sunday assemblies (after the 12:30 P.M. Spanish Mass) are well attended by a mixture of families and single men, all ready to sing, dance, and celebrate to the tune of an electric guitar, a bass, an organ, and a set of drums. Most of the animators at the assemblies are young men.

> Relations with the parish priests are cordial. At Sacred Heart, Father Marlon told us that we [the priests] try to visit them during their assemblies and prayer groups. Accompaniment is important to make things run smoothly because some groups like the Catechumenate try to do their thing and the result is not always beneficial. Some people from the Don Rúa Catechumenate came to tell me they wanted to form their own group here, that they wanted their own Mass. I said no, I will not celebrate Mass for just one group. Masses are public events. Anyway visiting each group in the parish is hard when you have many groups to take care of. Remember in this parish we have not just Salvadorans or Central Americans, but Haitians, Vietnamese, and African Americans.

We argued that in Don Rúa, the CCR provides both rupture and continuity;

it enables faithful Catholics to reinterpret life's vicissitudes within the framework of a progressive spiritual growth, especially through the notion of crecimiento. How does the CCR work for Salvadoran immigrants in Washington? The case of Jonas, a member of the Charismatic group in Our Lady of Lourdes in Takoma Park, can shed some light. Jonas, now in his early thirties, came to the United States in 1994 "to search for a better life and to help economically my family back home." Jonas reflects on his past experiences in El Salvador.

> I have lived a hard, hard life. Beginning when I was twelve years old, I was not able to sleep in peace at home. My father always had to take me out to the back country *[el monte]* to sleep because we were accused of being with the guerrillas. Those were tough times in El Salvador. One could not go out after 7 P.M. for fear of not coming back alive. And my life continued like that for ten years. I bounced around *[reboté]* quite a bit, because first I participated with the guerrillas. I did it because I liked it for awhile. But then I returned to civilian life, and that's when the army forced me to join them. So I have experienced both sides. Finally, I got out of the army, but my life didn't have any meaning or peace. And that's when I found the church.

While the church gave Jonas "more tranquility," he felt he had to leave to the United States to help his struggling family. His journey to the United States represents another "bounce" in his life.

> I bounced into the States as a wetback *[rebotando como mojado]*. First, I went to Guatemala. Then I traveled through Mexico with great hardship. The guy who was taking us to the border kept us going, hungry and all. Suddenly, the truck I was in, along with other twenty five people, got off to a dirty road and going at a high speed overturned. The whole group was thrown around. I thought we all would die. And there, the Mexican police came and arrested twenty one. Four or five of us hid behind some bushes and were not detected. But then we had to return by foot to the Guatemalan border because we didn't know how to keep going. Finally, we arranged another trip with some of the people in our first group. The Mexicans had dumped them at the Guatemalan border.

Like many Salvadoran immigrants, Jonas found that arrival in the United States does not automatically put an end to hardship. He continues:

> When I came here I forgot about the church. I met some friends and started to go the wrong way again *[me fui desviando]*. I drank and partied a lot. I was kind of alone, with no place to go, really. But one day I thought about

who I was, an undocumented person with no sense of responsibility, and decided to go back to church. There I found Jesus in a Charismatic retreat. I think my life is now more tranquil, more stable, meaningful. I don't make a lot of money, but I have my car and send money to my family in El Salvador. I also try to preach to other Salvadorans. There are so many of them lost and dirty in the streets just because of addictions. One has to be careful in this country. Unfortunately, many people just come here to work and by the weekend they have spent everything they've earned, and in the end they have nothing to show. But if you come to the church you learn how to value the good life without wasting all your money.

Jonas's life history is instructive on several levels. First, the growth that Jonas finds in the Charismatic group is an attempt to order and give meaning to a history of dislocation, dramatized by the idea of having "bounced through life." A particularly important bump in the road to life, as it were, was migration to the United States. In Jonas's own words: "I believe that all the vicissitudes I have experienced are part of a plan God has laid out for me to learn to be a better person. And finding Jesus in the *renovación* has been an especially important step." This discourse of progress mirrors that among Charismatics in Don Rúa and, to some extent, also echoes the notion of the *caminata* (the path), a central concept for progressive Catholicism. However, the meaning of crecimiento takes on different meanings in different settings. For Salvadoran women, the notion of crecimiento serves primarily to give structure to their lives in the face of changing gender roles. For Salvadoran immigrants in Washington, however, the concept offers a way to make sense of the traumas involved in the migration and acculturation processes. Charismatic theology offers a narrative of continuity that, while acknowledging change, places it in the context of a progressive self-improvement. This, again, reflects the Catholic character of the CCR.

Jonas's case is not unique. Time and again we heard similar stories for Salvadoran immigrants of diverse background. Another case in point is Lupe, a member of the Charismatic group at Sacred Heart.

Huy! If I only told you the story of my life! It is like a soap opera. Even before I was born I had problems. My mother denies it but other people who lived around her time told me. My mother, when she got pregnant with me took medicine, she hurled herself down the stairs to abort, but God didn't let her and I was born. My mother wouldn't take care of me when I was a baby, and I almost died from an intestinal infection. Finally, she took me to the hospital and abandoned me there. But God watched out for me and grandma got me from the hospital. She took me to my aunt and uncle's house . . . and there, as young as seven years old, my uncle tried to rape me several times. He drank a lot, you see. . . . When I was seventeen, a woman convinced me to go to Guatemala to earn some dollars. I thought I was going to work at a pharmacy, but it was really a house of prostitution. So I escaped with another girl. Then we were accused of stealing from the owner of the establishment. So we ended up at the police. And there another thing of God happened: I met my husband, a Guatemalan policeman. Everything was fine for a while, I had two girls with him. But one day I went back to El Salvador for a month, and when I came back found that my husband had gone with another woman. He was finally kidnapped because he was a spy *[oreja]* for the government. So I came to the States, found another husband with whom I'm happily married, and I have two children with him. But I want to tell you: all this is God's plan. He wanted things to be this way for me. And he has always been with me. He has always had pity for me *[ha sido misericordioso conmigo]*, down to giving me the change now to celebrate his glory with our [Charismatic] group. You don't know the joy that now fills me.

The second element worth emphasizing in both Jonas's and Lupe's testimonies is the dual theme of renewal and tranquility provided by their participation in the CCR. This echoes the reports of Charismatic women in El Salvador, as discussed by Peterson in chapter 1. Among Salvadorans in Washington, the CCR appears to function as Pentecostalism does for poor people in Latin America: inoculating males against street vices and thus preserving or even repairing family structures (Brusco 1995; Gill 1990; Mariz and Campos Machado 1997). Some scholars have argued that, because immigrants are far from their families and communities, they are particularly vulnerable to other social pathologies (Poblete and O'Dea 1960). This is certainly the case among young Salvadorans in Washington. Migrant men, in particular, are prone to engage in behaviors destructive to self and community (in both the sending and receiving countries). The CCR offers a way for immigrants to reorient self and reconstruct families and communities. Salvadoran immigrants can experience all the elements that go with personal renewal (that is, the sense of being cleansed and of being filled with joy) without having to break with Catholicism, which still strongly informs Salvadoran culture and everyday life. All this reinforces Hervieu-Léger's hypothesis that the movement is an instance of "controlled socialization," allowing adaptation to the contemporary social demands within a traditional Catholic framework.

Jonas provides an illustration of the paradox of change within continuity, of upheaval within tranquility that characterizes the CCR:

Now, I'm clean. You know: you feel like before you were dirty and after a good bath you are clean. You are different. It's funny; it's like you are still you but now with a completely different life. The church has thus helped me a lot. I have separated myself from vices and I have become committed to my family [in El Salvador] either by sending them money or even writing to them. Before I didn't even use to write, I didn't have time in between work and my weekend parties with friends. Now I recognize I was in the wrong. And the church helped me to reconsider *[recapacitar]* what I need to do and that has helped a lot.

Jonas's participation in the Charismatic movement at Our Lady of Sorrows has redirected his focus toward his relatives in El Salvador, which brings us to the subject of transnationalism. At the level of individuals, at both Sacred Heart and Our Lady of Sorrows, there is quite a bit of activity across national borders: people send remittances not just to help their immediate families but also to rebuild or beautify their villages (working as voluntary civic associations). In terms of religious life, Father Marlon comments that "many of the leaders of the Charismatic group at Sacred Heart come from Don Rúa. They come already with a strong training and background to animate the group here. And when they go back to visit, they always mention going to Don Rúa for the [Charismatic] assemblies." Despite this "grassroots transnationalism," it is not necessarily true that the CCR functions in a transnational way, at least organizationally. Unlike the Pentecostal churches seeking to convert gang members, Charismatic groups among Salvadorans are not deliberately oriented toward transnational missions. Rather, Charismatic groups function within global frameworks (the Catholic Church and, within it, the CCR as a worldwide movement) by, paradoxically, focusing on the local (as part of the parish structure). Thus, while Archbishop Saenz Lacalle can go to Sacred Heart to ask for contributions to finish construction work at the National Cathedral in San Salvador, all pastoral activity at Sacred Heart, including the CCR, is directed toward Salvadorans in Columbia Heights and Adams Morgan. To the extent that there is transnational ministry, as in the case of some Charismatic outreach among Latino inmates in Lorton, it results mainly from individual initiatives. The church, as represented by the two parishes, is both universal and local, but not transnational, meaning that the frame of reference within which followers weave their daily religious life is not focused simultaneously on the sending and receiving cultures.

Conclusion

While the Catholic Charismatic Renewal functions somewhat differently for Salvadorans in El Salvador than for those in the United States, important common elements help Salvadorans in both countries deal with their personal and local predicaments. One of the most important is the notion of crecimiento. In El Salvador, crecimientos offer opportunities for lay leadership development as well as a vehicle for middle-aged women to break the cycle of boredom, isolation, and domestic conflict. They provide a sense of personal accomplishment and a certain measure of rupture with the negative elements of their past lives. Such rupture does not require a break with the traditional Catholic gender roles. To the contrary, the movement reaffirms male authority within a context of simultaneous resignation and well-being for women.

For Salvadoran immigrants, the concept of crecimiento helps make their often harrowing migration histories meaningful by inserting them into a divine plan that leads to personal growth, health, and balance. Crecimiento helps control the initial chaos and anomie experienced by many immigrants. By redirecting their attention to self, family, and church, the CCR protects immigrants, particularly young, single men like Jonas, from the temptations of the street, which defeat the original purpose of coming to this country: to build a better life. In this sense, the lyrics "upward, never down," come to symbolize the struggle of Salvadoran immigrants to attain their small piece of the American dream. The optimism and controlled socialization offered by the CCR are all the more valuable as many Salvadorans find the American dream difficult to realize.

The notion of crecimiento reflects the CCR's distinctively Catholic identity. Despite many similarities in the style of worship, the CCR remains Catholic, offering a paradoxical blend of change within continuity that stands in contrast to Pentecostalism, with its more radical notions of break. Here, the CCR has more in common with the progressive notion of the *caminata* than with Pentecostalism's sharp dualism between the things of God and the things of the world. Another important difference between Pentecostalism and the CCR is in the scope of their mission. Pentecostalism often functions as a transnational religion, ministering to transmigrants through flexible networks, reminiscent of Castells's (1996) descriptions of the network society. In contrast, Catholic churches function more according to what Roland Robertson calls glocalization. The term originates from the Japanese *dochukuka,* adapting a global institution's practices to local conditions. Others have applied this concept to changes in industrial economies, seeking to illuminate the mutual implication of global and local levels. Thus Amin (1994) and Harvey (1989) have documented how, in the endless search for profits, rigid, corporatist economies of scale that produce for homogeneous national markets are giving way to flexible, decentralized production for diverse global markets. Glocalization, as Japanese corporations envisioned it, is precisely a set of flexible production strategies, which increase the "local content" of products, thus allowing for a rapid response to changing local needs, while facilitating the concentration of management and profits in "global cities" (Sassen 1998), where multinational companies are based. Although glocalization appears as a triumph of diversity and the local, it is also part and parcel of the global processes of capital accumulation.

Since religious markets are also becoming increasingly global and competitive, the concept of glocalization becomes helpful in understanding religion also. The parish, the cornerstone of Catholic pastoral work, tends to operate in a Fordist mode, as a religious economy of scale dispensing one-size-fits-all products. In contrast, the CCR reflects a post-Fordist model of religious production, introducing flexibility and context sensitivity to the parish structure without challenging established hierarchies. While practices are decentralized, put in the hands of lay leaders in various settings, the overarching symbolic power of the clergy is not just reproduced but enhanced through a quasi-militaristic discourse *(acatamos)*. Moreover, as we saw in El Salvador, the CCR cannot thrive without institutional and clerical support. This also holds true for CEBs.

In Don Rúa, the physical church is the central place where movements such as the CCR join Salvadorans from different areas. The CCR, thus, serves to extend the missionary and pastoral boundaries of the parish, creating a mega-parish. The process, however, does not completely erase parish boundaries, because pastoral work stresses personal renewal within the ritual and sacramental life of the church. This affirmation of the local, which was also clear in Washington, is not opposed to the global. Rather, the local comes to serve the interest of the global, since the CCR is ultimately part of the Vatican's attempt to build a "Christian culture of love," in John Paul's words, with the institutional church at its core.

The CCR and Pentecostal Protestantism represent two strategies to negotiate the dilemmas of globalization. Pentecostals bank on multiple, relatively horizontal networks of transnational churches, each dealing with the local effects of globalization. Catholics, in contrast, increasingly seek to balance the global and the local, centralization and flexibility, continuity and rupture, and renewal and discipline. This does not mean that the CCR has no transnational dimension. However, these transnational links represent individual initiatives at the level of the laity, such as the people who go back and forth between Don Rúa and Sacred Heart. These links are not part of a deliberate institutional strategy. This paradox of lay transnationalism within a structure anchored in geographically bound parishes is possible because Catholicism, as a global institution, is open to multiple forms of inculturation, allowing the laity to create new forms. In the United States, the demands placed on the clergy by large, multicultural parishes often give the laity more latitude to engage in their own practices.

It is difficult to discern, at this point, whether Catholic or Pentecostal pastoral strategies are more likely to succeed. There are signs that the CCR's model of flexibility within structure may ultimately be untenable. In the United States, priests active in Latino ministry often complain that the CCR is self-centered and detracts from the multiple ways of being Catholic in the parish. One non-Charismatic Hispanic layperson in Brooklyn explained:

> I don't understand Charismatics. They don't like to participate in parish activities like the feast of the patron saint or dances and cultural presentations to gather funds to rebuild the parish or help the needy. They say that to drink, smoke, and dance is a thing of the devil. Where is that written in the Bible? They claim to know the Bible, but they ignore the wedding at Canaan, where Jesus transformed water into wine so that the celebration could continue. And you know who asked him to do that, Mary, the mother of all Catholics. Anyway, not helping in or attending the feast of the various patron saints in the parish insults people. These are the occasions that we, as a group, as Hispanics, celebrate the various nations represented here. To reject this is, in a way, to reject our Hispanic roots.

In other words, for all its effort to bridge the global and the local, the CCR can increase, rather than ameliorate, tensions within the territorially bound and hierarchically organized parish, tensions that have been aggravated by globalization and transnational migration.

Notes

1. Interview with Zamora, May 6, 1992, Iglesia El Carmen, San Salvador, conducted by Philip Williams. Zamora's *campos de misión* (mission fields) closely resemble the Assemblies of God strategy of *campos blancos* (open fields), in which members establish prayer groups and new congregations, with support from the mother church (Williams 1996).
2. All quotations from individuals in El Salvador, except Zamora, are from interviews conducted by Francisca Flores, Ileana Gómez, Anna Peterson, and Norys Ramirez between June 1997 and December 1998.
3. All quotations from individuals in New Jersey and Washington, D.C., are from interviews conducted by Carmén Albertos, Carlos Ruben Ramirez, and Manuel Vasquez between June 1996 and December 1998.
4. Interviews in Brooklyn were conducted by Manuel Vásquez on December 10–12, 1999.

Chapter 10

Anna Peterson, Manuel Vásquez, and Philip Williams

The Global and the Local

The contributors to this book have explored some of the diverse ways that Salvadoran and Peruvian Christians, in their home societies and in the United States, negotiate the pressures generated by contemporary social, political, and cultural changes. We have focused on the ways that people draw on religious beliefs, practices, and organizations to build and sustain individual and collective identities in the face of transitions to democracy, economic restructuring, transnational migration, and other globalizing dynamics. In order to highlight some of religion's specific roles, we divided the book into three parts. Part 1 explored the varied and sometimes contradictory ways that religion intertwines with personal and local concerns, including changing gender relations, the redrawing of private and public spheres, and the redefinition of traditions and local identities. The chapters in part 2 showed how the infrapolitics of everyday life, in which religion plays a central role, can make lasting, albeit often subtle, contributions to the strengthening of civil societies and democratic institutions. Part 3 took an even wider viewpoint to explore the movement of religious discourses and practices across national borders, as Peruvians and Salvadorans in the United States sustain multiple relations in both their sending and receiving societies.

This tripartite division is useful for organizational purposes and to illuminate some of Christianity's distinctive social, political, and cultural roles in the Americas. However, the different levels of analysis are not separate and self-contained. Rather, personal, local, national, and global experiences are intertwined in complex, dynamic ways. To focus on just one level of analysis is to miss other aspects of religion's interplay with society, especially given the increasing fragmentation and interdependence brought about by globalization. In this final chapter, we hope to draw out some of the common themes that inform our case studies and link our different levels of analysis. More than just summarizing our findings, this conclusion underscores core theoretical and methodological issues that are raised by the changing place of religion in the Americas and thus suggests directions for future research on these themes.

Religious Pluralism

The chapters in this book demonstrate emphatically that there are multiple ways of being Christian in El Salvador, Peru, and the United States. Both Catholicism and Protestantism show a great deal of internal variation in terms of theology, practice, organization, and approaches to the predicaments of everyday life and politics. Within Catholicism, we found at least four major models or types of theology, pastoral work, and practice. The first encompasses the practices connected to traditional popular Catholicism. This model is strongly marked by the dialectic of penance and celebration built around patron saints and Marian apparitions. While this type of Catholicism is central to the construction and maintenance of community life in the countryside, it has also found its way to urban centers, both in Latin America and the United States, where it has helped strengthen collective identity in the face of dislocation. The second cluster of practices can be described as "reformed Catholicism." It is strongly influenced by the Second Vatican Council and especially the faith-life link. Within this way of being Catholic we can place groups like Catholic Action, *cursillos,* and marriage encounters, which stress lay leadership without embracing explicitly sociopolitical agendas. The third type is progressive or liberationist Catholicism, which has played an important role in opposition to conservative regimes in both El Salvador and Peru. The fourth tendency, Charismatic Catholicism, is growing rapidly throughout the Americas, largely because it combines small, intimate groups with sophisticated global communications and other technologies.

Even though a particular cluster might be dominant in a given setting, often as a consequence of local pastoral agents' priorities, all of these ways of being Catholic are present simultaneously in many parishes and dioceses. They do not simply compete but also enter into complex relations of accommodation and cross-fertilization. For example, several chapters show how individuals might sustain multiple engagements: they might participate actively in the celebration of the town's patron saint and later on read the Bible in a CEB or attend a Charismatic assembly. In other cases, believers might bring two or more clusters into dialogue, for instance, injecting a Charismatic style to liberationist initiatives, or attempting to transform devotional practices into explicit acts of social mobilization and resistance (turning the *via crucis* into an indictment of violence in the neighborhood).

Diversity within Catholicism is not just the result of theological and pastoral styles. The organization and degree of centralization in the parish also matter. The parish can be structured hierarchically around the priest or more loosely as a space where different movements meet, and this has consequences for local religious pluralism. We found that in both El Salvador and Peru, especially in urban parishes, there has been a trend toward greater decentralization of pastoral functions in an effort to engage laypeople more fully. For example, in the parish of Our Lady of Peace in Comas, the reorganization of the parish into eight Christian communities has fostered a variety of religious movements, some of which exercise a significant degree of autonomy. The parish of Maria Auxiliadora (Don Rúa) in San Salvador, on the other hand, functions as a kind of super-parish, where movements are the central organizational axes. Don Rúa brings people from various parts of the capital to attend Catholic Charismatic and Neocatechumenate activities. This strategy seems to be successful, as the parish struggles to deal with urban sprawl and to compete against nearby Protestant churches. In the United States, however, an emphasis on movements, especially those with national and transnational bases, can weaken the parish structure and intensify internal conflicts. In particular, the tension between the long-established *cursillo* movement and the upstart Charismatic Renewal can divide Latinos by generations and nationalities, undermining attempts to build multicultural parishes.

The issue of dissent and conflict takes us to a final aspect of the diverse ways of being Catholic: the tension between official and grassroots Catholicism. This relationship is complex, contradictory, and uneven. There is no sharp dichotomy between a hierarchical, clerical, and oppressive official Catholicism and an egalitarian, lay-centered, and emancipatory grassroots Catholicism. Rather, the relations between official and popular religion are fluid and contextual. Sometimes different parties enter into conflict, other times they avoid or ignore each other, and sometimes they cooperate. Neither official nor grassroots Catholicism is of one piece. Each category encompasses interacting levels of practice, and the logic of each can shape, and sometimes constrain, the other. Thus grassroots Catholicism includes local devotions as well as transnational linkages, and official Catholicism contains multiple layers of authority, including parish priests, bishops, national episcopal bodies, and ultimately the Vatican.

A similar diversity is found among and within Protestant churches. Historical denominations such as the Lutheran, Methodist, and Presbyterian churches differ significantly in theology and practice from Pentecostal and neo-Pentecostal churches. Pentecostal churches working among Salvadorans in the Washington area seek the personal conversion of gang members in their struggle against the devil. In the same neighborhoods, Lutherans try to organize immigrants to demand better housing, in a manner reminiscent of progressive Catholicism. However, there is also cross-fertilization among different Protestant groups. Many mainline churches have incorporated some aspects of evangelical style, and some Pentecostal churches have begun to address social concerns like urban services and racial discrimination.

As in the Catholic Church, variations in discourse and practice among Protestants often emerge out of the minister's leadership style and the church's structure. The size of the church matters, as does its degree of bureaucratization. A small storefront church built around a charismatic pastor necessarily differs from congregations that belong to large denominations, such as the Assemblies of God. Both, in turn, differ from media-driven churches like the Universal Church of the Kingdom of God. The degree of indigenization is another key variable shaping theology and pastoral action. For example, some Pentecostal churches in Peru articulate a strongly nationalistic message that may reaffirm indigenous and mestizo identities in ways that would seem totally inappropriate to middle-class Protestant Peruvians, for whom conversion to Protestantism means upward mobility and entry to modernity.

In sum, the various case studies contained in this volume demonstrate the complexity and multiplicity of lived religion in the Americas. This underlines our argument that the study of religion and society in the Americas must be comparative. We need to look not only at differences and similarities among various religions' traditions (in our case between Catholics and Protestants) but also at intra-church variation. These in-depth studies of the "varieties of religious experience," to use William James's phrase, should build on the strong existing tradition of detailed ethnographies in order to illuminate the complexity of lived religious communities, discourses, and practices in the increasing pluralistic context of the Americas.

Multi-Site Research

While it is important to continue sharpening our understanding of everyday, local religion, we need to go beyond phenomenological descriptions, however textured they may be. Globalization, and particularly transnational migration, has made it necessary to link the global and the local by setting up systematic comparisons within and between countries. One important axis for intranational comparisons is degree of urbanization. Throughout the Americas, religious life in the city differs from that in the countryside. For instance, community-building and maintenance concern Peruvians in urban locations like Huaycán and Comas and also in rural settings such as Yungay. However, in Huaycán and Comas, a major issue is the role of religious congregations in the sociopolitical mobilization to carve out and manage *pueblos jóvenes* (new settlements) at the periphery of sprawling Lima. In both cities, people who did not know each other previously, a mixture of poor migrants from the highlands and slightly better-off migrants from other areas of Lima, came together in a common quest to form community. The chaos of urban life, together with a shared sense of dislocation and marginalization, has a leveling effect, overriding class, ethnic, and geographic differences. In this context, the parish, with its multiple ways of being Catholic, offers the space and resources to articulate a strong sense of solidarity and collective identity.

In Yungay, in contrast, people from the same locality work to reweave old traditions in the face of drastic social and natural forces. However, the residents of Yungay must rebuild their community in a rapidly modernizing context that encourages disenchantment, social differentiation, and individualism. Paradoxically, despite the population's common origins, the new community is more fractured along ethnic and class fault lines, which the post–Vatican II emphasis of the Catholic parish has intensified. The situation in Yungay appears on the surface unrelated to, and even in contrast to, that in Huaycán and Comas. However, all are particular expressions of larger social processes, some of which are directly connected to globalization. Yungay is also embedded in the same processes of urbanization (particularly cyclical city-countryside migration) and modernization, which gave rise to Huaycán and Comas. This underlines the importance of not overemphasizing the city-countryside dichotomy. For instance, while the religious field in Morazán is not as fragmented as that in San Salvador, churches in both settings must respond to social dislocation produced by the civil war and its aftermath. More concretely, the problem of defending the family, dramatized by the plight of Salvadoran youths and the rise of gangs, is an overriding concern for Catholic and Protestant churches in both the city and the countryside.

Our study involves comparisons not only within but also between countries. Peru and El Salvador differ significantly in size and ethnic composition, but they also share a number of common processes and features. In both countries, the Catholic Church is shifting away from liberationist approaches that stress the link between religious life and structural social change and toward a stronger emphasis on the sacraments and personal spiritual renewal. In this context, progressive Catholics must renegotiate their self-understanding, pastoral methods, and place in the larger church. They also face changes in their political and social roles, given the end of the dictatorships and human rights abuses that unified moderate and liberationist Catholics. Further, economic changes, such as neoliberal restructuring, have made the physical and psychic survival of self and family a priority, placing serious obstacles to the type of grassroots collective mobilization envisioned by progressive Catholics. This concern for the survival, integrity, and well-being of individuals and their immediate kin has dovetailed with restorationist shifts in global Catholicism. The church today presents itself as an alternative to failed modernity, in both its socialist and capitalist expressions.

Despite progressive Catholicism's loss of hegemony, it is still very much alive in the form of more modest but perhaps more foundational, associational practices and self-help initiatives. Liberationist Catholicism has shed some of its reliance on collective agents like political parties and the state and has begun to address, at personal and local levels, the increasing fragmentation and dislocation produced by globalization (Brooks 1999). Our study also confirms Marjo De Theije's observations that the ideological difference between base communities and Charismatic groups has been overstated. She writes that "participation in religious groups has more to do with Catholic practice in general, with the continuity of 'being Catholic,' than with specific ideological characteristics of alternative groups . . . in the construction of everyday religion within those different groups, the interpenetration of ideological elements from different ideologies takes place with great ease" (De Theije 1999, 122). Thus, while the CCR might be ascendant in terms of visibility, liberationist discourse and practice have become an integral part of the Catholic repertoire. This discourse and practice can be re-radicalized in the future, if conditions require it.

A comparison of Peru and El Salvador also shows that evangelical Protestantism often plays a more nuanced and constructive political role than observers grant. In Morazán and Huaycán, both of which suffer from high levels of political and criminal violence, evangelical churches are helping to repair the torn social fabric. Here the effects of Protestant participation can go deep, to the very foundations of democracy and civil society: the formation of moral and peaceable individuals. Evangelical Protestantism remains contradictory, especially insofar as it sometimes reproduces the authoritarianism that has dominated Latin American politics. Still, Peruvian and Salvadoran evangélicos show that democracy is more than just elections, rationalized institutions, and legal procedures. It involves revisions in cultural and personal identity, transformations in local social relations, and greater participation in all dimensions of the public sphere. This means that religion, as the lingua franca of vast sectors of the population, must play a role if democratic transitions are to succeed.

In both El Salvador and Peru, religion is crucial in the changing attitudes and practices of women and in transformations in family life. Families help construct, alter, and legitimize particular conceptions of democracy and civil society. This dimension of family life takes on special import in the present context of fragile democratic transitions in much of Latin America. The links between family life and democratization are tied to the ways that families help form women's and men's ideas about gender roles and sexuality. Family life helps give meaning to sexual expression and reproduction and assigns roles to those who participate in the activities of child rearing. Women and men carry the attitudes and behaviors learned in the family into the larger society, and changes in gender roles within the family, especially trends toward greater egalitarianism, can contribute to larger processes of democratization.

While all kinds of religious participation influences understandings of and experiences in families, in recent years Catholic parishes have not received as much attention in this regard as evangelical Protestantism. The evangelical emphasis on the private sphere and on the strengthening of traditional family structures has, according to some observers, been a major reason for the growth of Protestantism in Latin America in recent decades. In the common interpretation, evangelicalism makes the family central to religious life and also reinforces the values and behaviors that sustain traditional families. Thus in the face of the multiple threats to individuals and families in the Americas today, evangelical congregations are appealing because they not only provide a refuge but also reinforce the family, that other "haven in a heartless world" (Lasch 1977). While some Protestant congregations in Latin America do indeed follow this model, we found that Protestantism is more diverse than this and that participation in other religious groups, specifically the Catholic Church, can also help strengthen families. Further, as some Protestant and Catholic women have argued, reinforcing traditional patriarchal forms is not the only way to strengthen or support the family. Our research in Peru and El Salvador suggests that both the family and civil society can be strengthened when religious institutions present alternatives to traditional perceptions of the family itself, of gender roles, and of the individual's social responsibilities.

This helps us refine Elizabeth Brusco's (1995) argument about the "reformation" of machismo. While Brusco focuses on evangelical Protestantism's role in curbing machismo, we found that Catholic pastoral involvement can also encourage both women and men to alter their gender identities and behaviors. In both progressive and relatively conservative parishes, Catholic pastoral programs can have many of the same consequences that Brusco and others have described for evangelical Protestants, such as domesticating men and generating more peaceful patterns of behavior. Catholic participation, however, places these private changes squarely in the context of larger communities, including not only the church but also the neighborhood and civil society itself. At least in Latin America, evangelical Protestantism sharply separates the things of God from the corrupting influence of the world. In contrast, Catholicism, especially but not only in the progressive form represented by Christian communities, insists that the things of God must live in and strive to transform the world itself. This theological and ethical principle is clearly evident in the concrete pastoral experiences of the laypeople we interviewed, most of whom viewed their personal changes in terms of a growing commitment to service and participation in the community. This commitment has diverse expressions, from small-scale acts of charity to explicitly political movements for social change. Evangelical Protestant attitudes toward the larger society also take diverse forms, and Protestantism, no less than Catholicism, encourages believers to interpret their daily lives in light of God's word.

Generally, however, Catholic pastoral participation encourages laypeople, especially women, to take leadership roles, develop public speaking skills, and organize groups. By empowering women, Catholic social teaching and participation in church initiatives often lead to a critique of machismo and male dominance in the family. Thus, like neoliberalism, postconciliar Catholicism challenges hierarchical structures and advocates individual assertiveness. Nevertheless, the agency built through the faith-life link is relational, in stark contrast to the atomistic individualism and consumerism that neoliberalism encourages. In other words, in the context of the economic changes wrought by globalization, religion can help bridge tensions between tradition and modernity and between the public and the private spheres.

This reference to globalization takes us beyond international comparisons to a transnational focus on religion's multiple roles in the Americas. The comparative study of immigrant congregations in the United States and churches in El Salvador and Peru has proven especially fruitful because it reveals the artificial nature of the divisions imposed by area studies. These divisions proved useful during the Cold War to understand the specificity of the Latin American case, either through modernization theory or through its nemesis, dependency theory. Today, however, the increasing interconnections generated by globalization and transnationalism have problematized the notion of American exceptionalism and the idea that Latin America is utterly separate from the north. If people's lived experiences and affiliations are simultaneously embedded in their home countries in Latin America and in the United States, then we must develop "bifocal" approaches to be able to make sense of this "in-betweenness" (Rouse 1991). As Ruíz Baía shows, anyone interested in the evolution of gender roles among Peruvian Catholics would do well not just to look at what is happening in Peru, including city-countryside cyclical migration, but also to consider events in Paterson, Washington, Miami, and other places in the Americas where Peruvian immigrants have concentrated. Ruíz Baía also shows that religion is crucial to the emergence of "hybrid identities and cultures" (García Canclini 1995), as Peruvians interact with other Latin American immigrants.

Micro-Macro and Local-Global Links

Implicit in the call to take an inter-American approach is the deeper issue of connecting everyday life to what Daniel Levine has termed "big structures," which include "institutional formations like church, state, or major economic groups." Everyday life and big structures are dialectically related. On the one hand, structures "control real resources, both symbolic and material, which they use to project messages and power over time, space, and social boundaries. Big structures find expression in everyday life as they shape the general contours of opportunity" (Levine 1992, 317–318). On the other hand, these structures are embodied, contested, and re-created in and through the experiences and actions of individuals in their daily struggles to construct and maintain their life world. "Institutions are more than just machines that allocate roles and statuses, that grind out a steady flow of rules, regulations, and edicts. They are also communities of identity and loyalty through which meaning and action are bound together" (1992, 350).

Building on Levine's work, we link grassroots ways of being Christian to large-scale dynamics in the economic, political, cultural, and religious fields. While all the chapters in this book build on specific case studies, they also share a common concern with religion as it is lived by individuals dealing with daily existential predicaments, especially in family and community life. We view local and personal experiences in the context of larger changes, which simultaneously shape and are shaped by what goes on at smaller scales. Unlike Levine, however, we do not see big structures as representing only or even primarily corporate, nation-bound institutions. The nature and place of the state in the context of globalization is the subject of ongoing debate. Some scholars speak of the demise of the sovereign state and its replacement by de-territorialized regimes (Held 1991; Keohane 1995). Others see the state not disappearing but undergoing major transformations that allow it to retain significant power in a simultaneously fragmented and interconnected world marked by a pluralism of authority (Arrighi and Silver 1999; Rosenau 1997). There is consensus, however, that the nation-state is no longer the only logical and natural unit of social analysis. We must also consider other large structures in multiple, interacting, and overlapping spatiotemporal scales, including not only national but also transnational, hemispheric, and global levels, each with its own set of dynamics, actors, practices, and discourses.

Using *big structures* as an umbrella term to capture diverse phenomena raises the danger of losing specificity and analytical rigor. This danger is particularly serious when it comes to characterizing globalization, which too often appears as an anonymous, baffling, and inexorable force that determines, in a single manner, all aspects of social life. As Mittelman (2000, 7) writes, globalization is less a rigid mold than "a domain of knowledge," an interpretive framework that "helps to explain the intricacy and variability of the ways the world is structured. . . . A rubric for myriad phenomena, a globalization framework that *interrelates multiple levels of analysis*—economic, politics, society, and culture. This frame thus elucidates a *coalescence of diverse transnational and domestic structures,* allowing the economy, polity, society, and culture of one locale to penetrate another." It is important to identify concretely the processes involved in globalization: economic restructuring, the crisis of socialism and the ascendance of liberal democracy, the emergence of transnational populations, the rise of global media, and changes in world Catholicism. Moreover, we need to specify the actors that spur and manage these processes, helping to embody them, in uneven and contradictory ways, in everyday life. These actors include multilateral organizations like the World Bank and the International Monetary Fund, multinational corporations, the state, national elites, nongovernmental organizations, global churches and their missionary and charitable initiatives, and even immigrants and their grassroots forms of transnationalism.

Despite their complexity and rapidity, global changes are not disembodied processes relevant only to cosmopolitan elites. These changes wield a powerful impact on everyday life, transforming gender roles, exacerbating generational conflicts, and limiting and creating possibilities for community life. Determination, however, does not go in just one direction. Everyday forms of citizenship fostered by religion, such as local, national, and transnational social movements, respond creatively to larger processes, helping individuals and their families and neighborhoods resist or accommodate.

This points to the importance of exploring the changing nature of local communities and their connections to global processes. As anthropologist Arjun Appadurai argues, locality is not what it used to be: "There are some brute facts about the world of the twentieth century that any ethnographer must confront. Central among these facts is the changing social, territorial, and cultural reproduction of group identity. As groups migrate, regroup in new locations, reconstruct their histories, and reconfigure their ethnic projects, the ethno in ethnography takes on a slippery, nonlocalized quality, to which the descriptive practices of anthropology will have to respond" (Appadurai 1996, 48). To respond to the reality that "groups are no longer tightly territorialized, spatially bounded, historically unselfconscious, or culturally homogeneous," Appadurai invites us to engage in a "cosmopolitan" or "macro-" ethnography, whose task will be "the unraveling of a conundrum: What is the nature of locality as a lived experience in a globalized, deterritorialized world?" (Appadurai 1996, 52). We have sought to construct a robust cosmopolitan ethnography of religion in the Americas. Thus, rather than collecting ethnographies of disparate and self-contained places, we tried to use our case studies to articulate flexible methodologies and theoretical approaches that make it possible to examine religion's roles in the globalization of the local and the localization of the global.

Toward a Robust Methodological Pluralism

Given the diversity of religious expressions and the intertwining of everyday life and big structures, and of the local and the global, it is increasingly difficult to analyze the role of religion by a simple appeal to a pathology model. This model has two versions. In the modernization-secularization version, religion is a desperate, mostly impotent response to the anomie generated by incomplete modernization or uneven development. In the crudest Marxist version, religion is just a reflection of contradictions in the economic base, an ideological tool to reinforce and reproduce class oppression. Even a more nuanced Gramscian reading of religion, which recognizes its potential role in building counter-hegemonies, still reduces it to class dynamics. As we have seen, religion in the Americas is polyvocal, operating at multiple social levels and interacting dialectically with small and large-scale economic, political, and cultural dynamics.

In light of the limitations of modernization and Marxist approaches to religion and social change in the Americas, new perspectives have emerged in recent years. In a recent edited volume, Prokopy and Smith (1999) have proposed two "new theoretical lenses." The first is the theory of religious economies, which has been strongly influenced by rational choice models. The notion that religious institutions, for all their claims of serving other-worldly goals, behave like economic firms seeking to maximize gains and minimize costs, particularly in competitive markets, can be traced back to classic theorists like Adam Smith and Max Weber.

Drawing more immediately from a tradition that has had a considerable impact in sociology of religion in the United States (Finke and Stark 1992; Iannaccone 1995; Young 1997), Anthony Gill seeks to understand changes in the Latin American religious field by focusing on the means-ends, strategic behavior of religious actors in competition to shore up and extend their clienteles. More specifically, Gill focuses on the decisions and choices made by Catholic bishops to deal with the rapid growth of Protestantism in the context of political changes in the 1960s and 1970s. According to Gill, "where competition for the souls [of] the popular classes was fierce, a pastoral strategy of a preferential option for the poor was adopted. . . . Where competition was minimal, bishops downplayed the preferential option for the poor and sought to maintain cordial relations with the military rulers so as to preserve traditional perquisites" (1998, 71). The key strength of Gill's approach is its comparative and synthetic nature, which allows scholars to formulate relatively simple hypotheses that can be tested with multiple sites and studies. Thus, Gill goes beyond the confines of the ethnographic work undertaken in the late 1980s and early 1990s, which often stress the specificity of a given site.

However, what rational choice theory gains in breadth, it loses in depth. Paradoxically, although the model borrows heavily from micro-sociological approaches such as exchange and game theory, it has thus far not been applied to lived, popular religion. The focus thus far has been on institutions such as church and state, to the exclusion of what happens at the grassroots. In fact, Gill assumes unproblematically that the religious field is determined by religious institutions. As our study shows, institutions like the national episcopal bodies are both embedded in large-scale transnational and global dynamics and also in dialectic relation to everyday practice. The configuration of religious field is the product of the complex interplay of local, national, hemispheric, and global spatiotemporal levels of activity. To privilege one of the levels impoverishes our understanding of religion and society in the Americas. However, even if we were to give Gill the benefit of the doubt and grant that institutions play a preponderant role, his reading of religious institutions is still too simplistic, because he makes them synonymous with religious elites. And in order to fulfill the demands of rational choice's methodological individualism, he construes these elites as a monolithic actor. This allows Gill to make the unwarranted assumption that the various episcopal bodies have unified sets of interests that single-handedly determine the course of action and configuration of national and even regional churches. Berryman (1999), Vásquez (1999), and Vásquez and Peterson in this book offer alternative, more nuanced understandings of the operation of religious institutions, taking into account their organizational structures, modes of leadership, theologies, habits, and internal tensions. Institutions, not just individuals, also reflect multiple ways of being Christian. In sum, rational choice theory tends to confuse the "representation of reality with the reality of the representation," as Bourdieu puts it (1984, 482), flattening the complexity of socioreligious reality to make it fit predetermined theoretical postulates.

The second main model that Prokopy and Smith identify is subcultural identity theory. In contrast to rational choice models, this theory directly addresses religious complexity and pluralism. A major strength of subcultural identity theory is that it does not make religious pluralism synonymous with secularization—that is, with the declining importance of religion in the public sphere. This resonates with what we stated in the introduction. Traditional religious actors such as the Catholic Church, particularly in its liberationist wings, are challenged by globalization, the transition to democracy, and the crisis of socialism. However, this has not translated into a retrenchment of religion from the public sphere. To the contrary, religion has become even more central at the everyday level, due to a combination of deregulation of the religious field and the growing micro-pressures generated by national, continental, and global changes. Subcultural identity theory argues that in highly differentiated social settings such as cities, people are compelled to distinguish themselves from others in order to maintain a sense of self. To define their uniqueness, people use markers, particularly religious markers, which help them order their surroundings and locate themselves within a special, sacred space. Greater social differentiation and religious pluralism increase the need to set and patrol sharply demarcated religious boundaries. Thus, subcultural identity theory provides elegant explanations to both why pluralization does not lead to secularization and why religious traditions with high symbolic thresholds (like Pentecostalism) succeed.

For all its attention to the role religion plays in the articulation of contested individual and collective identities, subcultural identity theory still offers a limited picture of the religious field in the Americas. The theory fails to explain the pervasiveness of religious cross-fertilization and syncretism that our case studies document. While there are analytically distinct ways of being Catholic, in real life there are no hard, fixed boundaries. Believers may engage in several ways of being Catholic or they might explore two or three of them in creative combinations, depending on the situation or the problem at hand. The Charismatic Renewal, which according to subcultural identity theory would have a high threshold, can be a separate movement that makes significant demands on members in terms of time and commitment and also a style that informs various parish activities such as *cursillos* and even CEBs. This issue of cross-fertilization also goes for interdenominational relations. Pentecostal Protestantism and Charismatic Catholicism have a tense, contradictory relationship that includes competition as well as accommodation and cross-fertilization.

In the post–Vatican II spirit of ecumenism, we also found cases like the Lutherans in San Salvador and Washington, where liberationist Catholicism has strongly influenced Protestant ministry.

These are not isolated examples. Indeed, a great deal of the pluralism, complexity, and heterogeneity in the religious field in the Americas emerges from the relative fluidity of religious practices, affiliation, and choices. And this does not just concern Christianity, since a range of different religious traditions, including African-based, indigenous, and New Age religions, not only compete but cross-fertilize each other. Some scholars go as far as to argue that all cultures and religions are syncretic (Rosaldo 1995; Stewart and Shaw 1994). Even without accepting that generalized claim, it is undeniable that Latin American religions are strongly syncretic, blending in various degrees Iberian, African, and New World traditions. Transnational migration and other global connections add more layers of hybridity and contribute to the region's growing religious pluralism. By overstating the strength and rigidity of religious boundaries, subcultural identity theory might thus be missing a significant dimension of the religious field in the Americas. Part of the problem with subcultural identity is that it attempts to build a general theory of religion in Latin America derived from the special case of U.S. evangelical fundamentalism (Smith 1998). Fundamentalism has shown remarkable resilience in the face of so-called secular humanism, precisely by drawing strong boundaries and opposing itself to the corrupt outside world. Despite its high visibility, though, U.S. fundamentalism appears rather atypical in a hemispheric perspective.

We have sought to offer a more comprehensive and flexible view of religion and social change in the Americas, one which can account for the differences and similarities within and among Christian traditions. We have also kept in mind the larger institutional and structural contexts in which local practices are situated. These big structures, particularly when it comes to institutions, are not monolithic, naked facts detached and standing over and against daily struggles to renew self and to build family and community life. This has been our main critique of the rational choice approach to institutional analysis.

We believe that our global-local approach, for lack of a better name, provides a more nuanced and synthetic analysis of the religious field in the Americas than other emerging perspectives. However, we also recognize that social and religious complexity in the hemisphere belies any attempt to construct a single totalizing theory. Thus, we want to suggest that scholars of religion in the continent adopt a robust methodological pluralism. Borrowing from philosopher of science Imre Lakatos (1999), we can describe the study of religion and society in the Americas as having multiple "research programs," multiple analytical clusters, each with its own social epistemologies and ontologies and its own methods and conceptions of what counts as significant social facts. Each cluster continues to develop as an ongoing project, attempting to refine its methodologies and expand its range of application, sometimes in competition and other times cross-fertilizing with other clusters, not unlike intra- and interchurch relations. For example, we may consider Gill's rational choice approach to church-state relations as a further refinement of the institutionalist research program first developed by Thomas Bruneau, Brian Smith, and Daniel Levine. Subcultural identity theory, on the other hand, can be seen as an extension of the grassroots research program exemplified by the work of John Burdick, Rowan Ireland, Elizabeth Brusco, Carol Ann Drogus, and others.

It is important to recognize the existence and validity of multiple research programs, each with its own range of application and its own strengths and weaknesses. No theory can account for all socioreligious facts. This acknowledgment of fallibility, however, is not in itself sufficient. Two dangers remain. The first one is an uncritical theoretical and methodological eclecticism that borrows piecemeal from various perspectives without regard to epistemological constraints. We should not assume that approaches are neatly reducible to each other or that they can be linked without rigorous theoretical and empirical work. On the other hand, the second danger is that of viewing different approaches as totally incommensurable. Rather, the aim should be to see how the various research programs can inform each other; how, for example, institutional perspectives help understand constraints, opportunities, and choices on the ground and how grassroots practices challenge or reproduce organizations. A focus on local and global links, with various levels in between, can help bring various approaches in the study of religion in the Americas into fruitful conversation.

Methodological pluralism is not methodological anarchy. It is not the case that anything goes at a particular juncture. As scholars of religion in the Americas, we should strive, however imperfectly, to assess various research programs on the basis of their simplicity, elegance, coherence, capacity to deal effectively with complexity and perceived anomalies, and potential for cross-fertilization with other models. In this way, we can gradually extend explanatory power to more and more areas of interaction among religion, culture, and society. Still, the aim is not totality or universality but rather comprehensiveness, flexibility, richness, and rigor.

Limitations and Prospects

In keeping with the claim that all research programs are fallible, we recognize certain limitations in our global-local approach. First, we began with a rather static conception of congregations. We assumed that we would encounter relatively homogeneous churches, sharply defined in terms of territory and composition. However, we quickly found that there is considerable diversity within any given parish, as the case of Yungay underlines. We also found cases like Don Rúa in San Salvador, where pastoral action was sustained mainly by movements that drew participants from far beyond the parish boundaries and that received resources and inspiration from national and transnational organizations. The idea that congregations have fixed internal and external boundaries also made it difficult to study Peruvian and Salvadoran immigrants in the United States. While Peruvians are the third largest Latino group in Paterson and are concentrated in certain parts of the metropolitan area, they worship with larger groups such as Puerto Ricans and Dominicans. In this sort of multicultural setting, it is sometimes difficult to identify national congregations. In Paterson, we had to study more congregations than we had anticipated in order to include enough Peruvian Protestants. In the case of Salvadorans, we had less difficulty identifying fairly self-contained churches, because they are the largest Latino group in the Washington area. However, tracing transnational links proved challenging, because many of the Salvadorans we interviewed in Washington came from small towns like Intipucá and Chirilagua, which were not among the sites selected in El Salvador. Another link we could not trace, but would have liked to, is the connection between a Salvadoran Pentecostal congregation in Washington and its sister church among Salvadoran agricultural workers in South Carolina, with whom it shares a back-and-forth movement of members and pastors. By the same token, a community of worship links Peruvians in Paterson with *hermandades* in Atlanta, Miami, Los Angeles, and even Montreal. Given the limitations of time and resources, we could not follow all these circuits to our satisfaction.

In light of these limitations, we would suggest that future global-local research go beyond the traditional ethnographic focus on a distinct locality, such as the congregation, and examine fluid, urban-rural and transnational religious networks. In order to embed the local in the global and study the local struggles to negotiate, reproduce, and contest the global, it is necessary to explore the ongoing interactions among various spatiotemporal levels. Focusing on situated but open-ended religious circuits makes it possible to study variations, cross-fertilizations, and evolutions across various points in the networks. Vásquez and Gómez use Castells's notion of network to understand the work of Pentecostal churches with Salvadoran youth gangs. Future work on religion and society in the Americas can benefit greatly from the emphasis in current social movement theory (Alvarez, Dagnino, and Escobar 1998; Keck and Sikkink 1998) on the role of grassroots networks in building national and transnational civil societies (Rudolph and Piscatori 1997).

A second issue is that of access to congregations. We had considerable difficulty in gaining access to some Pentecostal churches and to the Catholic Neocatechumenate in Peru, El Salvador, and the United States. A few examples will illustrate the kinds of obstacles we encountered. In Washington, one of our research assistants was rebuked in public by a Pentecostal pastor, insisting that she accept Jesus on the spot. When the researcher politely declined, she was unceremoniously kicked out of the church. In another small, independent Pentecostal church in El Salvador, our assistant was told, after several weeks of accompanying the group, that because "the devil works in mysterious ways," she had to leave. Similarly, researchers in El Salvador were shut out of the Neocatechumenate's special evening Mass in Don Rúa. In this case, the doors were literally closed in their faces.

These experiences raise at least two questions. First, which churches get studied? How representative are the Pentecostal congregations that have been studied by other scholars? The churches that permit access to researchers are not always the most representative. We met with Assemblies of God leaders in El Salvador and pursued various potential research sites. We chose the Assemblies church La Redención in part because its head pastor, Rev. Noé Pérez, was receptive to foreign scholars. In this and other respects, he is atypical of Pentecostal pastors. Pérez is a university-trained medical doctor, with liberal political views and some skepticism toward his denomination's leadership. Although his church is dynamic and fascinating, it does not exhaust the entirety, or even the mainstream, of Salvadoran Pentecostalism. On the other hand, the presence of an eclectic pastor does not always make the congregation itself less representative, and the surveys and interviews from the San Salvador parish did not differ widely from those of the Assemblies church we studied in San Francisco Gotera. Further, while the Assemblies pastor in Gotera was more typical of Salvadoran Pentecostal ministers in his education and political views, he was also much less open to sociological research. Thus he permitted our presence in the church and allowed us to conduct surveys and interviews, but he did not speak with us at any length or otherwise enrich our picture of the congregation. Pastor Pérez, in contrast, spoke with us at length on several occasions, greatly enhancing our understanding of his church and its place in both the local community and in the larger arena of Salvadoran Pentecostalism.

In sum, both researchers and readers should keep in mind not only that every religious community is distinctive but also that there is a certain amount of (sometimes unconscious) self-selection involved in the process of matching researchers to sites. Fieldworkers do not just select the ideal congregation or community for their work but rather negotiate their presence and participation every step of the way. This need not be only a limiting factor. Our close relations with pastoral agents and laypeople in some congregations provided mutual benefit, as when a research associate in El Salvador, Norys Ramírez, helped Pastor Pérez's congregation compile a history of the church. Our interviews provided the foundation for a document that has helped church members not only understand their collective history better but also reflect upon important social and theological questions.

In addition to the question of which churches get studied, researchers must raise the issue of who is permitted to study them. Clearly, the characteristics of the congregation and its leadership matter. So do the characteristics of the researchers, including gender, nationality, educational preparation, professional position, and religious affiliation. On several occasions, the presence of one of the principal investigators from the United States facilitated access to a church for researchers in Peru and El Salvador. In other cases, the opposite was true. For example, one pastor in Peru mistook one of the principal investigators for a foreign missionary attempting to "steal his flock." Moreover, both pastoral agents and laypeople relate differently to researchers from the United States and those from their own country, and these differences inevitably enter into interview responses. Our fieldwork, in other words, is reflective: the identity of researchers and their relations to the research subjects affect the outcomes, even prior to analysis. A crucial factor in this process is the researcher's religious identity. A number of questions are relevant here. There are both gains and losses when a researcher is part of the religious tradition she studies. Some evangelicals, in particular, believe that only an active member of the congregation under study should have the kind of intimate access required for fieldwork. Many scholars, on the other hand, believe that the researcher should maintain a certain distance from the community under study.

Another issue concerns the researcher's academic credentials. Does having a doctorate facilitate or hinder ethnographic work among religious congregations? In a working-class Latino church in the United States, for example, one of the principal investigators attended a Pentecostal *culto* in which the pastor, aware of his visit, asserted, "Here we are not doctors, lawyers, or intellectuals. Here we are all working class, busboys, waiters, gardeners, and construction workers. You see, diplomas will get you nowhere in the kingdom of God. Books, if they are not the Bible, will get in the way of your salvation by Jesus." These questions are part of the larger issue of the relation between researcher and subject and between outsider and insider. Too often, scholars of religion in the Americas have assumed that this relation is unproblematic enough to ignore when presenting data. If the goal is to map out the multiple roles religion plays in the articulation of everyday life in a globalized setting, we believe that it is necessary to examine the impact of this relation in the production of our knowledge.

A final and especially difficult challenge is dealing with power asymmetries between scholars based in the United States and those based in Latin America. All too often, Latin Americans work merely as research assistants, viewed by the principal investigators as, at best, junior partners with little to contribute to the crafting of the project, the analysis of the data, or the writing of the final product. This situation not only exploits the researchers but also impoverishes the process and the results of the research. Against this tendency, we included all members of the research team at various stages of the project, from planning meetings to the writing of this book, which includes a number of chapters written or co-written by Latin American researchers. This international, interdisciplinary approach presents logistical problems. No doubt we would have produced this volume more quickly if it had been written by the principal investigators alone. Given the strong push to publish or perish, this has consequences for young scholars who would like to work collaboratively but would also like to get jobs and tenure. On the other hand, the collaborative model is well-established in Latin America, where theses for the *licenciatura* degree almost always have two or more coauthors and where jointly written articles, reports, and monographs are the rule rather than the exception. This reflects not only a philosophical position in favor of collaborative work but also the practical fact that few intellectuals in Latin America can devote themselves full time to research and writing. In the face of limited time and few resources, it makes sense to combine forces. Even in the relatively flush situation facing North American academics, a collective approach can enrich the process and results of research in multiple ways. We end, then, with a final expression of gratitude to our coworkers and the hope that the process and the results of our collective efforts can provide some direction for further work on religion in the Americas.

Appendix

Research Sites

El Salvador

Mejicanos

Mejicanos, a working-class area a few miles north of San Salvador is both a suburb of San Salvador and a separately incorporated municipality, the third most populous in the department of San Salvador. Mejicanos had 130,000 residents in 1992, according to the government census (the entire San Salvador metropolitan area has a population of 1.8 million). Mejicanos was largely rural until the 1950s or 1960s, when it began urbanizing as a result of the arrival of migrants (from the countryside farther from San Salvador) seeking opportunities in the capital city. Of the present population, only about 20 percent are descendants of the original residents, and only about 10 percent of the residents currently live in the shrinking rural areas on the margins of the municipality. With urbanization has come cultural transformation, from indigenous communities to the *mestizaje* characteristic of El Salvador's cities. In the 1980s Mejicanos entered a stage of more rapid growth with the arrival of a large number of people displaced by the civil war. This most recent wave of migration helped give the municipality its high population density, which, added to the state's lack of will to attend to the metropolitan area, has contributed to a scarcity of basic services. Currently the problems that residents cite most often include delinquency, poverty, poor basic services, gangs, drug abuse, and violence.

Iglesia San Francisco

The main Catholic parish in Mejicanos is the Iglesia San Francisco de Asís. San Francisco was founded in the early 1970s, with base communities as the core of pastoral work. The political involvement of many parishioners led to persecution during the late 1970s and early 1980s, and in 1979 the parish priest, Octavio Ortiz, was assassinated by the National Guard. His replacement was killed less than a year later. This violence still marks the church's self-understanding and its commitment to social change. Pastoral work in San Francisco Mejicanos today, as in much of El Salvador, finds itself torn between a drive to regroup and strengthen the church as an institution and attention to the country's many urgent social problems. The parish is organized by zone and by *pastorales* (ministries), with activities on almost every day of the week. Passionist priests administer the parish, with assistance from about 150 lay pastoral agents in areas such as liturgy, catechism, social projects, base communities, women's groups, and ministries to the sick. Its traditional emphasis on CEBs has continued, albeit without the intensity and the political polarization of the 1980s and with a more "ecclesial" focus.

Iglesia La Redención

The Assemblies of God (Asambleas de Dios) is the largest Protestant denomination in El Salvador (and the largest Pentecostal denomination worldwide). Among several Assemblies of God churches in Mejicanos, one of the most successful is Iglesia La Redención: Expresión Máxima del Perdón (Redemption, Greatest Expression of Forgiveness). La Redención began in the 1970s in a different part of Mejicanos; it moved to its current setting in the Montreal district of Mejicanos in early 1996. From an average of fifteen to twenty-five adult members in the 1980s, the church has grown today to encompass several hundred regular participants in Sunday services and other activities. The church's core pastoral strategy is "family growth groups" *(grupos familiares de crecimiento),* which makes families the key unit of evangelization. The pastor and deacons hold educational and leadership activities every day of the week, and most church members are involved in at least one activity in addition to the Sunday *culto* (service). La Redención's pastor, Dr. Noé Pérez, grew up Pentecostal in western El Salvador and has been an Assemblies of God minister since 1980. After ministering to several other small congregations, Pérez came to La Redención in the mid-1990s and has overseen a large increase in both membership and activity level. More explicitly than many Assemblies pastors, Pérez seeks to unite progressive social concerns with an evangelical emphasis on church growth.

San Miguelito

San Miguelito is an established working-class and lower-middle-class barrio north of downtown San Salvador. It includes a large indoor/outdoor market, a number of small businesses, schools, offices of a number of nongovernmental organizations (including, at least for a time in the late 1990s, the FMLN), and many churches, including a number of small and large Pentecostal congregations. Most churches in the neighborhood draw the majority of their members from outside the immediate neighborhood, in part because it is easily reached by bus from other parts of the city.

Iglesia Don Rúa

The largest church in San Miguelito is the Roman Catholic parish of María Auxiliadora. The parish, commonly known as Don Rúa, was founded by Archbishop Luis Chávez y González in 1953, with the present church building inaugurated in 1969. The church, run by Salesian priests, attracts both nearby residents and people from other parts of the metropolitan area. Much of its appeal comes from the parish's reputation as a center for movements associated with the "new evangelization," especially the Catholic Charismatic Renewal and the Neocatechumenate. The parish also has active youth ministries and evangelization programs, mostly organized by lay leaders, including programs for youth, liturgy, families, "irregular" marriages (with the purpose of "regularizing" them), prayer and Bible study meetings, and social projects such as a clinic, a school (the Colegio María Auxiliadora), and sewing and cooking classes run by the women's group, the Damas Salesianas (Salesian Ladies). The parish is a center for the Neocatechumenate, which has around nine hundred participants involved in daily trainings and weekly meetings, and the Catholic Charismatic Renewal, which involves its hundreds of participants in step-by-step education as well as weekly liturgies.

Iglesia La Resurrección

The "historic" or "mainline" Protestant churches, which have been present in Latin America in small numbers since the nineteenth century, share many theological and historical features with Pentecostalism. Politically and liturgically, however, they have more in common with progressive Catholicism. Many maintain strong ties to churches in Europe and the United States. This is especially true of La Resurrección, the largest and oldest Lutheran congregation in El Salvador and the center for Lutheran administrative, educational, and pastoral activities throughout the country. La Resurrección was founded in 1972 as an affiliate of the conservative Missouri Lutheran Synod, from which it later separated, primarily over the issue of female ministry. The congregation's work on behalf of war refugees, victims of human rights abuses, and marginal communities, and its leaders' outspoken criticism of government abuses have both given the church its high public profile and drawn many of its members. This activism reflects the commitment of Bishop Medardo Gómez, who began denouncing human rights abuses and initiating programs to help victims as the civil war deepened in the 1980s and who spearheaded close ties to progressive Catholic groups and social movements in El Salvador and to development and solidarity groups in the United States and Europe. These international links helped publicize the church's work, provide funds, and protect its members at least partially from the threats and harassment that faced all progressive activists in El Salvador during the war. Much like progressive Catholics, Salvadoran Lutherans today face special challenges in adapting to a postwar situation. As part of the church's transition, leaders are working to adapt Lutheran theology and religious identity to the Salvadoran situation, particularly in the context of the church's commitment to social justice. Evangelization is also receiving greater attention; while La Resurrección remains the heart of Lutheran pastoral work in El Salvador, church leaders have made efforts to train pastors and found congregations elsewhere, particularly in smaller towns outside the capital.

San Francisco Gotera, Morazán Province

San Francisco Gotera is the capital of the department (province) of Morazán in northeastern El Salvador. The city has a population of about twenty thousand, which grew significantly during the late 1970s and 1980s as a result of the influx of refugees from rural areas of the province. Northern Morazán was a stronghold for the Ejército Revolucionario del Pueblo (ERP, one of five armies constituting the FMLN during the war) and a major battleground during the civil war. The presence of a large army barracks gave Gotera the appearance of a garrison town during the war. Today the town is peaceful, with most residents employed in small businesses and markets; surrounding villages are largely agricultural. The city of San Miguel to the south has been altered dramatically by the immigration of many residents to the United States and the influence of visiting immigrants and their money. Gotera reveals much less of this transnational flavor, although U.S. influence is evident in a number of ways, including the presence of youth gangs.

Parish of San Francisco

The parish of San Francisco Gotera today encompasses a blend of styles of Catholicism. Traditional Catholicism in the area focuses on fiestas for patron saints and similar rites. Beginning around 1970, however, several Sisters of St. Claire arrived and began forming Bible study groups and base Christian communities in the town and surrounding villages. The Clarisas lived in San Francisco Gotera but worked with residents of the numerous villages in the area. They also started educational and agricultural training programs with peasants, and social and political concerns became increasingly central to pastoral work in and around Gotera. Beginning in the late 1970s, political violence forced a sharp reduction in pastoral work in the area, although the Clarisas remained, primarily assisting communities affected by war and refugees from the north. The most active sectors of the parish currently are in the wards that emerged out of refugee settlements, where community organizations based on church affiliation have been created. Today, base communities and Bible study groups remain central to the pastoral work of the parish, which is still carried out largely by the Clarisas along with Franciscan priests.

Assemblies of God

Gotera served as a meeting point for many Pentecostals who had to flee their places of origin elsewhere in Morazán. The Assemblies of God in Gotera has served as a social base for evangelical families dispersed by the violence, although the church offered spiritual rather than material assistance (in contrast to the Catholic Church). The church began with 30–50 members, but presently has 400–500 steady members, due in large part to continuous evangelizing work carried out despite the war. At present, the Assemblies church in Gotera has become a vibrant center for evangelization and outreach to other parts of the province. Besides the traditional focus on personal conversion, the congregation has undertaken many social projects such as the expansion of the temple, building the children's church, and building a clinic.

Base Christian Communities of Ciudad Segundo Montes, Morazán Province

The part of Morazán province north of Gotera, across the Río Lempa, is populated mostly by small farmers and sharecroppers. The area was hit hard by the political violence of the late 1970s and early 1980s, and many villages were abandoned. The largest mass repopulation in Morazán occurred in January 1990, when approximately eight thousand refugees returned to the abandoned village of Meanguera, which they renamed in honor of Segundo Montes, one of the Jesuits killed by the army during the November offensive. The core of organized religious life in the repopulation is grassroots Christian communities, with most pastoral work undertaken by lay leaders. Ciudad Segundo Montes is divided into five sectors, and each sector is coordinated by a team of three to fifteen catechists. Their efforts include a variety of projects. Every

Sunday, pastoral messages are transmitted over the community radio for the entire repopulation, and progressive priests offer Masses at different intervals, perhaps every two weeks in the bigger sectors. When there is no Mass, delegates of the word offer celebrations of the word. There are also traditional celebrations of Christ the King (Cristo Rey) and Pentecost, as well as celebrations of the Vía Crucis (Stations of the Cross) and other celebrations during Lent and Holy Week. One of the most well-attended religious events in the community is the celebration of the anniversary of Romero's assassination on March 24.

Peru

Comas

Located in the Northern Cone of Greater Metropolitan Lima, Comas is one of the largest municipal districts in Peru, with a population of more than 400,000. The first migrant families arrived in Comas in the late 1950s, and the government officially created the municipal district of Comas in 1959. Since then, Comas has grown steadily in territory and population. During the 1970s and 1980s, struggles over property rights and basic services spawned an array of popular movements in the district, including the *comedores populares,* an effort to provide poor women with collective strategies for confronting their subsistence needs, which spread throughout Lima. In recent years, Comas has changed from a squatter settlement to a bustling municipal district, and the level of community participation has declined, although *comedores populares* and *vaso de leche* groups addressing subsistence needs remain numerous.

The Catholic Church

Our Lady of Peace parish, founded by Canadian Oblates in 1959, is the oldest parish in Comas. Its early pastoral initiatives emphasized family and community. In 1968 the Oblates introduced an innovative program called *paternidad responsable* (responsible parenthood) for parents wanting their children to take their First Communion. During the 1980s it was replaced by *catequesis familiar* (family catechism). Both programs increased lay participation and strengthened the sense of community among participants. In 1980 a plan to encourage the establishment of Christian communities divided the parish into eight sectors and made each responsible for organizing pastoral programs. To facilitate the decentralization, the parish also began training lay celebrants in 1986. The *celebrantes* received training in administering the sacraments, preaching, and liturgy. Many other lay leaders were active in local social movements throughout the 1970s and 1980s. In the 1990s the parish became less closely identified with popular movements but continued to promote social programs such as a medical clinic, fifteen *comedores,* a technical college, and free legal and psychological counseling.

Evangelical Churches

Evangelicals, among the first wave of settlers to Comas, became active in the district beginning in 1960. Early on, evangelicals worshiped together in their homes, some of them associated with larger "mother" churches in Lima. Today, there are eighty-seven evangelical churches in Comas, with evangelicals representing 5.6 percent of the district's total population (INEI, 1993). The larger denominations include the Assemblies of God, the Peruvian Evangelical Church (Iglesia Evangélica Peruana, IEP), and the Christian Missionary Alliance (Alianza Cristiana y Misionera, ACM). We also interviewed pastors and members of two smaller denominations, the Methodist Church and the Peruvian Evangelical Pentecostal Church (IPP), founded in the late 1950s after splitting from the Assemblies of God.

Huaycán

Huaycán was established on July 15, 1984, as a result of a "planned invasion" by 2,000 homeless families from several eastern districts of Lima. Despite conflicts with the municipal government, Huaycán grew rapidly from 22,000 in 1985 to some 70,000 by 1990. The population is young, with 63 percent of the population under twenty-four and less than 10 percent over forty (Centro Ideas, 1991). Despite their precarious economic conditions, most residents would like to stay in Huaycán while improving their living conditions. Some employment opportunities have developed in Huaycán, including micro-enterprises and a new industrial park, although the town remains a bedroom community. A local development agency was created in 1995 to provide support for small businesses and micro-enterprises and community banks.

The Catholic Church

The Catholic Church worked actively to build community and solidarity with the poor in Huaycán's early days. In 1992, in the context of growing violence and fear, the parish launched a five-year pastoral plan calling for the formation of CEBs, with a goal of decentralizing pastoral work in the parish and increasing lay participation. The plan called for the establishment of CEBs in all Huaycán's zones by 1998, but the shortage of trained lay leaders, combined with the growing economic crisis, kept progress slow and uneven. By 1997 CEBs were well established in a few zones, barely functioning in several, and nonexistent in others. Given the mixed progress in promoting CEBs, in 1997 the parish launched a new effort to establish CEBs by bringing them closer to people in their everyday lives, thereby facilitating the church's evangelizing mission and enhancing lay participation in the life of the church.

Evangelical Churches

The Protestant presence in Huaycán is not large, but the active participation of evangelicals in community organization has created the impression among Catholics that evangelicals are much more numerous. There is a wide spectrum of evangelical churches present in Huaycán. These include the larger denominations, such as the Assemblies of God and the Peruvian Evangelical Church (IEP), and a number of smaller denominations and independent churches. Today there are thirty-five evangelical churches in Huaycán. Of these, we visited fifteen and conducted interviews with members and pastors of three Assemblies of God congregations and three IEP congregations. Compared to their counterparts in Comas, which received support from their mother churches in Lima, in Huaycán, the presence of Sendero and the relatively small evangelical population made it difficult to attract support from larger churches in Lima.

Yungay

Yungay is located in the north-central Andes of Peru. The picturesque "old" Yungay was buried by an avalanche during the May 1970 earthquake. The process of reconstruction was a painful one, made slower by the inadequacies of government aid. Despite a number of setbacks, the town eventually regained its stature as an educational and commercial center and today has two schools, a police training facility, a small regional hospital, a bustling produce market, and a number of small businesses and micro-enterprises. By the 1990s, Yungay had recovered and surpassed its pre-earthquake size, with a population of 4,646 according to the 1993 census. Migration from surrounding communities has led to much of the town's growth, although 73 percent of the district's population still lives in rural areas, 27 percent in the urban area.

The Catholic Church

The parish of Santo Domingo de Guzmán is as old as the town of Yungay. Before the earthquake, the Catholic Church helped maintain the town's traditional domination over the surrounding rural communities through the indigenous fiesta system. Following the earthquake, the church participated actively in the process of reconstruction, supporting the desire of survivors to rebuild the town near its old location. The church's social role has been ambivalent, with two distinct pastoral orientations. Parish priests devote most of their time to administering the sacraments and giving religious instruction in the local schools. Their relationship with rural communities tends to reinforce the traditional pattern of domination by town authorities, and laypeople complain that the priests are uninterested in the plight of the *campesinos*. In contrast, a group of Franciscan sisters and, more recently, French Canadian brothers of San Viator, have trained lay leaders to evangelize rural communities and the urban area, support social projects such as a children's lunch program, and work with the Juventud Agraria Rural Católica.

Evangelical Churches

Although evangelicals have been in Yungay since before the earthquake, their population remains small, with only 4 percent of the population in 1993. There are a handful of small evangelical congregations in town, with most evangelicals concentrated in one rural hamlet, Musho, where about one-third of the population attends one of the Protestant churches. Because of their limited presence, we did not include evangelical churches in our research in Yungay.

United States

Washington, D.C.

Washington, D.C., has a large and diverse Latino population, which dominates service sectors such as child care, housekeeping, landscaping, construction, and restaurant and hotel services. Migration from Central America, particularly from El Salvador, started in the 1950s, when women came to work as maids and nannies for a growing diplomatic core. This migration grew most during the political violence of the 1980s. Many Salvadorans, particularly young men, used already established networks to come to Washington, swelling the number of Salvadoran immigrants in the greater metropolitan area to about 100,000 by 1987. A significant characteristic of Salvadoran migration to Washington is that whole towns have migrated, establishing regional cultural enclaves in specific neighborhoods. The great majority of Salvadorans in Washington come from the eastern part of the country, particularly from the departments of San Miguel and La Unión. Within Washington, Salvadorans have concentrated in Adams Morgan and Mt. Pleasant. Today both neighborhoods are undergoing gentrification, which, in addition to persistent poverty and lack of opportunity among Latinos, has intensified racial tensions. In 1991 a case of police abuse against a Salvadoran immigrant triggered widespread rioting. The Catholic Church played an important role in mediating between the Latino community and city authorities. In the aftermath of the riots, the mayor created the Latino Task Force, bringing together twenty-five organizations to address community concerns. Today many Salvadorans have moved outside the district to suburbs such as Takoma Park, Maryland, and Alexandria, Virginia.

The Catholic Church

THE SHRINE OF THE SACRED HEART

The parish of Sacred Heart, encompassing the traditionally Latino neighborhoods of Adams Morgan, Mt. Pleasant, and Columbia Heights, is under the care of a team of Capuchin Franciscans. The congregation of about four thousand is dominated by Central Americans, particularly Salvadorans, although there are sizable Haitian and Vietnamese communities. In addition to activities of the various ethnic communities, the parish has programs for religious education, baptismal preparation, and Bible groups, as well as a very active Charismatic group, which attracts many young Salvadoran men. There is also a parish council that meets every month to plan pastoral and social activities such as Sacred Heart annual festival.

OUR LADY OF SORROWS CATHOLIC CHURCH

Our Lady of Sorrows, in Takoma Park, has a congregation of about two thousand families dominated by Salvadorans who have recently moved to the suburbs. In the early and mid-1990s, the parish was served by a Salvadoran who was eventually replaced, not without some tension. Like Sacred Heart, Our Lady of Sorrows is nearly half Latino but also includes Haitian, African, and African American members. In addition, a core of Euramericans (18 percent) attend two English Masses on Sundays. Also like Sacred Heart, Our Lady of Sorrows celebrates multicultural Masses for special occasions. Parish activities include Charismatic, Bible, Neocatechumenate, and marriage encounter groups.

Protestant Churches

CHURCH OF APOSTLES AND PROPHETS

Founded in 1981 by Salvadoran immigrants from the eastern part of the country, La Iglesia de Apóstoles y Profetas (IAP) is an independent Pentecostal church with a membership of 350. Located in a predominantly white middle-class area in the northeastern corner of the district, the IAP is a commuter church, which sends vans to ferry members from Takoma Park and Silver Spring. The male members of the congregation work primarily in the janitorial and construction sectors, the women as maids, waitresses, or homemakers. The IAP has a strongly evangelistic thrust that has generated conflicts with the neighbors. It also sponsors a weekly radio program "Toward Heaven," linking Washington and eastern El Salvador. At the time of the study, the church was suffering considerable internal turmoil, which eventually resulted in a split.

AUGUSTANA LUTHERAN CHURCH

Augustana, founded in the 1920s by Swedish immigrants, is just south of Adams Morgans and close to Dupont Circle and U Street. This locale has given the congregation racial and socioeconomic diversity. The church serves as a meeting point for poor and working-class Latinos and African Americans (30 percent), and for well-off members of the large, mostly white gay community in the area (70 percent). Augustana started outreach to Latinos in 1989. Currently, this outreach is coordinated by a Salvadoran, a former Catholic priest in El Salvador who is working on education and social concerns, especially health and housing. This work has attracted many Salvadorans who feel that Sacred Heart is not addressing social questions directly.

Paterson, New Jersey

A city of about 141,000 and located about twenty miles west of New York City, Paterson, a once-thriving industrial center, has seen its industrial base shrink dramatically in recent years. Peruvian migration to Paterson began in the 1910s as skilled artisans came to work in the city's silk industry and continued through the postwar years. In the 1980s, political and economic crisis in Peru increased migration, including professionals, middle- and lower-middle-class urbanites, and an increasing number of Serranos (people from the highlands). Currently, there are about thirty thousand Peruvians in the greater metropolitan area. They participate in many religious and civic organizations, including the yearly celebration of a Peruvian week in July, which is inaugurated by the Peruvian ambassador and the mayor of Paterson.

The Catholic Church

SAINT JOHN THE BAPTIST CATHEDRAL

Founded in 1820 by Irish immigrants, the cathedral is the seat of the diocese of Paterson. Its core membership has included waves of Irish, Italian, Puerto Rican, and Dominican immigrants. Today, about 90 percent of the 5,000–strong congregation is Hispanic, with roughly equal numbers of Puerto Ricans, Dominicans, Peruvians, and Colombians. The cathedral has two Hispanic associate pastors and a Hispanic deacon and offers two Sunday Masses in Spanish, which each attract an average of 900 to 1,000 people. The cathedral also houses a wide range of activities, including Charismatics, Cursillos de

Cristiandad, and the Neocatechumenate, as well as catechists, ministers of the Eucharist, ushers, marriage groups, and a Latino chorus. Peruvians participate in all of the groups above, but their religious life tends to concentrate around the brotherhoods of El Señor de los Milagros and San Martín de Porres.

OUR LADY OF LOURDES

Founded in 1882 by Belgian immigrants, Our Lady of Lourdes serves about three hundred families, 90 percent of Hispanic origin. Like the cathedral and other parishes in the area, its composition has changed with the demographic shifts in the city's population. The parish is headed by an Italian American Capuchin priest who is fluent in Spanish. At Our Lady of Lourdes there are various parish groups, such as the original hermandad del Señor de los Milagros, the *cursillo* movement, and the youth group. The *cursillo* movement, with its weekly Ultreya meetings, consists of an evangelizing community of approximately fifty members. Participants represent a variety of age groups, with a multi-Hispanic membership dominated by Puerto Ricans and Dominicans.

The Protestant Churches

LA GRAN COMISIÓN

La Gran Comisión, the Great Commission, is the oldest Hispanic evangelical church in Paterson, founded in 1953. The congregation grew rapidly during the 1960s, and its current site in downtown Paterson holds one thousand people. The Gran Comisión is essentially a commuter church, serving about six hundred first-, second-, and even third-generation Latino immigrants. The church offers a variety of services, including Bible study groups, ministry to prisons, a pantry for the homeless, a kindergarten to seventh grade school, and a theological institute to train future pastors. Most members are Puerto Rican and Dominican, with a small but growing Peruvian population. In contrast to Puerto Rican and Dominican members, most of the Peruvians we interviewed had at least some university education and were employed in skilled professions such as food service managers, court clerks, and master carpenters.

References

Alder, Daniel. 1994. "Crime Gangs Replace Death Squads in El Salvador." *San Francisco Chronicle,* August 23, A9.

Altamirano, Teófilo. 1992. *Exodo: Peruanos en el exterior.* Lima: Pontificia Universidad Católica del Perú.

———. 1996. *Migración: El fenómeno del siglo.* Lima: Pontificia Universidad Católica del Perú.

Alvarez, Sonia, Evelina Dagnino, and Arturo Escobar. 1998. "Introduction: The Cultural and the Political in Latin American Social Movements." In *Cultures of Politics, Politics of Cultures,* ed. Sonia Alvarez, Evelina Dagnino, and Arturo Escobar. Boulder, Colo.: Westview.

Amin, Ash, ed. 1994. *Post-Fordism: A Reader.* Oxford: Blackwell.

Anzaldúa, Gloria. 1987. *Borderlands/La Frontera: The New Mestiza.* San Francisco: Spinters.

Appadurai, Arjun. 1996. *Modernity at Large: Cultural Dimensions of Globalization.* Minneapolis: University of Minnesota Press.

Arrighi, Giovanni, and Beverly Silver. 1999. *Chaos and Governance in the Modern World System.* Minneapolis: University of Minnesota Press.

Azevedo, Marcello. 1987. *Basic Christian Communities.* Maryknoll, N.Y.: Orbis Books.

Basch, Linda, Nina Glick Schiller, and Cristina Szanton Blanc. 1994. *Nations Unbound: Transnational Projects, Postcolonial Predicaments and Deterritorialized Nation-States.* Amsterdam: Gordon and Breach.

———. 1995. "From Immigrant to Transmigrant: Theorizing Transnational Migration." *Anthropology Quarterly* 68, no.1:48–64.

Bastian, Jean Pierre. 1993. "The Metamorphosis of Latin American Protestant Groups: A Sociohistorical Perspective." *Latin American Research Review* 28, no. 2:33–61.

Bates, Steve, and Charles W. Hall. 1995. "For Latinos, Struggles Don't End in the U.S." *Washington Post,* October 22, A1.

Becker, Penny Edgell, and Nancy L. Eiesland, eds. 1998. *Contemporary American Religion: An Ethnographic Reader.* Walnut Creek, Calif.: Altamira Press.

241

Bellah, Robert, Richard Madsen, William Sullivan, Ann Swidler, and Steven Tipton. 1985. *Habits of the Heart*. Berkeley: University of California Press.

———. 1991. *The Good Society*. New York: Random House.

Benítez Manaut, Raúl. 1988. "Guerra e intervención norteamericana." In *El Salvador: Guerra, Política y Paz*. San Salvador: CINAS-CRIES.

Berger, Peter, and Thomas Luckmann. 1966. *Social Construction of Reality: A Treatise in the Sociology of Knowledge*. New York: Doubleday/Anchor Books.

Berryman, Phillip. 1984. *The Religious Roots of Rebellion: Christians in Central American Revolutions*. Maryknoll, N.Y.: Orbis Books.

———. 1986. "El Salvador: From Evangelization to Insurrection." *In Religion and Social Conflict in Latin America,* ed. Daniel Levine. Chapel Hill: University of North Carolina Press.

———. 1994. *Stubborn Hope: Religion, Politics, and Revolution in Central America*. Maryknoll, N.Y.: Orbis Books.

———. 1996. *Religion in the Megacity: Catholic and Protestant Portraits from Latin America*. Maryknoll, N.Y.: Orbis Books.

———. 1999. "Churches as Winners and Losers in the Network Society." *Journal of Interamerican Studies and World Affairs* 41, no. 4:21–34.

Bird, Shawn, and Philip Williams. 2000. "El Salvador: Revolt and Negotiated Transition." In *Repression, Resistance, and Democratic Transition in Central America,* ed. Thomas Walker and Ariel Armony. Wilmington, Del.: Scholarly Resources.

Blondet, Cecilia. 1992. *En la tierra de nadie más*. Lima: Instituto de Estudios Peruanos (IEP).

Blondet, Cecilia, and Carmen Montero. 1995. *Hoy: Menú popular, comedores en Lima*. Lima: Instituto de Estudios Peruanos (IEP).

Bode, Barbara. 1989. *No Bells to Toll: Destruction and Creation in the Andes*. New York: Charles Scribner's Sons.

Bourdieu, Pierre. 1984. *Distinction: A Social Critique of the Judgment of Taste*. Cambridge, Mass.: Harvard University Press.

Brooks, Sarah. 1983. *The Catholic Charismatics: The Anatomy of a Modern Religious Movement*. University Park: Pennsylvania State University Press.

———. 1999. "Catholic Activism in the 1990s: New Strategies for the Neoliberal Age." In *Latin American Religion in Motion,* ed. Christian Smith and Joshua Prokopy. New York: Routledge.

Brusco, Elizabeth. 1995. *The Reformation of Machismo*. Austin: University of Texas Press.

Burdick, John. 1992. "Rethinking the Study of Social Movements: The Case of Christian Base Communities in Urban Brazil." In *The Making of Social Movements in Latin America,* ed. A. Escobar and S. Alvarez. Boulder, Colo.: Westview.

———. 1993a. *Looking for God in Brazil*. Berkeley: University of California Press.

———. 1993b. "Struggling Against the Devil: Pentecostalism and Social Movement in Urban Brazil." In *Rethinking Protestantism in Latin America,* ed. Virginia Garrard-Burnett and David Stoll. Philadelphia: Temple University Press.

Cáceres Prendes, Jorge. 1989. "Political Radicalization and Popular Pastoral Practices in El Salvador, 1969–1985." In *The Progressive Church in Latin America,* ed. Scott Mainwaring and Alex Wilde. South Bend, Ind.: Notre Dame University Press.

Cagan, Beth, and Steve Cagan. 1991. *This Promised Land, El Salvador: The Refugees of Colomoncagua and Their Return to Morazán*. New Brunswick, N.J.: Rutgers University Press.

Calderón, Julio. 1991. *Izquierda y democracia: Entre la utopía y la realidad.* Lima: CENCA.

Calderón, Julio, and Luis Olivera. 1989. *Municipio y pobladores en la habilitación urbana (Huaycán y Ladras del Chillón).* Lima: DESCO

Cameron, Maxwell. 1997. "Political and Economic Origins of Regime Change in Peru: The Eighteenth Brumaire of Albert Fujimori." In *The Peruvian Labyrinth,* ed. Maxwell Cameron and Philip Mauceri. University Park: Pennsylvania State University Press.

Carroll, Michael. 1996. *Veiled Threats: The Logic of Popular Catholicism in Italy.* Baltimore: Johns Hopkins University Press.

Castells, Manuel. 1996. *The Rise of the Network Society.* Vol. 1, *The Information Age: Economy, Society, and Culture.* Oxford: Blackwell.

———. 1997. *The Power of Identity.* Vol. 2, *The Information Age: Economy, Society, and Culture.* Oxford: Blackwell.

———. 1998. *End of Millennium.* Vol. 3, *The Information Age: Economy, Society, and Culture.* Oxford: Blackwell.

Cavendish, J. 1995. "Christian Base Communities and the Building of Democracy: Brazil and Chile." In *Religion and Democracy in Latin America,* ed. William Swatos. New Brunswick, N.J.: Transaction Publishers.

CEDES (Episcopal Conference of El Salvador). 1975. *Actas* 101 (July 7–11).

Centro Ideas. 1991. *Campaña periodística: Un ángulo positivo por el desarrollo de la comunidad urbana autogestionaria de Huaycán.* Lima: Centro Ideas.

Cleary, Edward L., and Hannah Stewart-Gambino, eds. 1997. *Power, Politics, and Pentecostals in Latin America.* Boulder, Colo.: Westview.

Cohen, Anthony P. 1985. *The Symbolic Construction of Community.* London: Tavistock.

Coleman, Kenneth, et. al. 1993. "Protestantism in El Salvador: Conventional Wisdom versus the Survey Evidence." *Latin American Research Review* 28:119–140.

Comblín, José. 1994. "Familia Popular en América Latina." *Pastoral Popular* 238:12–18.

Conaghan, Catherine, and James Malloy. 1994. *Unsettling Statecraft: Democracy and Neoliberalism in the Central Andes.* Pittsburgh, Pa.: University of Pittsburgh Press.

Constable, Pamela. 1995. "Moved by the Spirit." *Washington Post,* August 12, B07.

Coral, Isabel. 1994. *Desplazamiento por Violencia Política en el Peru, 1980–1992.* Documento de Trabajo No. 58. Lima: CEPRODEP.

Cortina, Adela. 1997. *Ciudadanos del mundo: Hacia una teoría de la ciudadanía.* Madrid: Alianza Editorial.

Cotler, Julio. 1994, *Política y Sociedad en el Perú: Cambios y Continuidades.* Lima: Instituto de Estudios Peruanos (IEP).

Crabtree, John, and Jim Thomas, eds. 1998. *Fujimori's Peru: The Political Economy.* London: Institute of Latin American Studies.

Csordas, Thomas J. 1980. "Catholic Pentecostalism: A New Word in the New World." In *Perspectives on Pentecostalism: Case Studies from the Caribbean and Latin America,* ed. S. D. Glazier. Washington, D.C.: University Press of America.

———. 1994. *The Sacred Self: A Cultural Phenomenology of Charismatic Healing.* Berkeley: University of California Press.

———. 1997. *Language, Charisma, and Creativity: The Ritual Life of a Religious Movement.* Berkeley: University of California Press.

Dagnino, Evelina. 1998. "Culture, Citizenship, and Democracy: Changing Discourses and Practices of the Latin American Left." In *Cultures of Politics, Politics of Culture,* ed. Sonia Alvarez, Evelina Dagnino, and Arturo Escobar. Boulder, Colo.: Westview.

Danner, Mark. 1993. "The Truth of El Mozote." *New Yorker,* December 6, 50–133.

Davis, Natalie Z. 1974. "Some Tasks and Some Themes in the Study of Popular Religion." In *The Pursuit of Holiness in Late Medieval and Renaissance Religion,* ed. Charles Trinkhaus and Heiko Obermann. Leiden: E. J. Brill.

Dayton, Donald. 1987. *Theological Roots of Pentecostalism.* Metuchen, N.J.: Scarecrow Press.

DeCesare, Donna. 1998. "The Children of War: Street Gangs in El Salvador." *NACLA Report on the Americas* 32, no. 1:21–29.

Deck, Allan. 1995. "The Challenge of Evangelical/Pentecostal Christianity to Hispanic Catholicism." In *Religion and American Culture,* ed. David G. Hackett. New York: Routledge.

Degregori, Carlos Iván. 1991. "Al Filo de la Navaja." *Quehacer* 73:26–29.

Della Cava, Ralph. 1992. "Vatican Policy, 1978–1990: An Updated Overview." *Social Research* 59, no. 1:171–199.

De Theije, Marjo. 1990. "Brotherhoods Throw More Weight Around Than the Pope: Catholic Traditionalism and the Lay Brotherhoods of Brazil." *Sociological Analysis* 50, no. 2:189–204.

———. 1999. "CEBs and Catholic Charismatics in Brazil." In *Latin American Religion in Motion,* ed. Christian Smith and Joshua Prokopy. New York: Routledge.

Diamond, Sara. 1989. *Spiritual Warfare: The Politics of the Christian Right.* Boston: South End Press.

Dietz, Henry. 1998. *Urban Poverty, Political Participation and the State: Lima, 1970–1990.* Pittsburgh, Pa.: University of Pittsburgh Press.

Dirección General de Estadísticas y Censos (DIGESTYC). 1996. *Encuesta de hogares de propósitos múltiples.* San Salvador. Ministerio de Economía.

Doughty, Paul. 1968. *Huaylas: An Andean District in Search of Progress.* Ithaca, N.Y.: Cornell University Press.

———. 1999. "Plan and Pattern in Reaction to Earthquake: Peru, 1970–1998." In *The Angry Earth,* ed. Anthony Oliver-Smith and Susanna Hoffman. New York: Routledge.

Drogus, Carol Ann. 1992. "Popular Movements and the Limitations of Political Mobilization at the Grassroots in Brazil." In *Conflict and Competition: The Latin American Church in a Changing Environment,* ed. Edward Cleary and Hannah Stewart-Gambino. Boulder, Colo.: Lynne Rienner.

———. 1994. "Religious Change and Women's Status in Latin America: A Comparison of Catholic Base Communities and Pentecostal Churches." Working Paper #205, Kellogg Institute, University of Notre Dame.

———. 1997a. *Women, Religion and Social Change in Brazil's Popular Church.* Notre Dame, Ind.: University of Notre Dame Press.

———. 1997b. "Private Power or Public Power: Pentecostalism, Base Communities, and Gender." In *Power, Politics, and Pentecostals in Latin America,* ed. Edward Cleary and Hannah Stewart-Gambino. Boulder, Colo.: Westview.

Edwards, Beatrice, and Gretta Siebentritt. 1991. *Places of Origin: The Repopulations of Rural El Salvador.* Boulder, Colo.: Lynne Rienner.

Elizondo, Virgilio. 1983. *Galilean Journey: The Mexican American Journey.* Maryknoll, N.Y.: Orbis.

Epstein, A. L. 1958. *Politics in an Urban African American Community.* Manchester: Manchester University Press.

Erikson, Erik. 1968. *Identity: Youth and Crisis.* New York: Norton.

Escobar, Samuel. 1981. *Las etapas del avance evangélico en el Perú.* Lima: Seminario Evangélico.

Fabbri, Enrique. 1994. "Democracias, familias, solidaridad." *CIAS: Revista del Centro de Investigación y Acción Social* 436–437:381–394.

————. 1995. "Familias ante sociedad en cambio." *CIAS: Revista del Centro de Investigación y Acción Social* 448:533–556.

Farah, Douglas, and Tod Robberson. 1995. "U.S.-Style Gangs Build Free Trade in Crime." *Washington Post,* August 28, A01.

Fernández de la Gala, Juan. 1994. *Diagnóstico de organizaciones poblacionales de Ate-Vitarte.* Lima: Centro Ideas.

Field, Karen. 1982. "Charismatic Religion as Popular Protest." *Theory and Society* 11:305–320.

Finke, Roger, and Rodney Stark. 1992. *The Churching of America: 1776–1990.* New Brunswick, N.J.: Rutgers University Press.

Fleet, Michael, and Brian H. Smith. 1997. *The Catholic Church and Democracy in Chile and Peru.* Notre Dame, Ind.: University of Notre Dame Press.

Flores, William. 1997. "Citizens vs. Citizenry: Undocumented Immigrants and Latino Cultural Citizenship." In *Latino Cultural Citizenship: Claiming Identity, Space, and Rights,* ed. William Flores and Rina Benmayor. Boston: Beacon.

Foley, Michael, and Bob Edwards. 1996. "The Paradox of Civil Society." *Journal of Democracy* 7, no. 3:38–52.

Galer M., Nora, and Pilar Nuñez, eds. 1989. *Mujer y comedores populares.* Lima: SEPADE.

García Canclini, Néstor. 1995. *Hybrid Cultures: Strategies for Entering and Leaving Modernity.* Minneapolis: University of Minnesota Press.

Garrard-Burnett, Virginia. 1998a. *Protestantism in Guatemala: Living in the New Jerusalem.* Austin: University of Texas Press.

————. 1998b. "Transnational Protestantism." *Journal of Interamerican Studies and World Affairs* 40, no. 3:117–125.

Garrard-Burnett, Virginia, and David Stoll, eds. 1993. *Rethinking Protestantism in Latin America.* Philadelphia: Temple University Press.

Gill, Anthony. 1998. *Rendering unto Caesar: The Catholic Church and the State in Latin America.* Chicago: University of Chicago Press.

————. 1999. "The Struggle to Be Soul Provider: Catholic Responses to Protestant Growth in Latin America." In *Latin American Religion in Motion,* ed. Christian Smith and Joshua Prokopy. New York: Routledge.

Gill, Lesley. 1990. "'Like a Veil to Cover Them': Women and the Pentecostal Movement in La Paz." *American Ethnologist* 17, no. 4:708–721.

Goizueta, Roberto. 1995. *Caminemos con Jesús.* Maryknoll, N.Y.: Orbis.

Gonzáles M., José Luis. 1987. "Familia y socialización religiosa. La transmisión de la religiosidad popular en el Perú." *Revista de la Universidad Católica del Perú* 15–16:56–80.

Gordon, Milton. 1964. *Assimilation in American Life: The Role of Race, Religion and National Origins.* New York: Oxford University Press.

Gordon, Sara. 1989. *Crisis Política y Guerra en El Salvador.* Mexico: Siglo XXI Editores.

Grasmuck, Sherri, and Patricia Pessar. 1991. *Between Two Islands: Dominican International Migration.* Berkeley: University of California Press.

Greeley, Andrew. 1988. "Defections among Hispanics." *America* (July 30): 61–62.

———. 1997. "Defection among Hispanics (Update)" *America* (September 27):12–13.

Griffith, R. Marie. 1997. *God's Daughters: Evangelical Women and the Power of Submission.* Berkeley: University of California Press.

Grompone, Romeo. 1991. *El velero en el viento.* Lima: Instituto de Estudios Peruanos (IEP).

Guarnizo, Luis, and Michael Peter Smith. 1998. "The Locations of Transnationalism." In *Transnationalism from Below,* ed. Michael Peter Smith and Luis Guarnizo. New Brunswick, N.J.: Transaction Publishers.

Guidos Béjar, Rafael. 1998. "Deliberación pública democracia." Suplemento Especial, *Plan de Nación apuesta para ganar. Diario de Hoy.* San Salvador: Tendencias Editores.

Habermas, Jürgen. 1996. *Between Facts and Norms: Contributions to a Discourse Theory of Law and Democracy.* Cambridge, Mass.: MIT Press.

Harline, Craig. 1990. "Official Religion-Popular Religion in Recent Historiography of the Catholic Reformation." *Archive for Reformation History* 81:239–262.

Harvey, David. 1989. *The Condition of Postmodernity: An Inquiry into the Origins of Cultural Change.* Oxford: Blackwell.

Heater, Derek. 1990. *Citizenship: The Civic Ideal in World History, Politics and Education.* New York: Longman.

Hegy, Pierre. 1978. "Images of God and Man in a Catholic Charismatic Renewal Community." *Social Compass* 25:7–21.

Held, David. 1991. "Democracy, the Nation-State, and the Global System." In *Political Theory Today,* ed. David Held. Cambridge, Mass.: Polity Press.

Hennelly, Alfred. 1993. *Santo Domingo and Beyond.* Maryknoll, N.Y.: Orbis Books.

Henríquez, Pedro. 1988. *El Salvador: Iglesia profética y cambio social.* San José, Costa Rica: DEI.

Hervieu-Léger, Danièle. 1997. "'What the Scripture Tells Me': Spontaneity and Regulation within the Catholic Charismatic Renewal." In *Lived Religion in America: Toward a History of Practice,* ed. David Hall. Princeton, N.J.: Princeton University Press.

Houtart, Françoise, and Geneviève Lemercier. 1989. *La cultura religiosa de las Comunidades de base en Nicaragua.* Managua, Nicaragua: UCA.

Iannaccone, Laurence. 1995. "Voodoo Economics? Defending the Rational Choice Approach to Religion." *Journal for the Scientific Study of Religion* 34, no. 1:76–88.

Instituto Bartolomé de Las Casas. 1996. *Encuesta nacional de valores.* Lima: Instituto Bartolomé de Las Casas.

INEI (Instituto Nacional de Estadísticas e Información). 1993. *IX Censo Nacional de Población y el IV Censo Nacional de Vivienda.* Lima: INEI.

———. 1995. *Compendio de estadísticas sociales, 1994–1995.* Lima: Dirección Técnica de Demografía y Estudios Sociales del INEI.

Ingham, John. 1986. *Mary, Michael, and Lucifer: Folk Catholicism in Central Mexico.* Austin: University of Texas Press.

Ireland, Rowan. 1991. *Kingdoms Come: Religion and Politics in Brazil.* Pittsburgh: University of Pittsburgh Press.

———. 1997. "Pentecostalism, Conversions, and Politics in Brazil." In *Power, Politics, and Pentecostals in Latin America,* ed. Edward Cleary and Hannah Stewart-Gambino. Boulder, Colo.: Westview.

———. 1999. "Popular Religions and the Building of Democracy in Latin America: Saving the Tocquevillian Parallel." *Journal of Interamerican Studies and World Affairs,* 41, no. 4:111–136.

IUDOP (Instituto Universitario de Opinión Pública). 1997. *Sondeo sobre la juventud organizada en pandillas.* San Salvador: IUDOP/UCA.

Jankowski, Martín Sánchez. 1991. *Islands in the Street: Gangs and American Urban Society.* Berkeley: University of California Press.

Jelín, Elizabeth. 1994. "Ciudadanía emergente o exclusión? Movimientos sociales y ONG's en los años noventa." *Revista Mexicana de Sociología* 56, no. 4:91–108.

———. 1996a. "Emergent Citizenship or Exclusion?: Social Movements and Non-Governmental Organizations in the 1990s." In *Politics, Social Change, and Economic Restructuring in Latin America,* ed. William Smith and Roberto Korzeniewicz. Miami: North-South Center Press.

———. 1996b. "Citizenship Revisited: Solidarity, Responsibility, and Rights." In *Constructing Democracy: Human Rights, Citizenship, and Society in Latin America,* ed. Elizabeth Jelín and Eric Hershberg. Boulder, Colo.: Westview.

———. 1998a. "Relevance and Prospects for Local Democracy." In *Understanding Globalization.* Stockholm: Swedish Ministry for Foreign Affairs.

———. 1998b. "Toward a Culture of Participation and Citizenship: Challenges for a More Equitable World." In *Cultures of Politics, Politics of Culture: Re-Visioning Latin American Social Movements,* ed. Sonia Alvarez, Evelina Dagnino, and Arturo Escobar. Boulder, Colo.: Westview.

John Paul II. 1991. *Carta Encíclica "Centesimus Annus."* Lima: Editorial Salesiana.

Juventud Agraria Rural Católica (JARC). 1997. "Historia de la JARC." Lima: JARC.

Kamsteeg, Frans. 1991. "Pastor y Discípulo: El rol de líderes y laicos en el crecimiento de las iglesias pentecostales en Arequipa, Perú." In *Algo más que opio,* ed. Barbara Boudewijnse, André Droogers, and Frans Kamsteeg. San José, Costa Rica: DEI.

———. 1993. "The Message and the People: The Different Meanings of a Pentecostal Evangelistical Campaign." In *The Popular Use of Popular Religion in Latin America,* ed. Susanna Rostas and André Droogers. Amsterdam: CEDLA.

Keck, Margaret, and Kathryn Sikkink. 1998. *Activists beyond Borders: Advocacy Networks in International Politics.* Ithaca, N.Y.: Cornell University Press.

Keohane, R. O. 1995. "Hobbes' Dilemma and Institutional Change in World Politics: Sovereignty in International Society." In *Whose World Order?,* ed. H. Holm and G. Sorensen. Boulder, Colo.: Westview.

Klaiber, Jeffrey. 1992. "The Church in Peru: Between Terrorism and Conservative Restraints." In *Conflict and Competition: The Latin American Church in a Changing Environment,* ed. Edward Cleary and Hannah Stewart-Gambino. Boulder, Colo.: Lynne Rienner.

Kselman, Thomas. 1983. *Miracles and Prophecies in Nineteenth-Century France.* New Brunswick, N.J.: Rutgers University Press.

———. 1986. "Ambivalence and Assumption in the Concept of Popular Religion." In *Religion and Political Conflict in Latin America,* ed. Daniel Levine. Chapel Hill: University of North Carolina Press.

———. 1991. "Introduction." In *Belief in History: Innovative Approaches to European and American Religion,* ed. Thomas Kselman. Notre Dame, Ind.: University of Notre Dame Press.

Lakatos, Imre. 1999. *For and against Method.* Chicago: University of Chicago Press.

Lalive D'Epinay, Christian. 1968. *El refugio de las masas: Estudio sociológico del protestantismo chileno.* Santiago, Chile: Editorial del Pacífico.

Lancaster, Roger. 1993. *Life Is Hard: Power, Intimacy, and Danger in the New Nicaragua.* Berkeley: University of California Press.

Lane, Ralph. 1976. "Catholic Charismatic Renewal." In *The New Religious Consciousness,* ed. Charles Glock and Robert Bellah. Berkeley: University of California Press.

———. 1978. "The Catholic Charismatic Renewal in the United States: A Reconsideration." *Social Compass* 25:23–35.

Lasch, Christopher. 1977. *Haven in a Heartless World: The Family Besieged.* New York: Basic Books.

Leon, Luis. 1998. "Born Again in East L. A.: The Congregation as Border Space." In *Gatherings in Diaspora: Religious Communities and the New Immigration,* ed. Stephen Warner and Judith Wittner. Philadelphia: Temple University Press.

Lernoux, Penny. 1989. *People of God: The Struggle for World Catholicism.* New York: Penguin Books.

Levine, Daniel. 1992. *Popular Voices in Latin American Catholicism.* Princeton, N.J.: Princeton University Press.

Levine, Daniel, and David Stoll. 1997. "Bridging the Gap between Empowerment and Power in Latin America." In *Transnational Religion and Fading States,* ed. Susanne Hoeber Rudolph and James Piscatori. Boulder, Colo.: Westview.

Levitt, Peggy. 1998a. "Local-Level Global Religion: The Case of Dominican-U.S. Migration." *Journal for the Scientific Study of Religion* 37, no. 1:74–89.

———. 1998b. "Social Remittances: Migration-Driven, Local-Level Forms of Cultural Diffusion." *International Migration Review* 32, no. 4:926–948.

Lewis, Jeanne. 1995. "Headship and Hierarchy: Authority and Control in a Catholic Charismatic Community." Ph.D. diss., University of Michigan.

López, Sinesio. 1997. *Ciudadanos reales e imaginarios.* Lima: Instituto de Diálogo y Propuesta.

López Vigil, María. 1987. *Muerte y vida en Morazán.* San Salvador: UCA Editores.

Macdonald, Mandy, and Mike Gatehouse. 1995. *In the Mountains of Morazán: Portrait of a Returned Refugee Community in El Salvador.* London: Latin American Bureau.

Mahler, Sarah. 1995. *American Dreaming: Immigrant Life on the Margins.* Princeton: Princeton University Press.

———. 1998. "Theoretical and Empirical Contributions Toward a Research Agenda for Transnationalism." In *Transnationalism from Below,* ed. Michael Peter Smith and Luis Guarnizo. New Brunswick, N.J.: Transaction Publishers.

Mainwaring, Scott. 1986. *The Catholic Church and Politics in Brazil, 1916–1985.* Stanford, Calif.: Stanford University Press.

Margolis, Maxine. 1995. "Transnationalism and Popular Culture: The Case of Brazilian Immigrants in the United States." *Journal of Popular Culture* 29, no. 1:29–42.

Mariz, Cecilia. 1992. "Religion and Coping with Poverty: A Comparison of Catholic and Pentecostal Communities." *Sociological Analysis* 53:S63–S70.

———. 1994. *Coping with Poverty.* Philadelphia: Temple University Press.

Mariz, Cecilia Loreto, and Maria Campos Machado. 1997. "Pentecostalism and Women in Brazil." In *Power, Politics, and Pentecostals in Latin America,* ed. Edward Cleary and Hannah Stewart-Gambino. Boulder, Colo.: Westview.

Martin, David. 1990. *Tongues of Fire: The Explosion of Protestantism in Latin America.* Oxford: Basil Backwell.

Marzal, Manuel. 1989. *Los caminos religiosos de los inmigrantes en la Gran Lima.* Lima: Pontificia Universidad Católica del Perú.

Massey, Doug, Luin Goldring, and J. Durand. 1994. "Continuities in Transnational Migration: An Analysis of 19 Mexican Communities." *American Journal of Sociology* 99:1492–1534.

Mazón, Mauricio. 1985. *The Zoot Suit Riots: The Psychology of Symbolic Annihilation.* Austin: University of Texas Press.

McClintock, Cynthia. 1993. "Peru's Fujimori: A Caudillo Derails Democracy." *Current History* 92, no. 572:112–119.

McClintock, Cynthia, and Abraham Lowenthal, eds. 1983. *The Peruvian Experiment Reconsidered.* Princeton, N.J.: Princeton University Press.

McGovern, Arthur. 1989. *Liberation Theology and Its Critics.* Maryknoll, N.Y.: Orbis Books.

McGuire, Meredith. 1982. *Pentecostal Catholics: Power, Charisma, and Order in a Religious Movement.* Philadelphia: Temple University Press.

Melucci, Alberto. 1996. *The Playing Self: Person and Meaning in a Planetary Society.* Cambridge: Cambridge University Press.

Menjívar, Cecilia. 1999. "Religious Institutions and Transnationalism: A Case Study of Catholic and Evangelical Salvadoran Immigrants." *International Journal of Politics, Culture and Society* 12, no. 4:589–612.

Menjívar Larín, Rafael. 1998. "Mesas de integración en Costa Rica." Suplemento Especial, *Plan de Nación apuesta para ganar. Diario de Hoy.* San Salvador: Tendencias Editores.

Mitchell, Clyde. 1956. *The Yao Village: A Study of the Social Structure of a Nyasa Land Tribe.* Manchester: Manchester University Press.

Mittelman, James. 2000. *The Globalization Syndrome: Transformation and Resistance.* Princeton, N.J.: Princeton University Press.

Montero, Víctor. 1992. *Huaycán: Un pueblo que construye lucha y celebra.* Lima: EDAPROSPO.

Montes, Segundo. 1989. *Refugiados y repatriados, El Salvador, Honduras.* San Salvador: IDHUCA.

Montgomery, Tammie Sue. 1995. *Revolution in El Salvador: From Civil Strife to Civil Peace.* Boulder, Colo.: Westview.

Moreno Rejón, Francisco. 1984. "Cuestionamiento a la ética teológica desde las familias marginales." *Revista de la Universidad Católica del Perú,* 15–16.

Nagel, Joanne. 1994. "Constructing Ethnicity: Creating and Recreating Ethnic Identity and Culture." *Social Problems* 41, no. 1:152–176.

National Conference of Catholic Bishops (NCCB). 1988. *National Pastoral Plan for Hispanic Ministry.* Washington, D.C.: NCCB/USCC.

Neitz, Mary Jo. 1987. *Charisma and Community: A Study of Religion in American Culture.* New Brunswick, N.J.: Transaction Publishers.

O'Connor, Edward. 1971. *The Pentecostal Movement in the Catholic Church.* Notre Dame: Ave Maria Press.

O'Connor, Mike. 1994. "A New U.S. Import in El Salvador: Street Gangs." *New York Times,* July 3, A3.

O'Donnell, Guillermo. 1993. "On the State, Democratization and Some Conceptual Problems: A Latin American View with Glances at Some Postcommunist Countries." *World Development* 21, no. 8:1355–1369.

———. 1994. "Delegative Democracy." *Journal of Democracy* 5, no. 1:55–69.

Oliver-Smith, Anthony. 1992. *The Martyred City: Death and Rebirth in the Andes.* Prospect Heights, Ill.: Waveland Press.

Oliver-Smith, Anthony, and Roberta Goldman. 1988. "Planning Goals and Urban Realities: Post-Disaster Reconstruction in a Third World City." *City and Society* 2, no. 2:105–126.

Ong, Aihwa, and Donald Nonini, eds. 1997. *Ungrounded Empires: The Cultural Politics of Modern Chinese Transnationalism.* New York: Routledge.

Opazo, Andrés. 1985. "El movimiento religioso, popular en Centroamérica: 1970–1983." In *Movimientos Populares en Centroamérica,* ed. Eduardo Camacho. San José, Costa Rica: EDUCA.

Otter, Elisabeth Den. 1985. *Music and Dance of Indians and Mestizos in an Andean Valley of Peru.* Delft, Netherlands: Eburon.

Pace, Enzo. 1978. "Charismatics and the Political Presence of Catholics." *Social Compass* 25: 85–99.

Padilla, René. 1991. *De la marginación al compromiso: Los evangélicos y la política en América Latina.* Argentina: Fraternidad Teológica Latinoamericana.

Paerregaard, Karsten. 1997. *Linking Separate Worlds: Urban Migrants and Rural Lives in Peru.* New York: Berg.

Palmer, David Scott. 1980. *Peru: The Authoritarian Tradition.* New York: Praeger.

———. 1992. *Shining Path of Peru.* New York: St. Martin's.

Park, Robert. 1950. *Race and Culture.* Glencoe, Ill.: Free Press.

Parroquia de San Andrés. 1997. "Plan Pastoral 1997." *Boletín eco-comunitario especial.* Lima: Parroquia de San Andrés.

———. 1998. *Plan pastoral parroquial, 1993–1998.* Lima: Parroquia de San Andrés.

Pearce, Jenny. 1986. *Promised Land: Peasant Rebellion in Chalatenango, El Salvador.* London: Latin American Bureau.

Peña, Milagros. 1995. *Theologies and Liberation in Peru: The Role of Ideas in Social Movements.* Philadelphia: Temple University Press.

Perea, Juan, ed. 1997. *Immigrants Out!: The New Nativism and the Anti-Immigrant Impulse in the United States.* New York: New York University Press.

Peterson, Anna L. 1995a. "Cultural Critique and the Left in Latin America." *Socialist Review* 3:129–144.

———. 1995b. "Religion in Latin America: New Methods and Approaches." *Religious Studies Review* 21, no. 1:3–8.

———. 1996a. "Religious Narratives and Political Protest." *Journal of the American Academy of Religion* 64, no. 1:27–44.

———. 1996b. "Religion and Society in Latin America: Ambivalences and Advances." *Latin American Research Review* 31, no. 2:236–251.

———. 1997. *Martyrdom and the Politics of Religion: Progressive Catholicism in El Salvador's Civil War.* Albany: State University of New York Press.

————. 1998. "Varieties of Popular Catholicism: A Parish Study." *Social Compass* 45, no. 3:399–415.

Peterson, Anna L., and Manuel Vásquez. 1998. "The New Evangelization in Latin American Perspective." *Cross Currents* 48, no. 3:311–329.

Poblete, Renato, and Thomas O'Dea. 1960. "Anomie and the Quest for Community: The Formation of Sects among Puerto Ricans in New York." *American Catholic Sociological Review* 21, no. 1:18–36.

Poewe, Karla. 1994. "The Nature, Globality, and History of Charismatic Christianity." In *Charismatic Christianity as Global Culture,* ed. Karla Poewe. Columbia: University of South Carolina Press.

Poloma, Margaret. 1982. *The Charismatic Movement: Is There a New Pentecost?* Boston: Twayne.

Ponce, Ana, and Marfil Francke. 1985. "Hogar y familia. Problemas para el estudio demográfico." *Hogar y Familia en el Perú.* Lima: Universidad Católica del Perú.

Pontes Sposito, Marilia. 1994. "Violencia colectiva, jóvenes y educación." *Revista Mexicana de Sociología* 56, no. 3:113–125.

Portes, Alejandro. 1996. "Global Villagers: The Rise of Transnational Communities." *American Prospect* 25:74–78.

————. 1997. "Immigration Theory for a New Century: Some Problems and Opportunities." *International Migration Review* 31, no. 4:799–826.

Portes, Alejandro, Luis Guarnizo, and Patricia Landolt. 1999. "Introduction: Pitfalls and Promise of an Emergent Research Field." *Ethnic and Racial Studies* 22, no. 2:217–237.

PROMIES. 1993. *La Iglesia Evangélica en Números.* Lima: PUMA-CENIP.

Putnam, Robert. 2000. *Bowling Alone: The Collapse and Revival of American Community.* New York: Simon and Schuster.

Quebedeaux, Richard. 1976. *The New Charismatics: The Origins, Development, and Significance of Neo-Pentecostalism.* Garden City, N.Y.: Doubleday.

Repak, Terry. 1995. *Waiting on Washington: Central American Workers in the Nation's Capital.* Philadelphia: Temple University Press.

Robertson, Roland. 1995. "Glocalization: Time-Space and Homogeneity-Heterogeneity." In *Global Modernities,* ed. Mike Featherstone, Scott Lash, and Roland Robertson. London: Sage.

Rohter, Larry. 1996. "A Church Asunder Awaits the Pope in Salvador." *New York Times,* February 5, 6.

Romero, Catalina. 1987. "Iglesia en el Perú: Compromiso y renovación (1958–1984)." *Iglesia y Sociedad.* Lima: Instituto Bartalomé de las Casas-Rimac.

Rosaldo, Renato. 1995. "Foreword." In *Hybrid Cultures* by Néstor García Canclini. Minneapolis: University of Minnesota Press.

Rosenau, James. 1997. *Along the Domestic-Foreign Frontier.* Cambridge, U.K.: Cambridge University Press.

Rouse, Roger. 1991. "Mexican Migration and the Social Space of Postmodernism." *Diaspora* 1, no. 1:8–23.

Rovaletti, M. L. 1992. "Desobediencia y cambio: Juventud y sociedad en América Latina." *Logos: Revista de Filosofia* 59: 117–124.

Rudolph, Susanne, and James Piscatori, eds. 1997. *Transnational Religion and Fading States.* Boulder, Colo.: Westview.

Safa, Helen Icken. 1995. *The Myth of the Male Breadwinner.* Boulder, Colo.: Westview.

Saldaña, Julio, Luis Alvarez, and Víctor Orosco. 1997. "Municipalidad de Comas: Datos estadísticos de organizaciones de la población, por su estructura orgánica y funcional. Comas, Peru: Unpublished report.

Sandoval, Moises. 1990. *On the Move: A History of the Hispanic Church in the United States.* Maryknoll, N.Y.: Orbis.

Santagada, Osvaldo D. 1975. "Pentecostalismo y renovación carismática." *Criterio* (November 13): 625–629.

Sara-Lafosse, Violeta. 1988. "La familia y la mujer en contextos sociales diferentes." Lima: Taller de socialización, Universidad Católica del Perú.

———. 1995. "Familias peruanas y paternidad ausente." *El Perú frente al siglo XXI.* Lima: Universidad Católica del Perú.

———. 1996. "Hacia dónde va la familia?" *Páginas* 140 (August): 12–17.

Sassen, Saskia. 1998. *Globalization and Its Discontents.* New York: New Press.

Siebers, Hans. 1999. "Globalization and Religious Creolization among the Q'eqchi'es of Guatemala." In *Latin American Religion in Motion,* ed. Christian Smith and Joshua Prokopy. New York: Routledge.

Slootweg, Hanneke. 1991. "Mujeres Pentecostales Chilenas: Un caso en Iquique." In *Algo más que opio: Una lectura antropológica del pentecostalismo latinoamericano y caribeño,* ed. Barbara Boudewinse, Andre Droogers, and Frans Kamsteeg. San José, Costa Rica: DEI.

Smith, Christian. 1995. "The Spirit and Democracy: Base Communities, Protestantism and Democratization in Latin America." In *Religion and Democracy in Latin America,* ed. William H. Swatos. New York: Transaction Publishers.

———. 1998. *American Evangelicalism: Embattled and Thriving.* Chicago: University of Chicago Press.

Smith, Christian, and Joshua Prokopy, eds. 1999. *Latin American Religion in Motion.* New York: Routledge.

Smith, Michael. 1992. "Shining Path's Urban Strategy: Ate Vitarte." In *Shining Path of Peru,* ed. David Scott Palmer. New York: St. Martin's.

Smutt, Marcela, and Jenny Miranda. 1998. *El fenómeno de las pandillas en El Salvador.* San Salvador: UNICEF/FLACSO.

Stein, William. 1961. *Hualcan: Life in the Highlands of Peru.* Ithaca, N.Y.: Cornell University Press.

Stewart, Charles, and Rosalind Shaw. 1994. *Syncretism/Anti-syncretism.* London: Routledge.

Stokes, Susan. 1995. *Cultures in Conflict: Social Movements and the State in Peru.* Berkeley: University of California Press.

Talavera, Carlos. 1976. "The Charismatic Renewal and Christian Social Commitment in Latin America." *New Covenant* 6:2–3.

Torazo Roca, Carlos. 1999. "La pluralidad y la diversidad de la participación." In *Las paradojas de la participación.* San Salvador: OXFAM.

Ugarteche, Oscar. 1998. *La arqueología de la modernidad.* Lima: DESCO.

Vásquez, Manuel. 1998. *The Brazilian Popular Church and the Crisis of Modernity.* Cambridge: Cambridge University Press.

———. 1999. "Towards a New Agenda for the Study of Religion in the Americas." *Journal of Interamerican Studies and World Affairs,* 41, no. 4:1–20.

Vigil, James. 1988. *Barrio Gangs: Street Life and Identity in Southern California.* Austin: University of Texas Press.

Vigil, James, and Steve Yun. 1996. "Southern California Gangs: Comparative Ethnicity and Social Control." In *Gangs in America,* ed. C. Ronald Huff. Thousand Oaks, Calif.: Sage.

Warner, R. Stephen, and Judith G. Wittner, eds. 1998. *Gatherings in Diaspora: Religious Communities and the New Immigration.* Philadelphia: Temple University Press.

Weffort, Francisco. 1992. *Quál democracia?* São Paulo, Brazil: Campanha das Letras.

Welch, Sharon. 1990. *A Feminist Ethic of Risk.* Philadelphia: Fortress.

Welsh, Patrick. 1995. "When Immigrant Students Find Poverty, Isolation, and a Life of Violence." *Washington Post,* March 26, C01.

Willems, Emilio. 1967. *The Followers of the New Faith: Cultural Change and the Rise of Protestantism in Brazil and Chile.* Nashville, Tenn.: Vanderbilt University Press.

Williams, Philip. 1997. "The Sound of Tambourines: The Politics of Pentecostal Growth in El Salvador." In *Power, Politics and Pentecostals in Latin America,* ed. Edward Cleary and Hannah Stewart-Gambino. Boulder, Colo.: Westview.

Williams, Philip, and Vilma Fuentes. 2000. "Catholic Responses to the Crisis of Everyday Life in Peru." *Journal of Church and State* 42, no. 1:89–114.

Williams, Philip, and Anna Peterson. 1996. "Evangelicals and Catholics in El Salvador: Evolving Religious Responses to Social Change." *Journal of Church and State* 38, no. 4:873–897.

Wolf, Eric. 1988. "Inventing Society." *American Ethnologist* 15:752–761.

Young, Lawrence. 1997. *Rational Choice Theory and Religion: Summary and Assessment.* New York: Routledge.

Contributors

ROSA CASTRO received her M.A. in sociology from the Catholic University of Peru. She is currently a researcher at the Instituto Bartolomé de las Casas in Lima, where she is actively involved in educating the urban poor, rural communities, and religious organizations on issues relating to democracy, citizenship, and popular images of the Peruvian nation-state.

ILEANA GÓMEZ is a doctoral candidate in the urban sociology program at the University of Alicante, Spain. She received her *licenciatura* in sociology from Universidad Centroamericana José Simeón Cañas in El Salvador, where she has also taught. She is currently a fellow at PRISMA (Environment and Development Research Program) in San Salvador. Her publications include *El proceso electoral de 1994* (FLACSO El Salvador, 1995) and "Procesos ambientales y actores en la Región Metropolitana de San Salvador" (PRISMA-USAID, 1998).

HORTENSIA MUÑOZ is professor of anthropology at the Comunidad Bíblico Teológica Wenceslao Bahamonde and at the Escuela Superior de Humanidades y Filosofía Antonio Ruíz de Montoya in Peru. Her research interests include human rights, culture, and popular religion. Her recent publications include "Human Rights and Social Referents," in *Shining and Other Paths: War and Society in Peru*; *Micro-empresarios: Entre demandas de reconocimiento y dilemas de responsibilidad* (with Yolanda Rodríguez); and a multiauthored book, *Los Peruanos que Vienen*.

ANNA PETERSON is associate professor in the department of religion at the University of Florida. She has written *Martyrdom and the Politics of Religion:*

255

Progressive Catholicism in El Salvador's Civil War; Being Human: Ethics, Environment, and Our Place in the World; and numerous articles on Latin American culture, religion and politics, and environmental ethics.

LARISSA RUÍZ BAÍA is a doctoral student in the department of political science at the University of Florida. A chapter of her master's thesis on U.S.-Dominican immigration policies has been published in the *Latinamericanist*. Her dissertation examines identity formation among U.S. Latinos in New Jersey.

MANUEL VÁSQUEZ is associate professor in the department of religion at the University of Florida. His publications include *The Brazilian Popular Church and the Crisis of Modernity* and articles in journals such as *Sociology of Religion, Journal of the American Academy of Religion,* and the *Journal of Interamerican Studies and World Affairs.*

PHILIP WILLIAMS is professor in the department of political science at the University of Florida. His publications include *Militarization and Demilitarization in El Salvador's Transition to Democracy* (with Knut Walter); *The Catholic Church and Politics in Nicaragua and Costa Rica*; and numerous articles in journals such as *Comparative Politics, Journal of Latin American Studies,* and *Journal of Church and State.*

Index